Searching f(

Searching for Socialism

The Project of the Labour New Left from Benn to Corbyn

Leo Panitch and Colin Leys

VERSO

First published by Verso 2020
© Leo Panitch and Colin Leys 2020

1 3 5 7 9 10 8 6 4 2

Verso
UK: 6 Meard Street, London W1F 0EG
US: 20 Jay Street, Suite 1010, Brooklyn, NY 11201
versobooks.com

Verso is the imprint of New Left Books

ISBN-13 978-1-78873-834-7
ISBN-13: 978-1-78873-851-4 (UK EBK)
ISBN-13: 978-1-78873-852-1 (US EBK)

British Library Cataloguing in Publication Data
A catalogue record for this book is available from the British Library

Library of Congress Cataloging-in-Publication Data
A catalog record for this book is available from the Library of Congress
Library of Congress Control Number: 2020934238

Typeset in Sabon by Biblichor Ltd, Edinburgh
Printed and bound by CPI Group (UK) Ltd, Croydon CR0 4YY

Contents

Preface

Each of the three great economic crises of the last century – the 1930s, the 1970s and the decade after 2008 – precipitated a crisis in the Labour Party. Each time, the crisis posed fundamental questions of ideology, organisation and unity, and ended up by propelling into the leadership a radical socialist MP from the party's left wing. In each instance this produced a sharp reaction aimed at blocking whatever potential the crisis had for taking the party in a new democratic-socialist direction. And in each case Britain's relationship with Europe played an important role.

The first instance was in 1931, at the onset of the Great Depression, after the Labour leader Ramsay MacDonald had formed a 'National Government' in order to impose massive cuts in social expenditure on the unemployed and the working poor. In the ensuing general election, the Labour Party, although it won 30 per cent of the vote, was reduced from 287 MPs to 52. In the wake of this, the radical socialist and pacifist George Lansbury was elected leader, and party policy took a sharp turn to the left. Yet, despite massive street demonstrations by the unemployed, most of the remaining Labour MPs were opposed to any except purely parliamentary measures, leaving Lansbury feeling, as he wrote, 'absolutely helpless' in face of the imposition of ever more draconian austerity. In 1935, after the party conference endorsed military rearmament in response to developments in Europe and the Soviet Union, Lansbury resigned. His successor, Clement Attlee, put the party in the hands of 'a much more professional team', but 'also a much more "responsible" one', as Ralph Miliband wrote in *Parliamentary Socialism*. This was the team that would later carry through Labour's major post-war reforms, while leaving unchallenged the capitalist economy, the inherited structures of the state and the country's place in the new American empire.

In the 1970s, as the Labour governments of Harold Wilson and Jim Callaghan responded to a new economic crisis by abandoning the Keynesian welfare state and restraining union militancy, a new Labour left emerged that was determined to democratise and radicalise the party; and soon after the party's defeat by Margaret Thatcher in 1979, Michael Foot, whose political formation was rooted in the Lansbury years, was precipitated into the leadership. But in the interest of party unity Foot allied himself with the centre-right of the parliamentary party against the Labour new left and its most prominent spokesman, Tony Benn, reasserting the party's commitment to traditional parliamentarism. This did not prevent a second heavy defeat, by Thatcher in 1983. Nor did the ruthless repression of Labour's new left by Foot's successor, Neil Kinnock, prevent two further electoral defeats. Instead it paved the way for 'New Labour', and the embrace of neoliberalism under Tony Blair and Gordon Brown. Throughout these years, too, the issue of Britain's relationship with Europe was a constant complicating dimension of the party's internal divisions.

The contradictions of New Labour in government, culminating in the financial crisis of 2007–08, first propelled 'Red Ed' Miliband to the leadership. But when he, like Foot, gave top priority to securing the unity of the parliamentary party, leading yet again to electoral defeat in 2015, the crisis finally led to the election as leader – this time by the whole membership of the party – of Jeremy Corbyn. His election, the surge in membership that accompanied it, and the support he received from the trade unions finally brought the project of the Labour new left to the top of the party's governmental agenda. The question now was whether the cycle of resistance and neutralisation would once again be repeated, or whether the Labour Party could after all become the agent of democratic-socialist advance in the UK.

Jeremy Corbyn and his most senior colleagues had been formed in the previous attempt to make this happen, in the late 1970s and early 1980s. In *The End of Parliamentary Socialism: From New Left to*

New Labour, published in 2000, we traced the record of that attempt, and its ultimate defeat by the combined forces of its opponents inside and outside the party. Our conclusion was that 'the route to socialism does not lie through the Labour Party'. This did not make us despondent. While accepting that 'the first reaction to disillusionment . . . is fatalism, in the face of what are presented as global forces beyond anyone's control', we thought that this mood would 'sooner or later change to resentment and anger, and a rediscovered will to act, to which a new socialist project must respond'. We did not foresee how soon, in reality, this would happen, in the reaction against the inequality, militarism and economic failure of the neoliberal project; nor that events would again propel a socialist into the leadership of the Labour Party and reopen the question of whether the party could yet be transformed into one capable of leading the socialist transition that the surge of activists into its ranks called for.

Although the enthusiasm behind the Corbyn leadership and the achievements of its first years were impressive, the obstacles the Labour new left project faced were if anything greater than ever. By early 2019 it was clear that its prospects of success had been severely whittled down, so that its eventual defeat in December was not a surprise. The country's relation with Europe played an even more critical role in this than in the past, but the continuities with what had blocked the Labour new left project since the 1970s, above all the fierce obstruction from within the parliamentary party and from the media, were once again evident in every aspect of the events which culminated in defeat in the December 2019 election.

We have therefore condensed the previous book into the first five chapters of this one. The six chapters that follow cover the last twenty years. For help in researching them, we are extremely grateful to all those people inside the party, at every level, from whose knowledge and insights we have learned so much, for the generous time and help they have given us. In all of our work on the project of the Labour new left, we have tried to point to its huge importance while at the same attempting to analyse as clearly as possible the obstacles to realising its potential. But, in whatever form, the drive for democratic socialism will continue. This book is intended as a contribution and a tribute to the purpose and vision of those who, in wanting the Labour Party to become a genuinely democratic-socialist agent of transformation, have done so much to recover the capacity to think ambitiously about social change.

1

Beyond Parliamentary Socialism: Transforming the Labour Party?

The first great economic crisis of the twenty-first century destabilised social-democratic parties everywhere: the assumption that capitalism would coexist with and sustain governments committed to social progress and a broad degree of economic equality was finally proved illusory. And socialist forces, to the left of social democracy, had become very weak. As a result, socialists have rarely been able to intervene effectively in the response to the crisis, which has redounded instead to the advantage of the far right.

Jeremy Corbyn's election as leader of the Labour Party in 2015 was one of the very few exceptions to this rule. His campaign for the leadership put back on the political agenda a democratic-socialist project that had emerged in the previous great crisis of capitalism in the 1970s. What that crisis had shown was that if you could not advance beyond the reforms achieved in the postwar period, you were in danger of losing them. In Britain those who grasped this truth became known as the 'new left'. Inside the Labour Party a new left current developed practical policies for a socialist alternative and organised to win support from the party and trade unions. Their project was eventually defeated, after years of struggle whose twists and turns prefigured much of what has been witnessed since Corbyn's election.

The new left in Britain had first emerged in 1956. It sought to launch a new democratic-socialist alternative to transcend the ever more apparent problems, limitations and disappointments of both communist and social-democratic parties. It never succeeded in spawning a new political party to act as the vehicle for this project, yet its leading figures were highly sceptical of any possibility of turning the Labour Party into such a vehicle. Ralph Miliband's critical study of the history of the Labour Party, *Parliamentary Socialism*, published in 1961, played an important role in defining the British new left's politics in this respect.[1] At times, Miliband even went so far as to declare that 'the belief in the effective transformation of the Labour Party into an instrument of socialist policies . . . is the most crippling of illusions to which socialists in Britain have been prone'.[2] His work showed that Labour's prevailing conception and practice of parliamentary socialism were based on three essential concepts: democracy as a contest between competing teams of elites; the extra-parliamentary party as, in the final analysis, a servant of the parliamentary team; and citizens primarily as mere voters, not as active participants in self-government.

Nonetheless, a significant current developed within the Labour Party in the 1970s which shared the new left's outlook, but took the view that there was no alternative but to attempt precisely such a transformation of the party. Yet unlike the Conservative Party at the time, which relatively quickly embraced 'Thatcherism', the Labour Party was extremely resistant to change. As Stuart Hall noted in a famous essay shortly before the 1979 election, most of its leaders were wedded to a conception of politics in which ordinary people were passive 'clients of a state' over which they had no real control, when what was needed was a party of 'a more broadly mass and democratic character'.[3] The Labour new left, with Tony Benn as its most prominent figure, proposed to make precisely that change – to make the party capable of shaping a progressive solution to the crisis, win support for it, and carry it through in office – as a prerequisite of changing the state.

In setting this as its goal, the Labour new left was ahead of its opponents in grasping the seriousness of the crisis of the postwar order. Even as sophisticated a thinker as Tony Crosland, for instance, believed in 1970 that 'no fundamental rethinking' needed to be made of the analysis of capitalism he had offered in the early 1950s. As late as 1974, he could write that there were no 'signs of a new and fundamental crisis' in the western economies.[4] Tony Benn, by contrast, saw as early as 1970 that a fundamental democratic reform of both the party and the state was needed in order to prevent the ascendancy of 'a new philosophy of government, now emerging everywhere on the right', dedicated to freeing business and controlling the citizen.[5] This was five years before the publication in 1975 of the Trilateral Commission's famous report on the 'governability of democracies', in which a group of American, European and Japanese capitalists, former bureaucrats and right-wing intellectuals argued that governments in capitalist societies had become 'overloaded' by claims to social justice and participation; governability and democracy were 'warring concepts'.[6] Indeed, as productivity growth faltered in the late 1960s, and international competition intensified, the postwar compromise between capital and labour had already started breaking down. Even social-democratic governments began shifting the burden of taxation from capital to labour in order to sustain capital's after-tax profits, while labour began to seek compensation through higher wages and improved social services. This led to a crisis in the postwar Keynesian welfare state everywhere.[7]

The Crisis of Social-Democratic Parties

In the late 1960s, the collapse of the postwar settlement was a critical turning point in the history of the capitalist countries of the West. The response of the 'new right' was to call for the removal of restrictions on private capital accumulation and capitalist culture, and as far as possible for the replacement of collective decision-making by the operation of markets. The new right soon gained the ascendancy within the conservative parties of the West, which allowed it to reach outwards as a coherent political force, gain office, and embark on the market-oriented reconstruction of social, economic and political life that has characterised the past four decades. The response of the new left, on the other hand, was to call for the socialisation of capital and the democratisation of the economy and the state.

In 1976, even the once all-powerful Swedish Social Democrats were defeated for the first time in forty years – though, simultaneously, the Swedish labour movement adopted the Meidner project for democratising industry through 'wage-earners' funds', and quite sober academic analysts expected this to lead to a 'transition to socialism' in Sweden when the Social Democrats eventually returned to power. In Germany, the Social Democratic (SPD) government of Helmut Schmidt explicitly abandoned Keynesianism after 1973; the German trade unions tried but failed to get the SPD to adopt an industrial strategy involving investment controls similar to those being proposed by Labour's new left in Britain. In the process, the SPD's Young Socialists, whose ideas about radically redrawing the balance between parliamentary and extra-parliamentary activity had many parallels with those of the Labour new left, were stifled; but this in turn contributed strongly to the subsequent emergence of the German Greens. In the Netherlands in the early 1970s, a movement very similar to the Labour new left emerged in the Dutch Labour Party, and made extensive gains. It called for greater control by activists over the process of candidate selection and for limits on the power of the party leadership to compromise on the party's declared policies when in office.[8] In Canada, a new left emerged in the New Democratic Party in the late 1960s; by 1971 it was able to make a strong bid for the party leadership, before being expelled in 1972. Meanwhile, France's socialist party, which had been out of office for a generation, revived strongly and adopted an economic programme even more radical than the one then being advocated by the left in the Labour Party. By the end of the decade, it was poised to achieve a stunning electoral victory under a leader, François Mitterand, who insisted that his project had 'nothing in common with the corrupt compromises of a Schmidt or a Callaghan'.[9] The Labour new left was thus part of a much wider response within parliamentary socialist parties to the crisis of the postwar order. What distinguished it from the others, however, was how much further it went in fighting for a radical reorganisation of the relationship between state and party, and between party and people.

The crisis of the system brought the contradictions within the social-democratic movements themselves into focus. The internal life of the social-democratic parties had undergone a serious decline as a result of their integration into the institutions of 'managed capitalism'. As the socialist vision gave way to the pragmatic management of capitalism, there was little scope or need for a party-based 'counterhegemonic' community. Party branches continued to serve an electoral function and play their allotted role at party conferences, but they had lost whatever significance they might have had – which of course varied from country to country – as centres of education and mobilisation oriented to an alternative way of life. In countries where mass socialist newspapers were marginal or nonexistent, as in Britain, there no longer appeared any need to develop any, since the leaders' corporatist and pragmatic ideology gained sufficient currency (even if not explicit editorial support) through the mainstream media. Where a socialist popular press did exist, as in Scandinavia, it could become increasingly 'catch-all' and ideologically anodyne. Individual membership ceased to be so crucial, and in fact tended to decline in almost all the social-democratic parties in Europe in the postwar era.[10]

The decline of intra-party life did not seem to matter much so long as it did not threaten the social-democratic parties' links with the trade unions, while their acceptance as 'parties of government' gave them the legitimacy they needed for periodic election successes. But their failure to resume their former active roles in class formation and socialist education meant that they increasingly depended for electoral success on short-term policy programmes and personalities. When the conditions that had made social-democratic management of national capitalist economies possible ceased to exist, this 'hollowing out' was suddenly revealed as a serious liability.

One indicator of the impending crisis in the social-democratic parties was the radicalisation of the student movement in the 1960s. As the image of the United States as a decoloniser was replaced by that of guarantor of military dictatorships, the 'Atlanticism' of Europe's social-democratic governments became a liability. But this radicalisation had deeper sources as well. What Ralph Miliband termed 'a state of desubordination' affected an entire generation.[11]

The rhetoric of 'social citizenship' that had accompanied the establishment of the welfare state no longer held strong appeal. It was no longer the social justice and political pluralism of social democracy that impressed, but rather the partial character of that justice and the elite nature of that pluralism. When they were confronted by the cry for 'participation', social-democratic ministers who had become immersed in the executive structures and parliamentary apparatuses of the state were either uncomprehending or condescending. When the cry extended to the no less vague but certainly more militant call to 'smash capital', they thought they recognised an old Cold War foe. But they were mistaken: a new generation had emerged whose politics could not be reduced to those polarities.

Moreover, it was not only students, women and a variety of newly activated minorities and causes, from gay rights to environmentalism; it was people in almost every segment of the population who were being prompted to new levels of political interest and activism as the contradictions of social democracy and Keynesianism came to a head. A counter-current was also flowing strongly, of course, in the mass consumerism which capitalist markets had generated under the conditions of world-wide economic expansion – 'the joyous ringing of capital's cash-tills'.[12] Which current would prove dominant in the resolution of the crisis was not a foregone conclusion, as the massive ideological effort on the part of the new right clearly showed. Throughout the 1970s the issue seemed, and perhaps was, still in doubt.

Meanwhile, a generation of workers was also caught in the conflicting currents of consumption and 'de-subordination'. Their discontent took apparently more mundane forms than the burgeoning radicalism of students and the new social movements, yet it was very evident in factories and offices, as well as in youth culture. These young workers did not remember the Depression or have any affinity with Cold War trade unionism. They had been raised in an acquisitive, affluent society in which, they were repeatedly assured, class barriers were being swept away. But the image of the 'high mass-consumption society' held up to them by television contrasted painfully with the reality of life on housing estates and the shop floor. To hope to live like the middle class, they had to act like militant workers: to go in for more militant collective bargaining, the one sphere in which they had some real power. The 'affluent society' thus produced neither an 'end of ideology' nor an end of class conflict. It is true that the two main streams of 'de-subordination' – the 'new social movements' and the militant workers – rarely coalesced, apart from very briefly during the heady days of May '68; but the socialist parties had lost most of their capacity to appeal successfully to either. The radical students, feminists, ecologists, gay rights activists and others mostly looked elsewhere, while the workers mostly treated politics as instrumentally as the social-democratic parties treated them.

The social-democratic parties – compromised as they were by their continuing dependence on private capital accumulation as the engine of economic growth, and by their own absorption into the structures and culture of the state – had lost their ability to resume the leadership of the anti-capitalist currents in society. Their only distinctive governmental strategy to cope with the crisis – corporatism – was consistently undermined by the industrial militancy that the contradictions of capitalism provoked.[13] And when they were in office they found themselves unable to contain the inflationary pressures, and the consequent threat to profits and the balance of payments, which this militancy in turn produced. In office, capital effectively vetoed what the unions demanded in return for the wage restraint that the social-democratic governments wanted to use to curb inflation: effective price and dividend controls, a significant role for unions in determining investment policy, and a redistributive fiscal policy. In the meantime, it became harder and harder to maintain the growth of the 'welfare state', which was in any case administered in a hierarchical and bureaucratic manner, and was often resented rather than loved by those most dependent on it.

It was to this increasingly barren prospect that the resurgent left wing in the social-democratic parties of the West was responding in the 1970s. Even just to preserve the gains of the 'golden age' of the

1950s and 1960s now meant going beyond the compromise that had produced them, and putting socialism back on the agenda. The extra-parliamentary parties of the Marxist–Leninist left – old and new – had failed to make any significant impression. But the social-democratic parties were themselves no longer capable of redefining their relations with the various social movements, or with the branches of the state responsible for both party and state. For this to be seriously contemplated, their structure and culture needed to be radically changed.

The Issue of Party Democracy

The originality of the British new left's initiative lay in emphasising the prime strategic goal: to create a new popular base for democratic socialism. In France, Mitterand's Parti Socialiste Unifié (PSU), in spite of its rhetoric of making a radical break with the 'errors of the past', followed highly traditional lines after it came to power in 1981, both in its relations with the state and in its internal organisation.[14] In Greece, the undemocratic nature of Andreas Papandreou's Panhellenic Socialist Movement (PASOK), from 1974 to 1981, became a byword, in spite of its democratic pre-election promises.[15] In Sweden, notwithstanding the country's relatively open and democratic culture and state practices, the proposal for wage-earners' funds put forward by the trade union movement was not backed by any popular mobilisation; the technocratic and pragmatic wing of the leadership of the Social Democratic Party (SAP) treated the scheme with suspicion, ensuring that it was referred to a series of commissions. During the three-year intervals between party congresses, its contents were diluted to the point where it became, in practice, little more than a forced savings scheme to provide employers with a new source of capital.[16]

What especially distinguished the Labour new left in Britain was its drive to link its version of such an agenda with an attempt to democratise the party – an attempt that Tony Benn argued was necessary in order to extend Labour's representative function so as to bring ourselves into a more creative relationship with many organizations that stand outside . . . to reconstruct the Labour Party so that a Labour government will never *rule* again but will try to act as a natural partner of a people, who really mean something more than we thought they did, when they ask for self-government.[17]

In raising this issue, the Labour new left was taking on the enormous problem that Robert Michels had identified at the beginning of the century: the tendency to oligarchy in mass socialist parties. Conservative parties were elitist and undemocratic too, Michels noted, but this was not a problem for them, since they existed to defend the existing social order. It was a very different matter for parties nominally committed to radical change, if their leaders were able to insulate themselves from pressures from socialist activists and the mechanisms of democratic control provided for in the party constitution.[18] But the issues raised by the Labour new left went further than those raised by Michels, incorporating the nature of democracy in the state itself. As Max Weber had seen more clearly than his pupil Michels, it was through the embrace of the state, even more than through inner-party oligarchy, that the socialist and democratic thrust of the mass working-class party was neutralised: 'In the long run', Weber wrote, 'it is not Social Democracy which conquers the town or the state but it is the state which conquers the party'.[19] In Britain, as observers from R. H. Tawney to Lewis Minkin have noted, the policy of Labour leaders in office quickly became 'to emulate *in toto* . . . the governmental practice of their opponents, playing not only to the existing rules of the game but with the same style as their opponents and, in rapidly increasing measure, for the same ends'.[20]

This assimilation to the routines and perspectives of the British state was the real source of the long-running debate in the Labour Party over the autonomy which the parliamentary party leadership always claimed from the party outside parliament, whose annual conference was constitutionally invested with the 'direction and control' of the work of the party. The leading student of British political parties, Robert McKenzie, advocated changing this provision in the party's constitution, because in his view it was inconsistent with the role the Labour Party had to play as a party of government under the existing rules of the British constitution.[21] Whereas McKenzie saw the passivity of the population between elections as facilitating the autonomy of the party's MPs from extra-parliamentary pressures, Ralph Miliband, in his critique of McKenzie, contended that the proper role of a democracy was to develop the electorate so that it would become 'capable of political initiative through organization, mainly political organization'. McKenzie's argument against party democracy rested on the fact that party members were only a minority of the population; Miliband responded that it was an 'odd notion of democracy that the active minority should be penalized for the apathy of the majority'.[22]

Consistently enough, when the Labour Party's constitution was amended in the opposite direction in 1980, on the initiative of the Labour new left – enhancing the powers of the membership and the conference vis-à-vis the parliamentary party – McKenzie condemned the change. What had to be recognised, he said, was 'that political parties are unique among political organisations in that their leaders must *escape* control of their followers if they are to fulfil their broader role as the principal decision-makers in the political community', which included being able 'to take into account all other interest group volitions and demands'.[23] The Labour left thought that the one set of interests that were not being taken into account with the abandonment of the postwar settlement were those of the working-class majority, and that only if the party was democratised could it act as a countervailing force against the volitions and demands of corporations and the international financial institutions. For McKenzie, of course, 'democratic government' meant the efficient management of the existing social order. For the Labour new left, the issue was whether a transition to socialism could be effected through extending and deepening intra-party democracy, in turn effecting a broader democratisation of society, economy and the state.

Significantly, it was Tony Benn's ministerial experience in the 1960s, and the restrictions Harold Wilson sought to impose on him as a minister, that led him to see the need for the party to concern itself with the construction of 'a different type of state'.[24] What seemed so threatening to the party leadership about the Labour new left's focus on the need for 'a different type of state' was not just whether the leadership would be left free to operate within the rules of the existing state system without having to answer to the extra-parliamentary party. Even more important was whether, as ministers (and even as potential ministers), they should continue to have no responsibility for mobilising popular support for new socialist measures, including measures to change the state – both to broaden its scope and to enlarge the public's role in it.

While the Labour new left's ideas about the changes needed in the state for a transition to socialism were mostly speculative and incomplete, some things were fairly clear. It became evident that public ownership of a good part of the financial sector would be necessary, and that this could not take the form of the mere legal transfer of banks from private to public hands: both the public and the banking workforce would need to have a different kind of relationship to publicly owned banks. At the time of the 1945 nationalisations in other sectors, demands for industrial democracy had been ignored: they now needed to be implemented across the board. This in turn required the party leadership not only to work out new models of public enterprise capable of providing this, but also to work actively to win public support for them. This was the precise opposite of what, following an overwhelming vote in favour of a publicly owned financial sector at the 1976 Labour conference, the government and the union leadership actually did, which was to do their best to discredit the whole idea and bury it. In general, 'a different type of state', related in a different way to a different type of party as well as to the public at large, called for a leadership with a commitment to a socialist project – one that did not see a modus vivendi with capital, with its corollary of a narrow, elitist conception of parliamentary democracy – as the first principle of government.

But what the Labour new left could actually achieve was constrained not only by the need to fight every inch of the way for a few structural reforms in the party – reforms that, far from being very radical, were already common in many Western parties – but also by the inexorable pressure the crisis placed on the Labour governments of the 1960s and 1970s. The leading figures of the new left were so intensely focused on the party that they often failed to think enough about what changing the state in the midst of this crisis would entail. Their focus on changing the party also meant they tended to treat the struggles of the new social movements as secondary. Moreover, the Labour new left contained, inevitably, some sectarian elements which, while never setting its agenda, tended to cause internal friction and limit its appeal. Nevertheless, its efforts led to some important practical examples of more democratic and inclusive forms of self-government, and many creative ideas about how ordinary people could be involved in, identified with and in control of the public sphere. To say this is already to point to a considerable achievement.

The Labour new left's objectives were bound to be bitterly opposed. The defenders of the status quo proved too deeply entrenched, and the struggle too traumatic, for the project to be carried through. Their energies, as powerful as they were shown to be through the 1970s and early 1980s, were exhausted by the mid 1980s; whatever they had to offer to the wider society was submerged in the intra-party conflict. Despite the fact that their attempt to change the party went further than the sceptics had thought possible, the seriousness of their attempt generated a bitter and often far from scrupulous resistance. This meant that, unlike the new right, the new left was unable to reach out beyond the party to the country, to define the crisis in its own terms, or to present a comprehensive alternative – much as some of the original new left had foreseen.[25] The electoral costs for the party were severe: divided parties do not win elections.

The Labour new left's original project was undertaken in favourable circumstances – in the context of a profound crisis of the ruling ideas, in which a significant mass of the population was exceptionally open to new thinking and aspirations. If it was doomed to fail, this was not because of any fundamental inappropriateness of the new left's analysis. In particular, new left thinkers in the Labour Party like Tony Benn and Stuart Holland understood well before their opponents how the globalisation of the economy from the late 1960s onwards was destroying the 'Keynesian capacity' of all nation-states, on which the social-democratic management of capitalism depended.[26] It was this that sealed their determination to try to change the party into one with a different conception of its task. Moreover, in the context of the 1970s – long before capital controls had been abolished anywhere – their proposals for import quotas and tighter controls on transnational company activities, and so on, were far from unreasonable. It is historically false to assert – as even a historian of left-wing sympathies such as Donald Sassoon did – that the Labour left were defeated because they were unaware of globalisation, in favour of a 'siege economy', and 'profoundly conservative' about national sovereignty.[27] Labour's new left had quite clear ideas about both globalisation and Europe; it was perfectly possible – as indeed it still is – to be against the 'Europe of the bankers' while being for strong cooperation among European countries to defend society against being undermined by global market forces. The Labour new left were well aware of the need for international support. But how was such support to be won without first securing it at home?

This kind of criticism avoided all the difficult questions which have to be confronted by those who place the problem of countering the power of international capital at the top of their agenda – and, inside the Labour Party, only the Labour new left did so. But it was not enough for the Labour new left to have rational ideas. The party leadership, besides being much slower to grasp the implications of globalisation, was more committed to the centralised and elitist state than to socialism, while most of the union leadership still believed in the possibility of corporatism. In their struggle against the new left, they had several decisive advantages. In beating back the new left's challenge, the Labour leadership had the wholehearted support of the state (the civil service and the Bank of England, the judiciary, the police and the military); of all sections of capital, from the CBI to the City; and, crucially, of the media. Not just the partisan tabloid press, but all the 'mainstream' media, including the supposedly neutral radio and television channels, were ranged unanimously against Labour's new left, pillorying it as communist, fascist, self-interested, naive and mad, all at once. As the struggle dragged on into the early 1980s, the Labour new left lost the advantage that international conditions had initially furnished. Throughout the industrial West the crisis was being resolved in favour of capital, and the British left could not be immune from the consequences. The international conjuncture was no longer encouraging, and the inspiration that had once also been offered by the examples of left-wing movements elsewhere gradually gave way to the depressing influence of their failures.[28]

For its part, the Labour new left contributed to its own defeat through some major weaknesses. The most important of all was, evidently, that, in concentrating on trying to change the Labour Party, it became trapped in that struggle. It never solved the problem of having to fight for its goals through unending party committees and conferences without becoming absorbed by them. For many it was a point of principle to try to win the party over to a new democratic-socialist project by persuasion and the fullest use of the party's existing democratic processes. But the bitterness of the right's resistance prolonged the struggle over so many years that the energies of almost an entire political generation were consumed in this way. Another problem was that the Labour left was not homogeneous or united in its thinking. There was no broad unanimity. Some elements were sectarian – and by no means only the Militant Tendency. These currents brought some strengths: activists who were class-struggle oriented, capable and tough. Too many of these, however, had undemocratic political habits; and they also tended to speak in terms borrowed from the Leninist or Trotskyist classical literature – a style that made even other activists feel excluded, and was incapable of reaching out to the many people who needed to be persuaded, as Benn could and did.

A related but somewhat different problem was the role of the unions. The Labour new left wanted to see the unions democratised and made into agencies of political education and popular mobilisation; but although they worked to encourage this in various ways, they did not get very far. Yet it is hard to envisage that any socialist project can make headway unless organised labour plays a major role in it. The problem was posed in a very poignant way by the intense industrial militancy of the 1970s: direct action, flying pickets, work-ins, and the like. How could these various actions have been made less defensive and more transformative?[29] Why was it left so much to Tony Benn to point up the links between the issues being pursued by industrial and non-industrial movements? In general, if the future of socialism depended on social movements taking on each other's agendas, what did this mean in practice? Was there any alternative to a political party of some sort taking on the task of fusing diverse issues and struggles into some sort of unity? If not, what kind of party might be capable of doing this, and be accepted in that role? The Labour left did not solve any of these problems; its achievement was only to put them on the agenda for the future more concretely than before.[30]

The project's lasting legacy, however, was its vision of a radical broadening of the public arena, tapping the talent and energy of ordinary people and bringing them into new positions of power and responsibility in the state. No doubt this vision was imperfectly shared, but there is also no doubt that when Benn articulated it he struck a powerful chord: if there was one thing more than any other that unified the drive to change the Labour Party – and, no doubt, also united the centre and right against the Labour new left – it was this intimation that people wanted, needed and deserved a more active role in the government of their lives, that it was no longer safe or acceptable to leave it to a small elite of professional 'representatives'.

Did this conception of democratic socialism expect too much of ordinary people? Did it imply 'too many committees', as Oscar Wilde complained it must? It is very possible that most people in the

Labour new left saw democratisation largely in terms of simply having elected delegates take over functions from bureaucrats.[31] But this was really secondary; what was crucial was to see that the key to any alternative to capitalism lay in rejecting the dominant ideology according to which 'activism' is considered something to be discouraged, and if necessary suppressed. What democratic alternatives there might be to periodic elections of representatives – what other forms of participation, openness and accountability, what alternative expectations and habits socialism might require – were questions that the Labour new left did not have the time or opportunity to resolve.[32] But they did show that finding new forms of democracy is an indispensable requirement for the renewal of the socialist project.

What they did not do was to consolidate their ideas and achievements in any enduring institutional forms. This was partly because they were unavoidably too focused on the Labour Party, which they failed to change; and partly because, whatever they did achieve inside the state – such as Benn's regime in the Department of Industry in 1974–75, and Ken Livingstone's at the Greater London Council – was ruthlessly extirpated. The consolidation of Thatcherism through the 1980s also radically altered people's perceptions of what could be achieved in the short run, underlining the urgency of trying to salvage as much as possible of what was left of the postwar settlement. This led some Labour new left figures, especially those who had always aimed at political careers, to align themselves with the 'modernisers' – a move sanctified by the cultural 'retreat from class' promoted by the Communist editors of *Marxism Today* – whose illusory new 'radicalism of the centre' offered itself as a 'counter-hegemonic' project. It led others, such as most of the Socialist Campaign Group of MPs that had formed around Benn at the height of the intra-party struggle in 1981, and which maintained a genuinely radical stance, to fall back more on those elements within the labour movement whose class politics made them reliable in the hard 'new times' – though often at the expense of side-lining their broader vision.

In 1981, when some of the elements in the party most actively opposed to the Labour new left, led by the so-called 'Gang of Four' former Labour cabinet ministers, went so far as to break away from the Labour Party to form the Social Democratic Party, they famously described their aim as 'breaking the mould' of British party politics. What they meant by this was that Labour and the Conservatives were being pulled towards more and more 'extreme' policies, whereas they stood for a new kind of politics of the centre. But the truth was that what the Social Democrats wanted was precisely to *preserve* the mould of parliamentarist politics, placing themselves in charge. It was the new left in the Labour Party, and the new right in the Conservative Party, who were proposing to 'break the mould' – and it was the latter, led by Margaret Thatcher, who succeeded in doing so.

Thatcher's project, radical though it was by comparison with the postwar regime, was still much less radical than the project of the Labour new left in at least three respects. First, the postwar settlement had left capitalist social relations substantially intact, and since the mid 1960s even Labour governments had been striving to restore the competitiveness of British capital, and, as a means to this end, to break the power of trade union militancy and curb state expenditure. It was under a Labour government, during the 'Winter of Discontent' of 1978–79, that official rhetoric against strikes rose to fever pitch: Labour ministers demonstratively crossed picket lines and suspended civil servants for refusing to do the work of low-paid public sector strikers; and it was a Labour chancellor of the exchequer, Denis Healey, who in 1976 replaced full employment by monetary restraint as the dominant goal of economic policy. In these respects Thatcherism was a continuation of already-established trends.

Second, Thatcher was able to tap into an already significant degree of public disenchantment with public services that were bureaucratic and unresponsive to consumers, as well as suffering from chronic underinvestment due to repeated government-imposed cuts in their spending programmes. There was also widespread alienation from the similarly pinched and too often patronising agencies of the welfare state, and a significant popular current of racism and national chauvinism, to both of which Thatcher successfully appealed. These were not new values, but old ones, tirelessly sustained by the right-wing press and Conservative Party propaganda, and not particularly difficult to exploit.

Third, Thatcherism represented no fundamental breaking of the mould of the British state. With the emasculation of local government and the enhancement of police powers in the 1980s, democratic life became even more exclusively confined to the practice of parliamentary elitism. The dominance of the prime minister's office and the Treasury became more pronounced, as the spending ministries were eviscerated through the transfer of staff and functions to quasi-autonomous, business-oriented 'executive agencies'. 'Atlanticism' became even more marked in foreign and military relations. In all of these areas, Thatcherism was not breaking the mould but reinforcing tradition. The Labour new left project, by contrast, involved breaking with tradition in each of these dimensions. As a precondition, this would require the mould of intra-party politics to be broken as well.

From New Left to New Labour

The defeat of this project by the early 1980s left a Labour Party still functioning, if somewhat convulsively, according to its traditional logic. Under Neil Kinnock's leadership the Labour new left (the 'Bennites'), were marginalised, and key Labour policy commitments – most notably full employment, nationalisation and unilateral nuclear disarmament – were dropped. Kinnock was able to push through these changes with the support of the trade unions, which were suffering a dramatic loss of members and the progressive dismantling of their legal rights, and with the reluctant but real consent of a significant portion of the activists among the party's individual membership, who feared that the scale of Labour's election defeat in 1983 could eventually spell Labour's elimination as a party of government. To save the situation, the party in effect conceded an unprecedented grant of authority to the leader.

But it was not until Tony Blair's election as leader in 1994 that a radical break with Labour's past was undertaken. Blair set in hand a much more radical revision of party policies, symbolised by his successful campaign early in 1995 to replace 'the common ownership of the means of production, distribution and exchange' with flattering references to 'the market' in a new statement of the party's principles. The resulting policy package was widely criticised as lacking any 'big idea', and consisting only of numerous minor reforms. New Labour's one big idea was to accept definitively that global capitalism, and the political power of global capital, was a permanent fact of life, so that 'socialism', if it still meant anything at all, was a set of values that should guide public policy *under* capitalism – nothing more. Yet it was difficult to see anything socialist at all in the proposals that New Labour put before the public; even the reform package offered by the party fell far short of confronting the severity of Britain's accumulated economic and social problems, which two decades of neoliberalism had aggravated, not resolved.

The Labour new left had understood that 'parliamentary socialism', after reaching its apogee in the postwar settlement, had come to an end. The new left wanted to replace it with democratic socialism; New Labour would replace it with parliamentary capitalism. The project of the Labour new left was far more radical in this respect – indeed one might say, far more modernising – than that of New Labour. Indeed, the reason New Labour was so anxious for the Labour new left project to be discredited and forgotten was precisely because of what vision of a better future it could still offer: the fact that a great many people had once refused to take it for granted that the rule of capital was inevitable, and that they could organise themselves politically to change their lives. This was not a message the New Labour leadership were anxious for people to recall. The Labour new left's social base, the characteristic backgrounds of its activists, their diagnosis of the crisis, and their ideas for solving it were misrepresented, caricatured and vilified.

Thus, according to what became the received account of the intra-party struggles that came to a head in 1981, they were caused by the attempt of a mendacious and undemocratic left-wing faction in the Labour Party, out of touch with public opinion, to capture control of the party and impose an impracticable extension of 'old-style social-ism', or 'centralised state socialism', on a profoundly unwilling electorate. These formulations, by Tony Blair and Peter Mandelson respectively, were typical. Blair rightly insisted that the story began in the late 1950s and early 1960s. But whereas he saw these years as the time when 'old-style socialism' became irrelevant, giving rise to the need for the kind of radical rapprochement with capitalism that he and his colleagues now called 'modernisation', it was in fact the new left in the Labour Party which grasped the need for a break with 'old-style socialism' – and a break, too, with the old-style practices of the British state and of the Labour Party itself. In their much-discussed book, *The Blair Revolution*, Mandelson and Roger Liddle described Blair's 'revolution' as a 're-invention' of the Labour Party, and wrote that 'the last time Labour reinvented itself was in the 1930s' (i.e. after the electoral disaster of 1931).[33] What this occluded was the fact the Labour new left had proposed a far more radical reinvention of the party in the 1970s, and that a right-wing faction in the leadership had pushed matters to a split precisely in order to prevent it.

What was at stake here was the rationale and justification for the project of the Labour 'modernisers'. If, as they intended, the legacy of Thatcherism was to be accepted as a kind of 'settlement' (akin to the Conservatives' accommodation to the legacy of the Attlee govern-ments in the 1950s), the Labour new left project of the 1970s and 1980s had to be made, if not historically meaningless, then at least a dead end. If people were to learn to be content with the minimal version of democracy that was all that such an accommodation with 'global market forces' would permit, the promise and significance of this period had to be forgotten. For the special importance of the Labour new left was that it envisaged a much more far-reaching, active and inclusive kind of democracy; it was this vision – which remained its most important legacy, its potential 'communication with the future' – that New Labour's 'modernisers' most needed people to forget.[34]

Although many, if not most, of New Labour's characteristics had been in evidence throughout the whole history of the party, in the past they had always been disputed. However much the party as an arena of class formation and a developer of popular democratic capacities might have atrophied over the decades, it remained the main forum of debate and contestation in Britain about what form the regulation of capitalism should take, and about the continuing relevance of a conception of socialism as another kind of society. The fact that the protagonists in these debates, on all sides, came to be dismissed as 'Old Labour' showed that what was above all regarded as antiquated was the party as an arena of democracy and an incubator of democratic capacities. After 1994, when Blair gained the leadership, it became inescapably clear just how high were the stakes in the internal fight over the party's redefinition as New Labour. The project for a much fuller democratisation of British state and society through a much fuller democratisation of the Labour Party had been decisively defeated. Every previous phase of the party's history had been characterised by struggles between the party leadership and recognisably distinct, organised and programmatically informed left oppositions. New Labour restructured the party so that no room for this seemed to be any longer allowed.

For all the language of 'values' and 'morals' that tripped off the tongues of New Labour leaders when it came to how families were supposed to behave, one of the things that was abandoned in the process of embracing the virtues of competition so fully was the ethical socialism that Labour politicians were always proud to insist had motivated them so much more than Marxism. But, more fundamentally, accepting the leading role of business also involved the abandonment of any aspiration to shift the balance of class forces. However moderate it had been, mainstream social democracy in the postwar era had retained some commitment to this goal; indeed, Anthony Crosland's *The Future of Socialism* was entirely predicated on the achievement of a relative equilibrium between labour and capital and the displacement of business from its predominant position in relation to the government. This strategic orientation had now utterly vanished from the thinking of New Labour's leaders – at a time when the balance was steadily shifting the other way.

This was closely related to New Labour's posture towards the party and the labour movement – which had troubling implications not only for social justice, but also for democracy. The history of modern democracy in Britain cannot be told without the Labour Party. The party could not have come into existence if the vote had not been extended to some working men; and, once formed, it played a major part in the struggle to extend the vote to the great majority of the population who were still denied it. Inextricably bound up with the realisation of democracy was the enhancement of working-class power through the building of institutions through which it could express itself. However parliamentarist the Labour Party's strategic conception was, the institutions of the extra-parliamentary party, with their organic links to the trade unions' own representative institutions, were where working-class people and their representatives met to debate and define the wide-ranging common interests of the class.[35] Under New Labour, the old idea and practice of the party as something separate from government was reduced almost to vanishing-point – a major blow to the substance and process of democracy.[36] The mass socialist and labour parties formed in Europe a century before created institutional means through which working people could develop the capacity to govern their lives collectively, to learn to be active participants in democracy.[37] Little trace of this tradition could now be found in any social-democratic party – least of all in 'New Labour'. The 'modernisers' still spoke in terms of developing capacities; but the capacities they explicitly sought to develop were those of 'entrepreneurship' and 'competitiveness'.[38]

On the other hand, New Labour's project was itself unstable in a world where market efficiency could not be squared with social justice, and where the absence of any real 'third way' meant that the contradictions of capitalism continually and painfully reasserted themselves. By the start of the new millenium, a sense of the need to go further than New Labour declared possible or desirable was spreading well beyond the ranks of Labour 'dissidents' (as the media tended to call Labour members with the temerity to disagree with the modernisers). Outside the ranks of market fundamentalists, there was growing unease in face of the growing social costs of 'market society', and a dawning realisation that defining a new social order in which the market would be re-subordinated to society, and finding a political route to it, was the new millennium's greatest challenge.

After all the hype, some popular disenchantment with New Labour was sooner or later inevitable. What was perhaps more significant was a deeper sense of disappointment that gradually came to the fore among so many of those who had been most enthusiastic about the 1997 election result. There was an emerging awareness that New Labour's break with the past involved repudiating concerns that had been central to the struggle for democracy and social justice in the twentieth century. Even if social democracy has always been mainly about regulating capitalism, the point of the earlier regulation was normally to oppose or limit the power of capitalists, the writ of the market, and the commodification of social life. The type of regulation New Labour engaged in, however, was based on capitalist criteria – or as Blair put it, 'working with the grain of the market'. Whereas mainstream social democrats traditionally saw competition as a constraint on their goals, giving rise to social costs and posing problems that needed to be managed, New Labour actively embraced enhancing market competitiveness as its own main objective.

By 2000, as this realisation grew, there were signs of renewed vitality on the left. When young people around the world, including Britain, who were engaged in mass protests against 'globalisation' increasingly came to style themselves 'anticapitalist', a Labour Party that had closed itself to the idea that there was any future but global capitalism began to look antiquated and incapable of engaging creatively with these new political forces. Given its nature as an elite management exercise, New Labour proved vulnerable to fatigue and loss of direction under the constant pressure of market forces. After 2008, when it became evident to everyone that the New Labour project had been centrally complicit in the making of the global financial crisis, the Labour new left's original project gradually came to be seen in a new light. In the wake of its defeat in the 1980s, many people had lost the capacity to think ambitiously about social change. Once this capacity was revived in the context of the new crisis, the purpose and vision of those who had wanted the Labour Party to become a genuinely democratic-socialist agent of transformation could be better understood and appreciated.

Though it had been roundly defeated, the Bennite left had not been eliminated. However few in number, the Socialist Campaign Group contained those MPs – and prominently among them Jeremy Corbyn, after his election to parliament in 1983 – who, in Alan Simpson's words, 'you would always find on picket lines, at trade union and social movement rallies, on anti-war marches and at the forefront of campaigns to restore rather than exploit the planet'. Looking back on his years in the Campaign Group after his retirement as an MP in 2010, Simpson remarked that it was 'the only bolt-hole of real political thought that I found throughout my parliamentary years . . . It is sad that neither the trade union movement nor the party had the courage to wrap itself around those holding out this bigger vision'.[39]

This lament was written just six months before Jeremy Corbyn's election as leader of the Labour Party. The Labour new left had had no idea how close to bearing fruit their decades of political work had come. There is more than a little irony in the fact that Campaign Group MPs, seemingly thwarted by an electoral system so inhospitable, and a Labour Party so hostile, to socialist renewal, should have ended up in 2015 leading the party. Elsewhere in Europe, as social-democratic governments also embraced neoliberal policies, proportional representation allowed other socialist groupings to recombine in new parties and secure electoral footholds (most notably Die Linke in Germany and Syriza in Greece).[40] Corbyn's leadership campaign, in contrast, would attract so many new members to

Labour that it would become Europe's largest political party. This would never have happened had this handful of socialist MPs abandoned ship and joined in any of the attempts that were made around the turn of the millennium to reconfigure the British left electorally. Alex Nunns's comment, in his remarkable book *The Candidate: Jeremy's Corbyn's Improbable Path to Power*, is apt:

> As they clung on to their place in the PLP by their fingernails, it often seemed scarcely worth the trouble. Many colleagues regarded them as irritants or worse; friends on the broader left thought they were deluded in their fealty to a lost party. But in preserving their political strand within parliament, the Campaign Group kept alive the microscopically small likelihood of a resurgence. Only in retrospect can the significance of their stubbornness be appreciated.[41]

2

The Roots of Labour's New Left: From Modernisation to Democratisation

Who now remembers that 'modernisation', far from being merely a Blairite slogan, was also the central theme of Labour Party discourse in the early 1960s? Or that the efforts of the new left to radicalise the party in the 1970s were themselves a reaction against the failures of that earlier modernisation? It is also easy to forget that the 1970s attempt to radicalise the Labour Party had its roots in a much broader radicalisation – one that the Wilson governments of the 1960s largely ignored or even sought to suppress. As Eric Hobsbawm wrote in 1981,

> Even at the peak of the affluent society and the great capitalist boom, in the middle 1960s, there were signs of real recovery of impetus and dynamism: the resumed strength of trade unions, not to mention the great labour struggles, the sharp rise in the Labour vote in 1966, the radicalisation of students, intellectuals, and others in the late 1960s. If we are to explain the stagnation and the crisis, we have to look at the Labour Party and the labour movement itself. The workers, and growing strata outside the manual workers, were looking for a lead and a policy. They did not get it. They got the Wilson years – and many of them lost faith and hope in the mass party of the working people.[1]

The theme of 'modernisation' emerged as the Labour Party attempted to cope with the three election defeats of the 1950s, and bring to an end the 'wasted years' of Conservative rule. The famous intra-party controversies over Gaitskell's attempt to excise the commitment to public ownership from Clause IV of the party's constitution, and the unilateralists' attempt to excise the commitment to the nuclear arms race from the Atlantic alliance, were set aside in the years preceding the 1964 election. Left and right in the party leadership combined to seek election by adopting a Kennedyesque technocratic modernism (anticipating Tony Blair's 'Clintonism' by thirty years), as well as by striking a corporatist incomes policy agreement with the unions. The Gaitskellite journal *Socialist Commentary*, previously at the forefront of the campaign to downplay Labour's working-class links, now sought to take advantage of the Tories' conversion to an incomes policy by arguing that Labour's modernist and managerial appeal 'can only prove superior if Labour can show that its close alliance with the unions is an asset, which it alone enjoys, and not a liability'.[2] This in fact defined the core of the Labour Party's political strategy under Harold Wilson. It was a vague and contradictory – but glossily packaged – blend of modernity and traditionalism.

Thanks to Harold Wilson's talent for double-talk, the Labour Party approached the 1964 election seeming to some to promise fundamental social change, to others efficient capitalist management, and to most both at once. There was the celebrated invocation of the 'white heat of technology'; there were virulent denunciations of the Treasury and the City; there was an appeal to corporatism ('We shall . . . as a national Party . . . be frank in condemning all those who shirk their duty to the nation. The professional fomenters of unofficial strikes . . . equally with businessmen who cling to out-of-date methods and out-of-date machinery because it yields them profits').[3] And there was a socialist appeal. Wilson promised to replace 'a system of society where making money by whatever means is lauded as the highest service',[4] and in a famous speech 'worked on by Tony Benn' proposed that the 'fundamental inspiration of our social life should be the age-old principle: from each according to his means, to each according to his needs.'[5] Left-wing union leaders like Frank Cousins initially accepted the socialist promise in the 'planned growth of incomes' policy on the grounds that 'Harold says this every time he gets the opportunity. He is wanting to be part of a team that is going to change the system, and the trade union function will change along with a change in the political function; it is bound to do so.'[6] Stalwart socialist intellectuals like Michael Barratt Brown, Royden Harrison and John Hughes in the pages of *Tribune* looked forward to an incomes policy serving as the cutting edge of a socialist strategy. They argued that 'to plan to advance real wages in line with production and at the expense of property-derived incomes is to embark upon the transformation of capitalism into socialism.'[7]

Perry Anderson was more sceptical:

> Wilson above all has offered a strategy to the Labour Party – it is this that has enabled him to temporarily cancel the divisions within it and dominate the party. A strategy for the Labour Party as it exists today, however, is one thing; a strategy for socialism is another. It is precisely in this that so much of the difficulty lies.

Yet even he was optimistic, hopeful that the new Labour government represented a creative new phase in which the liberal and working-class traditions in the party might potentially be brought together to

> touch one of the deepest chords in the British experience . . . the simple idea of democracy, understood in its largest and most explosive sense . . . One of the encouraging results of the new phase inside the Labour Party has been the release of the generous, creative potential of each of these traditions – personified perhaps in men like Benn on the one hand, and Cousins on the other, in the present Government.[8]

And the results of the 1964 and especially the 1966 elections did appear to give the lie to those who had earlier insisted that Labour's electoral base had withered beyond repair.[9] They seemed to confirm Goldthorpe and Lockwood's central thesis, in their famous study of the 'affluent worker' – namely, that there was no evidence for an irreversible 'embourgeoisement' of the working class, with ineluctably negative electoral consequences for Labour.[10] Rather, they argued, the 'instrumental collectivism' of the new working-class communities allowed for a new and potentially more radical working-class identification with Labour. A new generation of working-class voters had come onto the electoral rolls in the 1960s who were more class-conscious than voters who had first entered the electorate before 1929, and in the mid 1960s they did largely opt for Labour. But they were also less class-conscious than those who had become voters in the intervening thirty years, and it was primarily these same new working-class voters who, in great numbers, deserted the Labour Party in the 1970 election.

It was only with Wilson's defeat by Edward Heath's Conservatives in 1970 that a substantial portion of the working-class vote deserted Labour for the first time, with manual workers' support falling from 69 per cent in 1966 to 58 per cent in 1970 (where it stayed through 1974, falling still further, to 50 per cent, in 1979, after a second experience of Labour government). As Mark Franklin pointed out,

The Parliament elected in 1966 provided the first Labour majority in fifteen years that was large enough to have a chance to build upon the achievements of 1945–50. The Parliament of 1966 thus provided the first opportunity for young voters to become disillusioned with the prospects for a socialist Britain. The same election will also have provided the first opportunity in fifteen years for the party to prove to potential supporters from middle-class backgrounds that it was content to govern a mixed society. The latter objective was the one Harold Wilson espoused. Paradoxically, his very success in achieving this objective may have been what cost the party so much support among members of the working class. Young voters may have ceased to see any class difference between the parties during this period, and so become responsive to appeals that were not class-based.[11]

Of course, the Wilson government had little success in actually governing a 'mixed society'. Indeed, the fact that it was content to do no more than try to do so, and that it failed so miserably, was no doubt its – and the Labour Party's – undoing. When the overwhelming majority of 1966 gave Harold Wilson the opportunity to turn his ambiguous phrases into practical policies, the shallowness of his strategy was revealed. Despite all its modernist pretensions, his government displayed 'an almost pathological preoccupation with respectability'.[12] A foreign-relations orthodoxy grounded in Atlanticism and anti-communism was symbolised by the government's support for US policy in Vietnam, and by its readiness to blame strikes on Communist influence ('tightly knit groups of politically motivated men', as Wilson called them during the Seamen's Union strike). An economic orthodoxy inherited from the British Treasury (and policed by the US Treasury) ruled out devaluation until 1967, by which time the defence of sterling had already led to the replacement of the 'planned growth of incomes' by a draconian deflation and a statutory wage freeze. This in turn nullified the corporatist promise that the trade-union leadership would participate in running the economy. Instead, maintaining wage restraint and limiting strikes became the government's most prominent concerns, with dire long-term consequences. Indeed, a plausible case can be made that the seeds of Thatcherism were planted here. As Blackwell and Seabrook put it, 'The public admission by a Labour Government that the only thing wrong with Britain was its irresponsible working class set the tone for the 1970s, and indeed furnished them with their *leitmotif*.'[13]

As the meaning of Wilson's phrases became less obscure, those elements of the working class whose consciousness was 'instrumentally collectivist' drew harsh and cynical conclusions. This was inevitable when real earnings before tax fell in four of the six half-year periods between the 1966 election and the summer of 1969, when the much-vaunted price controls proved laughably ineffective in controlling inflation, and when increases in social benefits did not nearly compensate for the effects of wage controls, inflation and higher taxation on working-class incomes. For the first time in decades the party's opinion poll ratings fell to well below 40 per cent, and local elections proved nothing short of disastrous. Local councils that had traditionally gone together with Labour 'like fish and chips' slipped from the party's control.[14] In Labour's worst local election results in the postwar period, the Conservatives in 1967 took control of the Greater London Council, Bradford, Cardiff, Leeds, Leicester, Liverpool, Manchester and Newcastle, among other cities. In the following year, Labour obtained only 17 per cent of the seats in the London and provincial borough councils and urban districts, and the Tories not only consolidated their gains of the previous year but took Sheffield for the first time since 1932. Labour was left with only four of the twenty London boroughs it had once controlled. Moreover, there was an explosion of 'action group' protest and community-based politics explicitly divorced from mainstream party politics, while an industrial militancy not seen since the early 1920s swept through the working class, most notably among previously quiescent low-paid public sector workers. Although party loyalty, and fear of the sharp rightward shift that was beginning to occur in the Conservative Party, combined to effect a brief recovery in Labour's electoral standing, so that in the 1970 election the party retained 43.1 per cent of the vote, this only temporarily concealed the electoral rot that had set in under the Wilson government.

It was not surprising that a great many of the activists who stayed with the party through this debacle (and even more who subsequently joined it in the 1970s) thought that Labour could only recover if it adopted policies of direct and manifest benefit to working people, and also provided a definition and vision of socialism that would distinguish it from other parties and make it possible for people to identify with. Some of these activists arrived at this conclusion by rethinking (and romanticising) the history of the Labour Party, such as the origins of Clause IV of the Party Constitution of 1918, or the victory of 1945. Others read the *Communist Manifesto* (which by 1968 had acquired a new popularity), in which the immediate aim of all working-class parties was defined as 'the formation of the proletariat into a class' through socialist education and agitation. Probably most of them, like Ken Livingstone (who was nineteen in 1964), drew their conclusions from the best teacher of all – personal experience:

I trembled with excitement on the night of the '64 election. No one need get involved with politics; poverty and bad housing would be abolished in five years. And you would have believed that if you had grown up and never known what a Labour government was like . . . People like myself have shifted to the left not on any theoretical basis but because we have seen two Labour Governments in the 1960s and 1970s fail to deliver . . . The social democrats . . . believe that because they have been educated in middle class homes, gone to university with some sort of academic success, that they have some inalienable right and talent to run the country. And they have run it appallingly badly.[15]

The feeling was mutual. As Labour's new left gained strength through the 1970s and advanced an alternative economic policy – and, more fundamentally, an alternative conception of politics and political leadership – they were seen by the social democrats at the top of the parliamentary party, as Dennis Healey delicately put it in 1976, as 'out of their tiny Chinese minds'.[16]

Various elements converged to initiate the attempt to change the Labour Party after the 1970 defeat – none of them Chinese. Among the amalgam of old and new left activists who had stayed with the party, or joined it, in the early 1970s, very few were Maoists (as in Italy or France), or even middle-class 'polyTrots' or organised 'entrists'; and many of them were as 'organically' linked to the working class as any Labour Party 'intellectual' had ever been. Their social origins were often working class; they were often active members of, or at least had close ties with, a trade union (albeit increasingly a white-collar or public-sector trade union); their political base lay in the working-class communities in which they had grown up, or in which they participated as local Labour Party activists. Moreover, in their lack of deference to established party authority, they were often encouraged by left parliamentarians and trade union leaders. Indeed, to appreciate why so much space opened up for a new left to emerge within the Labour Party after 1970, as well as the constraints faced by that new left in its attempt to change the party, we have to take into account the impact on the party of changes that were already taking place in the trade unions.

'Watch the unions: that's my tip'

As early as the 1965 Labour Party conference, a seasoned veteran of the left like Ian Mikardo could sense a new political radicalism among the union delegations at party conferences and appreciate what this might mean for the party: 'Watch The Unions: That's My Tip', he told his readers in *Tribune*.[17] Hidden beneath the government's control of the conference through its domination of the party's National Executive, an important shift was occurring in the attitudes of the union delegates, which Mikardo had discerned by taking part in the conference's 'extracurricular and extramural sessions' in the bars. This shift led to the party leadership being defeated on many of the government's policies at subsequent party conferences in the late 1960s. During the Attlee years, the dominant right-wing trade-union leadership had often shared the sentiments of resolutions criticising government economic policy, but had always successfully instructed their delegations to vote against them. On this basis the government had been able to treat conference resolutions as votes of confidence and present themselves as taking them seriously. Now, with union discipline seriously attenuated, Labour ministers had to repudiate the authority of the conference, since they had no intention of 'taking instructions' from the extra-parliamentary party, even though it was the organisation that had put their 'team' before the electorate. 'The government must govern' became Harold Wilson's stock phrase, as he suffered a series of defeats at party conferences of a kind Attlee had never known. Significantly, in light of the ideological prison the Cold War had fashioned, the first major defeat concerned Labour's foreign policy. When the 1966 conference voted against the war in Vietnam, and against military commitments in West Germany and East of Suez, this was the 'first time in the history of the Party [that] a Labour Government suffered defeat on major questions of foreign and defence policy'.[18] This was followed at subsequent conferences by defeats on economic policy, above all on incomes policy – a defeat preceded by Frank Cousins's resignation from the cabinet over the statutory wage freeze of July 1966).

But it was not only the government's policies that were being challenged. Also brought into question were the authoritarian manipulation of the unions' block votes by their leaders, appeals to an old mechanical 'loyalty' to the parliamentary leadership, and the notion that the only 'good conference' was one that was well under the control of the 'platform' – which was then still deeply ingrained in the trade-union movement. The shift of much of the union leadership from the defensiveness of the post–General Strike era (subsequently politically reinforced by the Cold War) to the militancy of the 1960s and 1970s had many facets. Not the least of these was the challenge to the old notion that centralised discipline and deference towards the leadership constituted the primary meaning of solidarity.

This change gradually found expression at the level of the unions' national leaderships. Left-wing union leaders were elected in the late 1960s in four of the six largest unions (Jack Jones, Cousins's successor, in the TGWU; Lawrence Daly in the NUM; Richard Seabrook in USDAW; and Hugh Scanlon in the AEU). All four were noted for their respect for shop stewards' autonomy, as well as for having broad sympathy with notions of independent working-class power. This also coloured their political orientations: at conferences of the Nottingham-based Institute for Workers' Control they were critical of 'top-down' models of public ownership, and open advocates of industrial democracy. Faced with the disappointments of the Labour government, new alliances had emerged in some unions between the Labour left and the Communists (most notably in Scanlon's victory in 1967 over the right wing of the Engineering union). Eventually – albeit not until the mid 1970s, as the new left-wing union leaders were careful not to upset traditional voting arrangements between the various unions – this process produced a left-wing majority on the party's National Executive Committee.[19] But even before this, the emergence of 'a new breed of capable left-wing Labour union leaders ... had an immediate impact on the political atmosphere', weakening the intolerant and tightly disciplined power structure – what Eric Shaw aptly called 'social-democratic centralism' – that had prevailed in the Labour Party throughout the postwar period, to the benefit of the right-wing parliamentary leadership.[20]

One immediate effect of the union delegations' new pattern of behaviour at Labour Party conferences was to give a greater political salience to resolutions in favour of public ownership, which, as Minkin has shown, union conferences had continued to pass right through the 1950s and 1960s – albeit somewhat mechanically and with little passion – despite the domination of the Croslandite 'revisionists' in the party.[21] Now, suddenly, during the 1968 conference debate on incomes policy, a resolution was nearly passed declaring 'that the policies of this Government have been and are being dictated by the monopolies and the big financial interests to the detriment of the needs and desires of the working class', and calling for 'taking into public ownership the 300 monopolies, private banks, finance houses and insurance companies', and for a 'socialist plan for production, democratically administered, involving the trade union and Cooperative movement, shop stewards and housewives' committees, scientists, teachers, technicians, doctors and the whole spectrum of working people of Britain'. So little was this resolution taken seriously by the leadership that Barbara Castle, responding for the NEC (and the government), did not even bother to instruct the delegates to vote against it.[22] Yet trade-union support for radical socialist resolutions now became common at party conferences.

This was accompanied by a wave of unofficial strikes throughout the country in the late 1960s, as just one instance of the broader wave of 'direct action' demonstrations that marked the political conjuncture. It expressed a popular mood of exasperation. As real wages fell and unemployment doubled during the late 1960s, and mass redundancies then loomed large in the face of Heath's initial determination in the early 1970s to let 'lameduck' industries go to the wall, and to establish legal controls over worker militancy, direct action escalated beyond strikes over wages. It became political, but primarily in the anarchic sense of 'bugger your laws'. This was reflected in TUC-staged demonstrations against Heath's Industrial Relations Act, and even more in the determined illegality of the 'Pentonville Five' Dockers in 1972, and the sympathy they inspired among activists throughout the labour movement. Even more telling of the mood was the famous occupation at Upper Clyde Shipbuilders in 1971 over threatened closure, the massive support this received, and the fact that it was followed by over a hundred similar occupations between July 1971 and February 1974.[23]

All this fell far short of being a coherent movement for political change. Whether it would have this effect depended very much on the outcome of an attempt to change the Labour Party, which at this point had barely begun. The political significance of the party's vast trade union membership had always been questionable. The number of union members indirectly affiliated to the party had doubled from 2.5 million to almost 5 million when the 1945 Attlee government reintroduced the law requiring individual trade unionists specifically to 'contract out' of paying a political levy as part of their union dues, if they did not wish to pay it. The number then stayed virtually constant until the mid 1970s, hovering around 5.5 million (thereafter rising to nearly 6 million as union membership grew apace in the late 1970s). But this only reflected the steadiness of the unions' institutional link with the party, concealing any trends in the level of individual trade union members' support for, or activity in, the party. Throughout the late 1960s, it was common to see reports of branches voting to disaffiliate from the party because of the actions of the Labour government.[24]

Union journals and conferences were replete with appeals from leaders to their members and branches not to show their displeasure in this negative fashion. Writing in *Tribune* as part of a campaign initiated in May 1968, Jack Jones argued: 'If we were to allow Government policies to destroy the assumption of working people that Labour is *their* party, the result would be ... to put the clock back one hundred years'. Instead, the unions should rely on their industrial bargaining power, so as to 'associate Labour with high wages and high efficiency in industry, not low wages and stagnation'.[25]

And this was the course the union leaders took, as they increasingly declared what had previously been unofficial strikes official. They tried to protect the Labour Party by calling for workers to vote for it, and above all by continuing to finance it; but they also entered into open conflict with the Labour government by at least indirectly supporting 'direct action' industrial militancy.

Not even the controversy over the Wilson government's 'In Place of Strife' proposals in 1969 was enough to spark open conflict between the unions and the party, however. This White Paper, which recommended the introduction of ballots for all strike action and an industrial relations board to manage industrial disputes, was an attempt to curb unofficial strikes, although it was eventually dropped by the government. Even then, the union leadership were concerned to contain the conflict. The 'solemn and binding agreement' they struck with Wilson and Castle over 'In Place of Strife' was specifically designed to avoid a 'civil war' in the party. After 1970, what the union leaders came to insist on was that the corporatist 'partnership' that Wilson had promised in 1963–64 should really be adhered to next time. Cousins had enunciated this in his last speech to the House of Commons, in October 1966: 'I am a representative of a very large union and of a large number of workers who want to help this country out of its economic difficulties . . . They are willing to be partners, but partners whose voice is heard, understood and respected and a voice to which regard is given.'[26] The union leadership did not see themselves as rivals for political leadership of the labour movement, even when they had sharp strategic as well as policy disagreements with the leaders of the Parliamentary Labour Party (PLP). And although many union delegations would eventually come to support constitutional reforms to make MPs more accountable, even left-led unions still respected the autonomy of the party leadership, seeing the way forward in terms of a more effective 'elite accommodation' between the industrial and political leaderships.

This is not to say that the unions were unconcerned with the substance of policy – although public ownership was nowhere near the top of their list of concerns. From 1968 onwards, the TUC had begun to produce its own comprehensive annual Economic Review, in which it set out the rationale of a Keynesian reflationary policy, insisting that government economic planning must extend to external trade and financial flows and embody detailed forecasts and specific requirements for the investment decisions of large firms. On this basis, the TUC was prepared to cooperate in a voluntary incomes policy. It was Jack Jones's insistence on not being sold a pig in a poke, as in 1963–64, together with his spirited commitment to the closing of wage differentials and to strengthened shop-floor bargaining arrangements, which made the parliamentary leadership's independence from the extra-parliamentary party and the broader labour movement look more contingent than ever before.

This insistence came to be institutionalised in the creation in January 1972 of the TUC–PLP–NEC Liaison Committee as the effective final arbiter of party policy. It was this insistence on a real 'social contract' from the mid 1970s that would give Michael Foot his prominence in the next Labour government. As the leading Bevanite to be left out of Wilson's 'team' in the 1960s, Foot's opposition to the incomes policy from 1966 onwards had been based not on opposition to the principle of statutory wage restraint, but on concern over the breach it had created with the left union leadership after Cousins's resignation.[27] Foot became in the 1970s what Tony Benn accurately called the parliamentary leadership's 'link and buckle with the industrial wing of the trade union movement';[28] and Foot's retention of this politically crucial role into the 1980s proved, as we shall see, critical to the ultimate defeat of the new left's attempt to change the Labour Party.

The priority that even the left trade union leadership still attached to securing a 'real' partnership with the parliamentary leadership placed limits on how far change in the party could go in the 1970s. Nevertheless, their pursuit of this goal and their general ideological outlook encouraged both rank-and-file activists and the left in the PLP to make their own mark on the party. The ties between the left trade union leaders and the left-wing Tribune Group of MPs were close. The unions' refusal to allow a pre-election incomes policy

agreement to be offered as an electoral reassurance to 'received opinion', as most of the leadership would have liked, meant that a more
comprehensive economic programme had to be fashioned instead,
and this helped to undermine the policy hegemony of the parliamentary leadership. Perhaps most important, however, was the new union
leaders' greater tolerance for dissent in the party, based on their view
that radical socialist activists were part of the labour movement's
'family' – rather than its enemies, as the revisionists and right-wing
leaders in their own unions had for so long insisted.

The New Activists

By the end of the 1966–70 Labour administration it was obvious
that the Labour Party was in the throes of a severe membership
crisis.[29] Until then it was by no means clear that the party had been
in worse trouble than other European social-democratic parties.
Only the Swedish and Austrian parties managed to maintain a significantly higher ratio of party membership to the total electorate
throughout the postwar era.[30] To be sure, it was a sign of the bank-
ruptcy of Labour's leadership that the staggering membership growth
between 1945 and 1952 (when individual membership more than
doubled to 500,000) had not been used to establish anything like the
social-democratic hegemony achieved by these two sister parties in
the political life of their respective countries. The leadership barely
concealed its view that the membership was an increasingly bother-
some and antiquated device for electing its team of parliamentary
leaders. Crosland had said as early as 1960 that 'the elan of the rank
and file is less and less essential to winning elections. With the growing penetration of the mass media, political campaigning has become
increasingly centralised; and the traditional local activities, the door-
to-door canvassing and the rest, are now largely a ritual.'[31] By the
1990s, such a view would become widespread, yet the scale and
speed of the collapse of membership that occurred in the mid-to-late
1960s could not be treated so lightly.[32] Patrick Seyd and Lewis
Minkin's view is hard to dispute: 'The greatest depletion took place

in 1966–70, during the Wilson government ... A combination of social change, neglect and political disillusionment almost destroyed the Labour Party as a mass party. In terms of ward and committee attendance – and electoral work – activity was the lowest in living memory.'[33]

The important point, however, is that this decline in Labour Party membership and activism did not mean a decline in political activism generally. On the contrary, there was a virtual explosion of activity at both national and local levels.[34] From squatters' to tenants' associations and Shelter, from community action groups to the Community Development Projects, from the Vietnam Solidarity Campaign to the Irish Civil Rights Solidarity Campaign, from local student activism in schools and universities to the Radical Students' Alliance and the Revolutionary Socialist Students' Federation, from the sixty local women's groups federated in the Women's Liberation Workshop to the National Joint Action Campaign for Women's Equal Rights, from AgitProp to CinemaAction, from Black Voice to the Gay Liberation Front, from *Black Dwarf* to Poster Workshop – and, not least, from the International Socialists to the International Marxist Group and Big Flame – the new politics were everywhere to be seen. Marjorie Mayo's retrospective view of this frenetic period of radical politics was apt:

> Amongst the new left radical intelligentsia there was at the time a mood of often totally unrealistic optimism about the possibilities of radical change ... coupled with a pervasive scepticism, not only about the nature of the state and officialdom, but also about traditional organizations and political parties of the left ... Simultaneously, there was a tendency to romanticize and overidealise the 'poor' and their possibilities for radical action ... Student politics and then the women's movement were seen, along with community action ... as short cuts to creating a new radical movement whilst bypassing the struggles of the traditional parties and the organizations of the working class and the labour movement.[35]

Nevertheless, a discernible drift towards joining the Labour Party did begin in the early 1970s, especially among young community activists who started to take a more pragmatic view of alliances with trade unions in anti-cuts campaigns, and to develop a more sophisticated view of the state than the term 'cooptation' allowed for. As the limits of 'direct action' and sectarian politics became clearer, and as the technocratic planning and limited participation of local Labour council administrations in the early 1970s quickly produced disappointments, a more radical and determined set of activists joined the Labour Party. It is true that most of these new activists were also 'new middle class', although they tended to be teachers or social workers (or studying to be such) rather than in management or public relations. But, like the two-thirds of Labour's middle-class voters who had working-class origins,[36] so did most of the new activists.

The orientation of the new activists produced varying reactions at the top. In 1969 Ron Hayward had been appointed the party's national agent, following Sara Barker's twenty-seven years of authoritarian rule in this key position. It was an appointment that signalled a shift to the left on the NEC, and a more open and tolerant intra-party regime. It was further strengthened when Hayward was appointed general secretary of the party in 1972. In January 1971 Hayward wrote a fascinating editorial in *Labour Organizer*. It began by relating a conversation he had had with 'Old Bill', chairman of a ward party, who had complained about a new member in his party. 'The first time I set eyes on him I knew he was up to no good', said Old Bill, 'you can't trust him, never ought to be in the Party, he's a ruddy Leftwinger ... First time he came to the Ward meeting, he questioned my ruling on selecting our local government candidate and he's been throwing questions at me ever since.' Hayward, with his long experience as a party organiser, recognised a general syndrome:

We all pay lip service to recruit new members into the party ... But, if we are going to 'tie labels' around their necks at first sight or after hearing their first views, then we ought not to pretend that we believe in 'democracy', 'communication' and 'liaison' ... We should encourage the cut, thrust and parry of debate. We should talk more politics at our meetings and not spend so much time on Minutes, Matters arising, jumble sales and Any Other Business ... The clobbering of a member usually new to our ranks, is the only bit of life this type of party shows from year to year.[37]

The call for working instead to defeat 'our political opponents who are *outside the ranks of our Party*', which Hayward made here, would become a familiar refrain on the centre and right of the party in the years to come. But if we are to understand the history of the attempt to change the Labour Party, we need to remember that the call was first issued in support of new left-wing activists joining the party in the face of resistance, offered by the old guard at both the national and local levels, to the pressures that began to be exerted by constituency activists in the 1970s.

The case that became most visible in the early 1970s (and that, incidentally, set a new pattern for media bias against constituency activists) was the conflict between the Lincoln Constituency Labour Party and its MP, Dick Taverne. The immediate issue was Taverne's stand in favour of Common Market entry, and his having voted with the Conservatives for it in the Commons in 1971 along with sixty-eight other Labour MPs, in defiance of both Conference and PLP policy. But what was involved here was far more than just an isolated case of the 'individual conscience' of an MP. The way Taverne had first been adopted, in 1961, as Lincoln's parliamentary candidate, itself spoke volumes about the hypocrisy of the Gaitskellites in their attacks on the left's allegedly undemocratic factionalism. Taverne had been a prominent member of the Gaitskellite Campaign for Democratic Socialism, which had worked undemocratically behind the scenes to ensure the selection of a number of Gaitskellite MPs throughout the 1960s.[38]

Nobody on the left was proposing that Taverne should be drummed out of the Labour Party for his role as a factional organiser, but his constituency party had had enough of him as their MP. After the 1970 election, fierce arguments between Taverne and his local party had already broken out over the Conservative government's new Industrial Relations Bill. After he defied the Labour whip on the Common Market, his GMC finally voted in June 1972 to ask him to retire at the next general election. Taverne was in fact the *only* one of the sixty-nine MPs who had voted with the Tories to be dismissed by his local party, although many other CLPs were extremely upset by their MPs' behaviour. But the media, as well as much of the PLP, played up the Taverne case as proof of the 'intolerance' at the base of the party. This was already a strong indication that the subsequent attempt to subject sitting Labour MPs to reselection would be treated as 'undemocratic' – an attitude that would prove a major barrier to the effort to change the Labour Party.

Nevertheless, the case set an important precedent. Taverne's resignation as MP in October 1972, forcing a by-election in which he stood successfully against the Labour candidate, revealed to many activists and trade unionists that the party loyalty of right-wing MPs was highly conditional, to say the least. Perhaps more importantly, however, the Taverne case showed that it was by no means only the old 'entryists' or even new party activists alone who were going to challenge their MPs. The Lincoln constituency was led by long-standing party members, many with impeccable trade union credentials. They had experienced at first hand the 'social-democratic centralism' that had governed the party through the postwar era. 'Not surprisingly', as Shaw remarks, 'the sudden fervour with which disciplinarians from this period embraced "tolerance", "the rights of minorities" and "the rights of dissent" when *they* found themselves in the minority was treated with cold scepticism by left-wing veterans of the Bevanite wars.'[39] As the new left inside the party made common cause with political activists of all kinds outside the party through the 1970s, it became increasingly clear that they were a force to be reckoned with – even before their politics found a voice in the person of a leader with vision and talent.

Tony Benn: Articulating a New Socialist Politics

In the early 1970s, the politics of the new left activists in the Labour Party were still relatively inchoate. The movement had not thrown up any nationally recognised leaders of its own, or developed any independent organisational focus. But one political leader heard what the new left was saying and expressed it in a way that gave it a clearer shape and purpose. What enabled Tony Benn to do this – to become the pre-eminent spokesperson and interpreter of Labour's new left – was his remarkably early perception of the political forces that would eventuate in Thatcherism, his understanding of the limits of parliamentary socialism as practised by the Labour Party, and his articulation of an alternative conception of socialist practice. It is a mistake to put too much emphasis on the role of any one individual; but it is also a mistake to deny it when an individual's significance is exceptional – and not least when such an individual, and the politics he articulated, have been systematically misrepresented. Even sympathisers with the Labour new left have tended to misrepresent it in retrospect as merely 'clinging to the old formulae'.[40]

Although Benn played the leading role in articulating the Labour new left's politics and getting its agenda debated in the cabinet and shadow cabinet, as well as in the party executive and its committees, the main organisations that composed the Labour new left were not built around him.[41] Even in parliament, no 'Bennite' faction of MPs emerged, as the 'Bevanites' had in the 1950s. Benn's role was not as the organiser but as the tribune of the Labour new left – its 'prominent voice'.[42]

Benn had always been an iconoclast in relation to both the traditional left and the traditional right of the parliamentary party, but he had hardly been seen previously as a dissident, much less as a radical socialist. He had stayed in the 1964–70 governments throughout, first as minister for the Post Office and then in the more senior office of minister of technology. But by 1968, in a series of speeches, he had already begun to show clear signs of his passage from radical liberalism to radical socialism by an unusual route: experience of the limitations and frustrations of high government office. As he began articulating with great clarity – and, as it soon turned out, with great commitment – what was at stake in changing the Labour Party, and through it the British state, it was not his espousal of more state intervention (or of Clause IV) that made an impression on the new activists. If this was all there had been to it, he would have appeared indistinguishable from the old Tribune left, or from the Communist Party. Perhaps only someone who had precisely *not* been integrated into the traditional Labour left could have understood so clearly not just that socialism was the necessary extension of democracy, but also that, *if* democracy was to fulfil its radical promise, then 'our long campaign to democratise power in Britain has, first, to begin in our own movement'.[43]

In this respect, it was already significant that, whereas Wilson seemed proud to assert that he had never read Marx, Benn was ashamed that he had not done so to any significant extent, and would try to remedy this in the 1970s, even while a minister – reflecting the view he came to by 1973 that a socialist party without Marxism 'really lacks a basic analytic core'.[44] Two decades later, in reaction to a 'New Labour' leader in the 1990s who peppered his speeches with sneers at Marx, Benn commented: 'When Labour leaders have said that Marx is dead, it's a bit like saying Galileo is old hat, or Darwin got it wrong, or Freud muddled things up'.[45]

But Benn's experience as minister in the first Wilson governments did not make him a Marxist. What it did was to make him increasingly uncomfortable with the contradictions between his radical liberal and democratic populist orientations and the technocratic strategy he had helped to construct as part of Wilson's team. He was finding it increasingly hard to escape the conclusion 'that parliamentary democracy, which is our proudest boast, is not working in this country'. As minister for the Post Office, Benn had encountered strong opposition (on even such a minor if imaginative proposal as 'establishing a Fellowship to study the way the Post Office might provide a link between the social services and those in the community who need their help'), not just from officials in his own department, but also from an alliance of officials across several departments. Coordination between Labour ministers could overcome such networks of bureaucratic reaction, he was convinced. But this involved first having

a really dynamic political party that is elected knowing the difficulties that will face it and determined to get control of the Whitehall machine and really use it to carry through fundamental changes. I just don't believe that this impetus exists within the Labour Party or within the Labour Cabinet ... We are going to go on floating, governed by civil servants with Ministers from the two parties coming in and out by a curious quirk known as the electoral cycle.[46]

There was still a further problem, beyond the absence of policy direction in the cabinet and bureaucratic resistance in Whitehall, and this was the incapacity of the state in relation to the structures of the economy, including not only the City of London but also manufacturing industry. This had already been recognised by Frank Cousins, who, shortly after he resigned his post in the Wilson cabinet in 1966, expressed his frustration to the House of Commons that as a minister he had had very little power over private corporations, not least because he depended on them for the information that determined state policy: 'I saw the type of planning we did ... I could get better facts related to the growth prospects of some of the major companies through my position as General Secretary of the Transport and General Workers Union.'[47] Benn eventually came to the same conclusion.

It was for these reasons, and not because of any dogma, that Benn also followed Cousins in becoming much clearer and more determined about the necessity of public ownership of the 'commanding heights' of the economy. Yet there was a still-deeper lesson that each of these two men had learned from their experience at the top of the state – namely, that their role in managing the economy precluded them from continuing to act as political leaders of the class that had put them in office. Any attempt to defend that class in its struggles ran fundamentally against their function as ministers. It was when he saw this clearly on the issue of wage controls that Cousins had resigned. Benn felt he was forced to face up to it when he was required to deal with the obstreperous employees of the firms he was so 'hooked' (as he put it) on merging in order to produce the internationally competitive corporate giants the government saw as the salvation of Britain's export and productivity ills:

> I have never forgotten the day I was sent by the cabinet up to UCS ... I got up at four in the morning, and I got there before light and went to the shipyard, and it was a foggy day and I climbed on one of the cranes and addressed the people, because I always liked to do it direct. I said 'look we're pouring money in and you've got 18 per cent absenteeism'. And some guy shouted at me: 'If you had to stand in an open yard with cold metal on a foggy morning like this you'd be absent most of the time.'[48]

Benn set out his thinking in 1970, in a Fabian Society pamphlet entitled *The New Politics: A Socialist Reconnaissance*. Unlike the Tribune MPs who focused on Clause IV, Benn preferred to leave the question of economic policy aside for the moment. For him, the real issues had to do with democracy – not only how to fashion intra-party democracy so as to ensure that leaders, once elected, still played the role of party leader while they were in government, but also how leaders, both inside and outside the state, could help to build the kind of mass popular support for and involvement in radical social change. Benn's starting point was the extra-parliamentary militancy of so many new activists, and the meaning this had for democracy. He thought it had been triggered not only by the heightened expectations produced by the rising incomes and collective bargaining strength of the postwar boom, but also by the higher levels of education and training that had improved people's analytical capacities, and by the media revolution that had given people an unprecedented mass of information about current affairs and exposure to alternative analyses of events. He repeatedly pointed to 'the thousands of . . . pressure groups or action groups [that] have come into existence: community associations, amenity groups, shop stewards' movements, consumer societies, educational campaigns, organizations to help the old, the homeless, the sick, the poor or underdeveloped societies, militant communal organizations, student power, noise abatement societies . . . ' He saw in them 'a most important expression of human activity based on issues rather than traditional political loyalties, and [they] are often seen as more attractive, relevant and effective by new citizens than working through the party system'.[49]

But he recognised at the same time that this was only one side of the picture. Far in advance of later commentators, Benn noted as early as 1970 an

> alternative philosophy of government, now emerging everywhere on the right, [taking] as the starting point of its analysis that modern society depends on good management and that the cost of breakdowns in the system is so great that they really cannot be tolerated and that legislation to enforce greater and more effective discipline must now take priority over other issues. The new citizen is to be won over to an acceptance of this by promising him greater freedom from government, just as big business is to be promised lower taxes and less intervention and thus to be retained as a rich and powerful ally. But this new freedom to be enjoyed by big business means that it can then control the new citizen at the very same time as Government reduces its protection for him.[50]

This was a most serious reaction, Benn contended, to a situation where people were showing that, by banding together collectively in a myriad of new organisations with clear objectives, they could win surprising victories on given issues against large and centralised corporations and governments that were increasingly vulnerable to dislocations. But without a radically different kind of democracy, the structures of power would remain intact: 'If the people have so much potential power why do those who enjoy privileges seem to be able to hold on to them so easily? The awful truth is this: that it is outdated concepts of parliamentary democracy accepted by too many political leaders in Parliament and on Local Authorities, which have been a major obstacle ...'.[51]

It is important to remember that, throughout the ensuing struggle, Benn continued to insist that he 'passionately' believed in parliamentary democracy, and that all the great achievements of the left had come about by pressures from below which had made 'the parliamentary system serve the people rather than the vanity of the Parliamentarians'.[52] While he showed throughout the 1970s and 1980s that he was prepared to support direct action against laws hampering democratic or egalitarian pressures, he insisted that this did not entail a break with parliamentarism. He was convinced that 'the debate between extraparliamentary violence versus parliamentarism ... is highly diversionary'. Where there was no democratic route to change, there was a moral right to revolt; but where democratic popular organisation and parliamentary change were not prohibited, socialist strategists could not pretend these means were ineffectual – to do so was to adopt 'the pessimism of the ultra-left', which he refused to share:

> My criticism of those who call themselves revolutionaries is that they speak as though reform had been tried and failed. Reform hasn't been tried ... I don't think there are any real revolutionaries in Britain. There may be dreamers, but there is nobody on the left who is actually planning and preparing themselves on the assumption that the transfer of power will come by revolution.[53]

Meanwhile, following Labour's 1970 election defeat, the main focus of the Tribune Group of MPs, and particularly of Michael Foot, was raising the issue of public ownership again. They returned, in other words, to reviving the old debate of 1959–60 over more or less nationalisation, which Wilson had bypassed by attaching the Labour Party to his vision of the 'scientific revolution'. But, in so far as the left-wing Tribune MPs were determined to make a call for more public ownership in the next manifesto the key issue, the question

was not about the number of firms to be targeted for public ownership, but how Foot's promise that the conference would force the
PLP to 'do it' could be realised. Mikardo, Frank Allaun and Jim
Sillars wrote a Tribune Group pamphlet in July 1972 which took up
the issue of the accountability of Labour representatives at all levels,
including as its 'most important proposal' the election of the leader
by the whole party at the annual conference, not just by the PLP.[54]
This broad line of argument was endorsed by thirty-eight other
Tribune MPs, but Foot's name was conspicuous by its absence from
the list; this was because he was already in the process of trying to
mend the left's fences with the parliamentary leadership. He strongly
opposed an inquest after 1970 into the mistakes of the Labour
government.[55] As he explained in 1972: 'It was a dangerous moment.
The Left within the Labour Party could have demanded a grand
inquest on all the delinquencies of 1964–70, could have mounted a
furious attack on the leadership.'[56] From the moment when he
became shadow leader of the house, in 1972, his crucial role became
that of repairing the frayed bonds of trust between the parliamentary and trade union elites. His objective was to prevent dissension
within the party, so as to present a united parliamentary front
against Heath's government, which he saw as the 'most hardfaced
Conservative government since Neville Chamberlain'. This overarching concern with party unity led him to oppose, not encourage,
the forces that now began to try to change the Labour Party.

Benn, as we have seen, took the opposite tack. He had come to the
view that it was necessary to reconceptualise the role of the Labour
Party in relation both to the explosion of organisational activism in
the country at large, and to the new conservatism that he believed
heralded something more profound and more dangerous than a
throwback to the Tory Party of the 1930s, let alone than what Heath
represented. In so far as most of the new progressive forces had
developed outside the Labour Party, this had much to do with the
fact that the party's internal democracy was 'riddled with the same
aristocratic ideas as deface our national democracy'. He therefore
saw the problem of achieving greater party democracy as crucial.

Most of the reforms proposed in the 1972 Tribune Group pamphlet Benn had already raised in his October 1971 Fabian Society lecture. All the sensitive constitutional issues were there: the process for selecting parliamentary candidates; who should elect the leader and deputy leader; and the accountability of cabinet members, MPs, local Labour groups, councillors, and trade-union delegations ('those who exercise this massive voting power should be accountable to their own members for the use they make of it').

The series of speeches Benn now embarked on making to as many groups as possible, inside the party and beyond it, were to become a hallmark of his style of political leadership. He kept an annual tally of the hundreds of meetings at which he spoke, and it seemed that he partly judged his success as a politician in these terms. This was consistent with the role of motivator and educator, rather than legislator and decision-maker, which he now ascribed to political leadership. His leitmotif was giving people a sense of their own power and encouraging them to use it. Many of the new activists were suspicious of his 'conversion', given his association with the previous government. Similarly, when Benn spoke at trade union conferences in this period, his insistence on applying the principle of democratisation to their own structures produced some discomfort among his audiences. At the 1972 Trades Union Congress, Benn made the following argument, hardly one the union delegates were accustomed to hearing from a chairman of the Labour Party bearing fraternal greetings to their annual congress:

It is simply not good enough to blame the Labour Government or the Parliamentary Labour Party entirely for our defeat in 1970. The Trade Union Movement, with all its virtues, must also accept its share of responsibility. Until very recently, the unions have hardly made any serious effort to explain their work to those who are not union members, even to the wives and families of those who are. You have allowed yourselves to be presented to the public as if you actively favoured the conservative philosophy of acquisitiveness. The fact that the Trade Union Movement came into being to fight for social justice, as well as higher wages, has just not got across. If the public opinion polls prove nothing else, they certainly prove that. Finally, neither the Party nor the TUC has given sufficient support to other movements of legitimate protest and reform . . . The lower paid, the unemployed, the poor, the old, the sick and the disabled, *expect* the Labour and Trade Union Movement to use its industrial and political strength to compensate for their weakness.[57]

But Benn went even further in challenging the unions. In his 1971 Fabian lecture he had explicitly connected the issue of union democracy to that of party democracy. The 'same thread of accountability' applied to the unions as to party representatives, and the 'same question should be asked about the representative system within the trade union movement in respect of the big political decisions in which they participate in annual conference'.[58] For a Labour politician to tread onto the sensitive ground of the defects of the unions' internal organisational structure, let alone their economism, was dangerous indeed. Yet in doing this he was to some extent taking his cue from key union leaders. Jack Jones, in particular, was a very vocal advocate of democratisation in the party in the late 1960s and early 1970s, and did not dissent when Benn pressed him on the undemocratic nature of the block vote that the unions still exercised at the party conference, whereby a single union leader cast the votes of all the union's party-affiliated members.[59]

As the Heath government drew to an end in a direct political confrontation with the unions over 'Who Governs Britain?', Benn again revealed the sharp divergence between his strategic approach and that of the rest of the Labour leadership, now including Foot. The shadow cabinet scrambled to get a last-minute form of words from the unions that would promise a clear commitment to voluntary wage restraint. This would have made it easier for them once again to run an election campaign that deflected attention from the underlying issues by merely claiming that Labour would secure industrial harmony and price stability where the Tories could not. Benn's own approach was very different. He sided with the unions in insisting that wage restraint should have binding conditions attached, to the effect that in return the government really would prosecute socialist policies. This was the very thing that made the rest of the senior Labour leadership most defensive in the face of the press and Tory charges that they were beholden to the unions. Benn simply refused to adopt this defensive posture. What Benn had come to see was that, on the ideological terrain of politics conducted through the mass media, the Labour Party simply could not pretend, in the context of the industrial militancy of the 1970s, that it was not a working-class party. An apologetic and defensive approach to the attack on the unions might work in the short run, but was bound to make it even more difficult to evolve an adequate long-term political strategy. The search for such a strategy was thus the essential next step for the Labour new left.

3

The Limits of Policy:
Searching for an Alternative Strategy

According to conventional wisdom, the most significant aspect of the shift to the left in the Labour Party after the 1970 election defeat was primarily on economic policy.[1] The policymakers in the eighty-odd committees and study groups that toiled at Transport House (which was then still the headquarters of the party, as well as of the Transport and General Workers' Union) between 1970 and 1974 were indeed mainly preoccupied with the hitherto underappreciated power of multinational corporations; and this question did eventually play a key role in defining the thrust of the Alternative Economic Strategy (AES), which was an important part of the Labour new left's programme. But what was most original in its thinking was that – however hesitantly, and initially in an uncoordinated manner – it began to address the structure of power in the party.

The left, through the party conference, was trying to get the leadership to develop a radical strategy, in terms of not only an economic programme but also an outward-looking campaign to mobilise support for it. In response to Roy Jenkins's claim that 'Socialism is just a slogan',[2] Brian Sedgemore (then a councillor in Wandsworth, elected as an MP in 1974), captured the orientation of the extra-parliamentary party when he told the 1971 conference that there was indeed 'a crying need in this party for someone to translate the abstractions of economic control into concepts that people can understand – growth, leisure, participation, responsibility, the environment – and to translate them in such a way that makes them not just moonshine, but something which is eminently and imminently practical'. But how could this be done when the party's own leadership was not interested in a socialist strategy, considering it irrelevant or even harmful?

How could public ownership possibly become popular with the electorate, Sedgemore asked, 'when our own leadership steadfastly refuses to discuss, still less to support . . . such ownership?'[3]

It was not a fetishisation of the conference, but an attempt to overcome this problem that led to a new struggle to assert the sovereignty of the conference over the PLP. This is why the most important issues brought onto the Labour Party's agenda in the early 1970s pertained to the adequacy of the vehicle, not just the adequacy of the policy. And it was Tony Benn who was to play a leading role in this. As chair of the NEC he was a key player in the selection of Ron Hayward as general secretary in January 1972. Hayward had told the NEC that adherence to Clause IV and the power of the conference would be his dominant considerations. Benn himself also ensured that the NEC's 1972 programme proposals went out to delegates so they could frame resolutions in light of it. That this was an innovation said a great deal about the traditional centralist workings of the party.

That said, it is important to stress that, at this time, 'the preliminary agenda of the party conference with its approximately 500 resolutions and amendments was remarkable for its spontaneous character'.[4] But few groups inside the party attempted to stimulate or coordinate resolutions from the constituencies; and without concerted action and an organised means of monitoring and publicising what happened to the resolutions that were passed, or of keeping the pressure up with further resolutions and intra-party mobilisation in support of them, successful radical resolutions, even if they enjoyed apparent NEC endorsement, could be watered down if not simply ignored. It was left to the closed meetings of the NEC and its committees, and the particular balance of left and right within them − where the 'left' was in any case not necessarily the same sort of 'left' that had produced the conference resolutions in question − to determine party policy. Indeed, a motion at the NEC by Benn, calling for NEC motions and votes to be published as minutes in the party's Annual Report, was set aside − after being attacked vehemently by Michael Foot.[5]

One group that did organise to ensure that certain resolutions reached the conference agenda at this time was the Militant Tendency.[6] It was smaller than rival Trotskyist organisations on the British left, but its steadfastly 'entyrist' determination to work within the Labour Party (the 'mass party of the working class') had given it a presence in a few CLPs, and in the leadership of the Labour Party Young Socialists. When the NEC finally dropped its List of Proscribed Organisations in 1973, formally ending the Cold War regime in the Labour Party, this gave Militant more room within the party, but it remained quite small in relation to the Labour new left. It also had a purpose and practice that were very different. Militant saw the industrial strategy of Stuart Holland and Benn as the merest reformism, in contrast with the revolutionary intent of its own resolutions, calling for the nationalisation of the top 250 corporations, which it consistently managed to get onto the conference agenda. The cynicism with which Militant leaders regarded Benn was indicated by their frequent designation of him as 'Kerensky'. Unlike most of the Labour new left (but rather like Scargill or Ted Knight), Militant's leader, Ted Grant, had no time for notions of industrial democracy, or for seeking links with pressure groups and social movements. Indeed, Militant's doctrine (what Hilary Wainwright termed its 'Marxism pickled in Labourism') contradicted almost everything that defined Benn's 'new socialist politics'.[7]

The Debate over Economic Policy

The primary strategic concern of the left on the NEC, led by Benn and Mikardo, was to use the resolutions on socialist policy passed by the conference to strengthen their hand in relation to the parliamentary leadership in the preparation of the party's programme. It is important to stress that the resolutions on public ownership and industrial democracy were not, for the most part, advocated in terms of returning the party to its tradition, but, like the constitutional reforms, were concerned to pull the party out of the failed patterns of its past behaviour in government. The emphasis on industrial democracy was very much propelled by a critical attitude towards the statism of Labour's public ownership tradition. The tone of the debate at the 1971 conference was set by Brian Sedgemore, who addressed not only the problems of the 1964–70 governments, but also the mistakes of 1945, when, almost by accident, Clement Attlee's government modelled the nationalised industries on Herbert Morrison's water boards.

> Was it any wonder that what we got was not what people wanted or expected, but centralised bureaucracies run by broken-down generals, bankrupt private industries bailed out by the taxpayer, and managements responsible neither to workers, consumers or Parliament? Public ownership suffered a blow from which it has never recovered and, worse, the Party ran scared and has continued to run scared ever since.[8]

But after the 1972 conference the left on the NEC's Industrial Policy Committee also proposed that twenty leading manufacturing companies, one of the major banks, and two or three of the leading insurance companies should be brought into the public sector. This proposal, along with others for an 'industrial powers enabling act' to be administered by a powerful Trade and Industry Department, and for an 'industrial commissioner' who might be put in to assume control of a company that sought to frustrate the objectives of the government, was incorporated into the draft of *Labour's Programme 1973*, which passed the Home Policy Committee and went to the NEC in May of that year, despite vociferous opposition from Tony Crosland and others.

It is important to understand clearly what impelled the left to specify the twenty-five companies as a minimum figure for public ownership. The reason for doing so was the knowledge that the social democrats in the PLP were opposed to pursuing an electoral or governmental strategy that even remotely reflected the spirit of the party conference in this period. The aim was to try to tie down the leadership and oblige it to comply with the general direction of policy established by the conference. As Mikardo explained at a Tribune rally at the 1973 conference:

> The fact is that those who wanted twenty-five companies written into the policy were not really advocating the nationalization of just twenty-five companies. In normal circumstances one would have said that the proposed National Enterprise Board has got to take a big slice of the economy and continue to add to it. Why did anyone seek to quantify at all? It was there because there was a lack of confidence in the leadership.[9]

And with good reason. The predominant feeling on the shadow cabinet was not only that the programme would ensure an electoral disaster, but that rejecting Keynesianism in favour of direct impositions on capital represented an 'ideological' throwback to a bygone era. In the shadow cabinet, Benn alone offered a strong defence of the document. Given that he, along with Mikardo and Hart on the NEC, made the case not in terms of a specific number of companies, but in terms of the need for a commitment to a strategy of quick and broadscale intervention, the majority in the shadow cabinet thought the NEC would drop the twenty-five companies from the programme. Such a calculation may well have been partly based on the fact that, in a very important indication of what was to happen under the next Labour government, left-wing union leaders put no pressure on the party leadership on this issue. Indeed, Jack Jones told Benn that he ought to concentrate on pensions rather than this 'airy-fairy stuff' of nationalisation, and that it was too late to try to convert the Labour Party into a socialist party. This was a remarkable volte-face, given the positions he had previously taken and supported at both party and union conferences. It led Benn to conclude that Jones had 'settled down into a central position which could at best be described at the moment as the Healey stance'.[10]

Yet, despite being willing to offer some concessions to the new left, such as over the National Enterprise Board, Wilson was unwilling to accept the twenty-five companies proposal. In the end, however, it was saved by the Conference Arrangements Committee, which, in the run-up to the 1973 conference, and following a long-standing practice of selecting the most far-reaching and radical resolution in order to minimise the chances of a specific commitment being passed, put together an amalgam of Militant-inspired resolutions that specifically endorsed the twenty-five companies proposal, but attached it to an additional call to nationalise 250 major monopolies. The left had been outmanoeuvred. Benn, in the unhappy position of replying to the debate for the NEC, had to endorse the two general resolutions and oppose the Militant one, which he did on the grounds that the 250 companies figure 'confuses strategy with tactics'. In his speech Benn tried to use this episode to offer a reminder of what the attempt to change the Labour Party was all about:

If we are only concerned to win the votes we shall never mobilise the strength we need to implement the policy ... We are offering much more than legislation. We are offering a perspective and a vision which will transform the political atmosphere of cynicism which has developed in recent years. Without a vision people will turn to their immediate and narrow self-interests. With some sense that they are part of a change in our society we shall be able to draw much more from them. We must mean what we say and say what we mean and not run for cover when Fleet Street turns upon us. I must say this quite seriously to conference: if it looks tough now it is as nothing to the roaring attack that will descend on us as we seek to carry through this programme ... We are saying, at this conference, that the crisis that we inherit when we come to power will be occasion for fundamental change and not the excuse for postponing it ... In light of that, it is not the drafting but the will that matters.

He forbore to add what he very well knew: that as far as the parliamentary leadership was concerned, the will was not there.[11]

Containing the New Left in Government

The closest Labour's new left ever came to occupying a key strategic position in state power was in the first fifteen months after the February 1974 election, when Wilson was returned to Downing Street as prime minister of a minority government (a second election in October gave Labour a bare majority of just three seats). Benn became minister of industry, with Eric Heffer as his minister of state and Michael Meacher as his parliamentary undersecretary. Francis Cripps, Stuart Holland and Frances Morell – all leading members of the new left – were appointed as political and economic advisors. The way they operated in the department in some ways also provided a model for later Labour new left policies in local government. But the Labour government as a whole had a very different complexion. The composition of the new cabinet reflected that of the shadow cabinets which immediately preceded it, with the centre-right in the majority. Although Benn hoped for some support from ministers who were already called 'soft left', like Foot, Peter Shore and Eric Varley, he knew that most of the cabinet would oppose all his proposals, and he soon felt as isolated as he had been in the shadow cabinet before the election.[12]

As a result, Labour's election victories in 1974 (such as they were – even the second 1974 election in October did not give Labour a secure majority in the Commons) made it possible for those who had stood on both sides of the debate in opposition to claim electoral plausibility. After all, the two election manifestos of 1974 had in fact faced both ways: beckoning towards the Labour new left's policy while at the same time defending the old Keynesian compromise as the way forward. The Labour new left's view – increasingly strengthened through the 1970s as Margaret Thatcher moved up in the opinion polls with her own radical reaction against consensus politics – was that the old policies could not work, and that it was on the basis of their failure that Labour would end up being judged electorally. Survey evidence provided support for this, as Paul Whiteley remarked in pointing to the strong correlation between a declining

Labour vote and rising levels of unemployment and inflation (especially the former) under Labour administrations:

> Solemn declarations in the party manifesto and resounding declarations during elections may influence some voters, but for most the Labour party performance is what counts. If radical socialist policies were to bring performance successes, particularly in the economic field, they would become electorally popular. If centrist policies fail, as they have done for the most part during Labour's tenure in office, no amount of moderation will bring electoral success. Butskellism in practice has been tried and found wanting, and it remains to be seen whether the alternative strategy of the left, if given a chance, can bring the success the party needs if it is to survive.[13]

But the bulk of the parliamentary leadership were determined not to give it a chance. They could not quite hide the new left's project from view, but neither were they prepared to do more than attach it, as a weak addendum, to the last chance they briefly gave to Keynesianism before they abandoned even that. The policy symbols associated with the social contract and the industrial strategy were retained as a minimal index of the government's ties to the party and the unions; but once in office the Labour leadership framed and administered these policies in a way that emptied them of all radical content.

The fate of the Labour new left's industrial strategy then depended on Benn's determination to maintain his freedom to campaign on key issues despite being a cabinet member. If the strategy was to have the slightest hope of making an impact, it had to be popularised – especially among workers. Benn had explained this to the 1973 conference, as we have seen, and his argument there was underscored by the fact that a subsequent poll commissioned by the party just before the election showed that the National Enterprise Board proposal commanded the clear support of only 6 per cent of Labour voters. On the general question of more nationalisation, the poll gave more hope (37 per cent in favour), but this paled beside the degree of support for pension increases (74 per cent).[14] It was obvious that the majority of the cabinet would use such polling figures to confine the interpretation of the social contract to the narrowest redistributive terms. It was thus crucial for Benn and his team in the Department of Industry to use the legitimacy and the resources that state office provided to spread the word about the industrial strategy, and to build support among the unions and in popular opinion, if a decision by a cabinet hostile to its spirit was to be avoided. It might not work, but it had to be tried: why else were they ministers, and what else were they in the Department of Industry to do? In any event, the industrial strategy was party policy and in the election manifesto. Benn was minister of industry, charged with implementing it. The question was only how far he would be able to use his mandate to accomplish any really significant change.

Virtually the first change Benn sought to inaugurate in his department was to complement its previously exclusive ties with business with close ties with the unions. He was appalled at the ignorance of his officials regarding the union bureaucracy, let alone the shop stewards' movement. (One of his favourite stories was of their blank look when he made a reference to consulting the CSEU – the Confederation of Shipbuilding and Engineering Unions, perhaps the most powerful union body in industry). His goal was to make his department's ties with the unions as comprehensive as those of the Department of Employment, and he immediately appointed a trade union adviser to be available to all his ministers and officials in the department. He made it clear in a paper on the industrial strategy, submitted to the Labour Party–TUC Liaison Committee in May 1974 ('A Note on the Current Work of the Department of Industry'), that his intention was to cleave very closely to Labour's 1973 programme – and that discussions with the unions on their role in making and administering planning agreements, and on experiments in industrial democracy, would be central to developing a framework for what he clearly intended to be the first really serious effort at economic planning in Britain since the war.

But to leave matters here, however much it might have strengthened the British state's previously weak and unstable corporatism
and brought it closer to Sweden's, was inadequate and potentially
even counterproductive. A close association with the union leadership alone would give the appearance of trade union power without
necessarily developing enough mobilisation behind it to make the
unions an effective force in support of the industrial strategy. So
Benn's paper also stressed the need for a national political campaign that had to go well beyond discussions with leaders of the
TUC and CBI:

> The policy changes outlined above, when carried through, will
> represent such an important development of policy that *there is no
> chance of success without a long period of public explanation,
> debate, consultation and development.* Apart from highly political
> comments in the context of the Labour Conference and the General
> Election, very few people really know what the programme says or
> what the argument is all about.[15]

Overcoming this would involve meetings throughout the country
with representatives of local trade unions and employers' associations, with local authorities, and with 'shop stewards and gatherings
of working management whose support is essential if our policies are
to succeed'. Only in this way would it be possible to 'isolate real
opponents from others who might not be opponents'. At the Liaison
Committee meeting, while Jack Jones and Hugh Scanlon 'sat silent',
Wilson declared that a public campaign based on Benn's paper was
'certainly not a vote winner'. Benn retorted that, while he did not 'for
a moment think we shall have the support of our opponents', he had
personally fought the election on this.[16] Although his cabinet colleagues would not say so in front of the union leaders, the legitimacy
that Benn derived from quoting the party's election manifesto, or
from pre-election speeches by Wilson himself, cut no ice with most of
them. According to Benn, Jim Callaghan told him later, in the privacy of the Cabinet Industrial Policy Committee: 'You can't write a

Manifesto for the Party in opposition and expect it to have any relationship to what the Party does in Government. We're now entirely free to do what we like.'[17]

Wilson's response to Benn's attempt to initiate a public campaign on the industrial policy was to take direct control over the cabinet committee that would receive the Green Paper being prepared in Benn's department by Eric Heffer's working group. When it was submitted, enshrining all the major policies of *Labour's Programme*, and somewhat further radicalised in tone by Benn, it was promptly rewritten, to become the very different document published in August 1974 as a White Paper entitled merely *The Regeneration of British Industry*.[18] The new hand was Michael Foot's – writing, as Wilson put it, 'within the parameters we laid down', so that it was no longer 'a sloppy and half-baked document, polemical, indeed menacing, in tone, redolent more of an NEC Home Policy Committee document than a Command Paper'.[19] The new version was actually far more half-baked, but it was certainly no longer menacing. The planning agreements were to be only voluntary as far as companies were concerned, and in any case they were to play a less prominent role than the National Enterprise Board, which was itself scaled down in terms of the finances it would command, and above all in terms of having to operate, as Wilson had demanded, within normal 'Stock Exchange procedures', so that it had 'no marauding role' via powers of compulsory acquisition. As for its tone, *The Regeneration of British Industry*, whatever else it was, was certainly not a campaigning document for mobilising a working-class assault on the prerogatives of capital. In this way the battle over the industrial strategy was effectively lost in the summer of 1974.

From this point on, the role of the new left ministers in the Department of Industry, and of Benn in the cabinet, was effectively one of damage-limitation. This lasted until Heffer and Benn were removed from the department by Wilson in the spring of 1975. The occasion (or more accurately the pretext) for this was their stand on the Common Market. Although the idea of holding a referendum on the issue was Benn's, the tactic of concentrating the Labour left's

stand on the issue of opposing the Common Market was characteristically Foot's. Foot was prepared to sacrifice the industrial strategy
in the hope of holding the Labour leadership to withdrawal from
the Common Market, and that his hope of doing so was based on
the extensive support this had within the PLP itself. But the compromise that was struck on this, whereby Labour committed itself
to renegotiation of the terms of entry, to be followed by a referendum, had worn thin by the time of the October 1974 election result.
It was clear that Wilson and Callaghan's conception of renegotiation did not extend to challenging any of the provisions of the
Treaty of Rome.[20] When the renegotiated terms were announced in
March 1975, leaving the basis of Britain's membership substantially unaltered, only seven cabinet members announced that they
would publicly dissociate themselves from these terms in the referendum campaign (Foot, Benn, Castle, Shore, Silkin, Varley and
Ross), while the other sixteen would line up in favour. The junior
ministers split evenly, as the PLP very nearly did itself, with 137
Labour MPs voting with the Tories in favour of staying in, and
145 against.

All this spoke volumes about the weakness of the Labour left –
old *and* new – vis-à-vis this government. Foot and the 'soft left' had
refused to join Benn and Heffer in a campaign on the industrial strategy, but Benn and Heffer were ready to join Foot and the soft left in
a campaign against the Common Market. In relation to the struggle
for extending democracy that was so much a part of the Labour new
left's agenda, it was very much to the point to address critically
'the democratic deficit' that marred (and still mars) Europe's
political institutions. The apparent victory the anti–Common Market
forces secured when a special party conference voted two-to-one in
favour of the No campaign was more than offset by Wilson's successful veto against the party throwing its organisational resources
and electoral machine into the campaign. Wilson's insistence that
'the party machine must remain neutral' was challenged by Benn
alone; Foot and Jones demurred.[21] With the dissenting ministers left
mainly to their own organisational resources, with the 'Britain In

Europe' campaign outspending the anti–Common Market 'National Referendum Campaign' by more than ten-to-one (the largest donation to the NRC came from the TGWU: the princely sum of £1,377), and with Labour supporters confused by the division in the party, the outcome was scarcely surprising.[22]

Nor was it surprising that it was interpreted inside the cabinet as legitimating the complete marginalisation of the Labour new left inside the government, despite the fact that the campaign had obscured rather than clarified differences over economic strategy. Wilson had already sacked Heffer for speaking in the Commons against the renegotiated terms in advance of the campaign, and immediately after the referendum Benn was dismissed from the Department of Industry.[23] Both Foot and Jones urged Wilson not to do this. Jones had warned Wilson publicly that this would be 'a grave affront to the trade union movement'; but, as with so much else that had gone before, in the event neither Foot nor Jones did anything to mobilise party or union opposition to it.[24] Still convinced of the futility of resignation, Benn accepted Wilson's decision to switch him to the Department of Energy, while Eric Varley replaced him at the Department of Industry.

But Benn's demotion had little to do with the Common Market, as the contrary fate of the other dissenting ministers, and notably Varley, clearly showed. Rather, it had everything to do with the way the centre-right of the cabinet, the senior civil service and business circles saw Benn's socialist commitment. With the spectre of another sterling crisis taking shape from the beginning of 1975, 'whispers from the Treasury's contacts grew stronger', as Joe Haines tells it. 'Only if Tony Benn was sacked, it was said, would the confidence of British industry be restored. If confidence was restored then industrial investment would begin again.' Haines, no great left-winger himself, added: 'It is astonishing that this sort of naivety is expressed by otherwise intelligent men.'[25] Neil Kinnock angrily warned in *Tribune*: 'The appeasement, like most appeasements, won't work. Those who demand the change will simply ask for more. But we are now in the extraordinary and dangerously undemocratic situation where our foes have a direct influence on the selection of Labour Ministers.'[26]

In March 1976 Wilson resigned. In the PLP leadership ballot for his successor, the right-winger Callaghan emerged victorious over Foot, while Benn obtained only 37 votes before throwing his support behind Foot in the second round. This outcome registered several facts. The new left's project had been sustained in the cabinet only by Benn, whose influence on policy was effectively neutralised by Wilson (with the support of the rest of the cabinet), the civil service, and media and business opinion. Crucial to this outcome was the fact that the union leadership had failed to give serious support to the industrial strategy. It was becoming more and more clear that, without a democratisation of the party – and the unions – this was the logic of Labour's parliamentary socialism in practice.

But, contrary to the judgement of contemporary observers like the *Guardian*'s Peter Jenkins, the defeat of the left inside the parliamentary party did not mean that the social democrats had triumphed. On the contrary, what the social democrats inside and outside the cabinet had yet to grasp was something that both Labour's new left and the Thatcherites, from very different perspectives, had already understood – namely, that the postwar mode of social-democratic regulation, combining Keynesian fiscal policy with a corporatist 'social contract' between business and labour, had become unsustainable. In the month before Wilson passed the torch to Callaghan, the government had announced the freezing of public expenditure in a White Paper detailing the most extensive cuts in social spending ever undertaken at that point in the country's history. Not only would this be followed by two further packages of massive cuts in public expenditure by the end of the year; the new leader would also bluntly tell the 1976 party conference, in what would immediately be seen as a 'defining moment' speech, that public expenditure, once seen as the solution to economic crises, had now become their cause. Burke and Cairncross, in their study of the 1976 IMF crisis, effectively described the illusion under which the social democrats were labouring:

By March 1976 ... the moderates and right-wingers in the Cabinet ... felt they had made hard decisions and choices and were now on the path to recovery. What they were on the brink of was a major exchange crisis, as a result of which the markets virtually refused to lend money to the Government. This combination of crises would ultimately force the government to make a public recantation of some cherished economic and political beliefs.[27]

In other words, it would force them to abandon Keynesianism.

Contesting Labour's Abandonment of Keynesianism

It is important to distinguish between the government's rejection of the Labour new left's economic strategy and its reluctant but definitive abandonment of Keynesianism. The 'hollowing out' of the left-wing policies that successive party conferences had endorsed cannot really be attributed to resistance from the opposition parties, senior civil servants, the CBI, the City, the IMF, the American state, the media, the Treaty of Rome and the Brussels bureaucracy, or even the anonymous international financial markets, although such resistance there certainly was. Most of the Labour leadership had always anticipated such resistance, and long before incorporated it as part of their justification for persisting in the 'art of the possible'. But when maintaining this accommodation with capital involved them having to renege on their Keynesianism, most of them were not anticipating powerful forces, but yielding to them, and they knew it. Indeed, they found it hard to credit that things had come to such a pass.

While rejecting and even ridiculing radical left alternatives directed at challenging these forces, the leadership helped to make credible Thatcher's claim: 'there is no alternative'. Their acceptance of defeat by the monetarists also precipitated a new and far more determined effort by the new left in the Labour Party to tackle the causes of their marginalisation in government. The abandonment of Keynesianism, even more than the rejection of the new left's policies, was what accounted for the tenacity and increasing sense of urgency with which the Labour new left mobilised right through the 1970s – and even while the government was in office – to attempt a fundamental redefinition of the relation between leaders and activists.

It was in the wake of Wilson's resignation – at the height of the 1976 IMF crisis, in the context of renewed and widespread selling of sterling – that his replacement, Jim Callaghan, issued a fulsome proclamation of the death of Keynesianism. That he did so at the Labour Party conference was seen on all sides – and not least by bankers in the City of London and on Wall Street – as having particular significance:

> For too long, perhaps ever since the war, we postponed facing up to fundamental choices and fundamental changes in our society and in our economy ... We used to think that you could spend your way out of a recession, and increase employment by cutting taxes and boosting Government spending. I tell you in all honesty that that option no longer exists, and that in so far as it ever did exist, it worked on each occasion since the war by injecting bigger doses of inflation into the economy, followed by a higher level of unemployment as the next step ... Now we must get back to fundamentals.[28]

There should be no underestimation of the contribution this Labour government made, as it sought to justify its policies, to legitimating the notion that 'there is no alternative' to monetarism, both within Britain and internationally. It did so, above all, by burying the fact that an alternative existed which Benn had repeatedly put forward to the cabinet right through 1975 and 1976. This 'Plan B' drew not only on the industrial strategy developed through the party's policy committees in the early 1970s, but also on the broad debate that had already emerged among socialist economists and other intellectuals on the nature and viability of an alternative economic strategy. As Andrew Gamble put it two decades later, it was 'the first clear sign for a generation that serious strategic thinking about socialism had re-emerged on the British left'.[29]

On 25 February 1975, after organising a large meeting of officials and advisers at the Department of Industry in January, Benn presented to the cabinet's Ministerial Committee on Economic Strategy a paper drafted by Francis Cripps. Entitled 'A Choice of Economic Policies', its Strategy 'A' described all too presciently the path the government was about to follow: it comprised 'tax increases and public spending cuts; some form of enforceable pay restraint; and the further transfer of cash to the company sector', which would lead to 'heavy deflation, rising employment, cuts in real wages and the withdrawal of support from the Government by the TUC and the Labour Movement'. Strategy 'B' outlined the famous Alternative Economic Strategy in twelve points, the first of which certainly was in political terms the most important: '1. A full explanation by the Government to the nation of the reason for the crisis – that is to say it is a world slump related to a failure to invest, and not just the fault of the unions.'[30] Among the specific policy proposals that followed the key ones were (a) selective import restrictions and the rationing and allocation of some imported materials, and (b) the extension of controls on capital outflows and control over banks and other financial institutions.[31] In light of the need for import and capital controls, Benn invited his colleagues to consider whether the Common Market was, as Roy Jenkins believed, 'a life-raft or whether we were being tossed into the deep in a straightjacket'. He recognised that strategy B would 'strain international relations, strengthen middle class opposition and impose some stress on relations between the Labour movement and the Government'. But the course the government had embarked on would 'merely deepen the existing social divisions'. As he undoubtedly expected, the paper did not receive a warm response from Healey and Wilson.[32]

The AES also took shape publicly in February 1975, in the form of a Spokesman pamphlet, *An Alternative Economic Strategy for the Labour Movement*, written by three leading members of the Institute for Workers' Control, John Eaton, Michael Barratt Brown and Ken Coates. They had all been 'involved in urgent discussions about the need for, and content of, an alternative strategy for the labour movement to that being pursued by the present government'. While very similar in content to what Benn had presented to the cabinet committee, the pamphlet made it clear that the strategy was not being presented to the movement as 'a policy statement', but was being proposed as a 'line of march' and as 'a basis for discussion, amendment and urgent appraisal'. The centre-right inside and outside the party alleged that the strategy was a recipe for a 'statist economy'; but its authors actually saw it as a response to the crisis that would lay the basis for a 'democratically controlled economy' involving popular participation at all levels through the unions, as well as 'workers' organisations in production and many other forms of people's organisations in the communities and at the grass roots ... supported by research teams from Universities, Polytechnics and other institutions of higher education and, to a limited extent, schools.' This presumed that the capacity could be developed for a 'new kind of economic management' that would entail extensive institutional change (not least, it was stressed, in the unions) and 'a considerable amount of supporting "educational" activity ... with Government backing'. It did not shy away from insisting that the 'main cost of a democratically controlled economy is active involvement of people themselves everywhere', but argued that this cost would come to be recognised as a benefit when 'social production is made thereby a much more stimulating activity and much less a drudgery of work'.[33]

Aided by more detailed papers drafted by Cripps, Benn continued throughout 1975 and 1976 to make the argument in the cabinet that the course the government was following – involving both wage restraint *and* accelerating cuts in public expenditure – would guarantee that there would be no return to full employment within its term of office, and that this 'economic nonsense' would lead to 'political suicide', which could be temporarily staved off only by recourse to a coalition government. Even soft-left ministers referred to this disparagingly as his 'familiar theme'. Benn, said Foot at a key meeting at Chequers in June, was 'dodging the issue' that the country's main problem was inflation, and the best way to defend the unions was for them to have a policy that worked to stop it.[34] Benn, of course, was not opposed to an egalitarian incomes policy (including wage restraint by those sections of the working class best placed to secure money wage increases in the crisis).[35] He also accepted that 'public expenditure may need to be re-planned in the full employment context and even cut back, especially where high import content may be shown to exist'.[36] But what Benn understood (and what the published versions of the AES at the time also made explicit) was that a policy of deflation through a fall in real wages and public expenditure cuts, besides being unjust, could not solve 'the deep-rooted and many-sided sickness of the economy', and would have the long-term political effect of making the unions and public expenditure scapegoats for the economic crisis.

Without endorsing Benn's alternative strategy, Foot, Shore and Crosland would eventually take up the demand within cabinet for restrictions on imports. The economic case for this was being strongly advanced at the time by the 'New Cambridge' group of economists associated with Lord Kaldor, Francis Cripps and Wynne Godley.[37] It accepted the need for a reduction in the budget deficit (mainly by means of tax increases), but insisted that import controls were required to prevent unemployment from rapidly rising even further, and to limit what would otherwise have to be a severe deflationary policy that depreciation of the exchange rate on its own would not be sufficient to offset. The problem was political, not technical, as Kaldor indicated when, after resigning 'dispirited and disillusioned' from the Treasury in August 1976, he leaked the information that the Treasury had – 'locked away in a cupboard' – a complete plan (known as 'the unmentionable') for exchange as well as import controls.[38]

One could not proceed very far with an alternative strategy, in other words, without confronting the power of the City, the Treasury and the Bank of England over the issue of control over financial markets and banks. Addressing this not only gave greater coherence to the Labour new left's alternative strategy, but went to the heart of an alternative *explanation* of the crisis by linking the analysis of

Britain's industrial decline, to which the radical industrial strategy was a response, to the diminished ability of states to control the burgeoning new financial markets. Although Benn spared no effort in trying to put this kind of alternative before the cabinet, he was under no illusions that he could carry the argument at that level. It was not only a matter of trying to take on the Chancellor, who had the whole technical and statistical apparatus of Treasury behind him (as well as the key support of the prime minister throughout); the whole make-up of the Cabinet was against it. While branding Benn's AES unrealistic, because it would not get through the cabinet, Foot had to admit that even his own limited proposals on import controls were very unlikely to get through either. Benn later recalled having told Foot a month before the run on sterling that 'monetarist ideas had embedded themselves in the heart of the government'. Foot lamely disagreed, saying the problem was not having a working majority. Benn replied:

> Look, it isn't because we haven't got a majority, Michael. You know that as well as I do. It's because the Cabinet doesn't believe in the policy. If we had a majority of a hundred we wouldn't implement it . . . The position is really this. We can't expose our strategy fully because in fact our strategy is to fight inflation by increasing unemployment, to pretend that we're keeping prices down when we're really trying to get prices and profits up, to pretend we're defending the public sector when we're really trying to cut it back.[39]

The problem was compounded by collective cabinet responsibility, prohibiting the promotion in public of any alternative explanations of the crisis – explanations which Crosland and Benn understood to be crucially important for the mobilisation of support for alternative policies. As early as February 1975, Wilson had forbidden any minister from speaking publicly about import controls. Even to write an article that included reference to the 'anarchy of capitalist markets that had developed after 1970' was considered inappropriate for a government minister.[40] And the problem was made even worse by the fact that the TUC – despite the resemblance of its annual economic reviews to much of the AES, not to mention overwhelming Congress votes for resolutions calling for import and capital controls – did little or nothing to explain or popularise the ideas behind these policies.

In February 1975 Benn had expressed the hope that the extra-parliamentary party would be able 'to use this crisis to break out of the circle of deception which lies at the heart of parliamentary labourism'.[41] Eighteen months later he told the 1976 conference that the Labour government's failure was not just one of policy and administration. It was a failure even to attempt to articulate a social-ist discourse that would explain the crisis of capitalism through which working people were living, and identify the forces that were resisting a progressive solution. In saying this, Benn was once again expressing the view of many activists who were organising them-selves within the party to challenge the autonomy of the parliamentary elite, and also trying to practise a new kind of politics at the munici-pal level. As energy minister during the final years of the 1976–79 Labour government, Benn certainly tested the doctrine of collective cabinet responsibility to the limit, and beyond, by using his chair-manship of the NEC's Home Policy Committee to vigorously promote alternative policy proposals.[42] And while he had to be care-ful not to dissent too openly on economic policy, he defied censure in a great many public speeches, calling for freedom-of-information legislation and curbs on the security apparatus to break through the impenetrable wall of secrecy behind which political and administra-tive decisions were taken. This increased the hostility of his cabinet colleagues. Callaghan, like Wilson, was more than once on the verge of firing him, but held back in view of the political risks entailed in making him 'a martyr in the cause of inner party democracy on such a key issue'. Benn's public campaign for 'open government' as the only way of making the state accountable to a democratic public certainly reinforced the lesson that many activists drew from the practice of this Labour government on the importance of intra-party constitutional reform.

Encouraged, no doubt, by the actions of Benn and the NEC during the course of the 1974–79 Wilson and Callagan governments, the feeling among party activists was not one of disillusionment and despair, as it had been in the late 1960s. On the contrary, there was a new mood of determination which, for the first time in many years, focused the broader left's attention on the possibility of changing the Labour Party. But with Thatcher having so effectively articulated an 'authoritarian populist' market ideology, precious time had been wasted. Many of those working-class voters who had opted for Labour in 1964 and then abstained in 1970 (see Chapter 2, above) had by 1979 responded positively to Thatcher's definition of the causes of their frustration and alienation. While the Labour new left's attempt to formulate an alternative economic strategy was an achievement, and deserved the attention it received, the political conditions for realising such a strategy were not in place. The formation of the Labour Coordinating Committee in 1978, by a group close to Benn, was undertaken with the explicit purpose of popularising the AES, while the Conference of Socialist Economists became linked through a number of working groups with the party's research department, with the result that in 1978–79 the contours of the AES were considerably elaborated. What was crucially important about this elaboration was its explicit concern not only with economic policies but also with the development of strategies for engaging in struggles 'in and against the state' – struggles which would be directed at democratising state services and agencies.[43] The development of this strategic orientation formed part of a broader attempt on the part of a remarkably creative British Marxist left at the time to transcend the limits of both Labourist parliamentarism and Trotskyist and Leninist vanguardism.[44]

But this was hardly sufficient to offset the Labour Party's incapacity to act as an effective vehicle for articulating and popularising an alternative strategy. The lesson many activists learned from the limited turn to the left that had taken place in the early 1970s was thus that the party had to be made into such a vehicle before anyone could plausibly expect fundamental change from a future Labour government. Even before the Labour Party went into opposition in 1979, the activists' determination and organisational capacity to bring this about were stronger than they had ever been. But they overestimated the significance of the changes they would be able to secure in the party's constitution, and underestimated the strength and determination with which parliamentary paternalism would be defended, and the lengths to which the parliamentary elite were prepared to go rather than concede anything to the new politics.

4

A Crisis of Representation:
The Conflict over Party Democracy

The Campaign for Labour Party Democracy (CLPD) – which for a decade became the core organisation of perhaps the most determined movement for radical intra-party reform yet seen in any social-democratic party – was set up in June 1973 in direct response to Harold Wilson's public declaration that the shadow cabinet would 'exercise its veto' immediately after the NEC's vote to include a commitment in Labour's 1973 *Programme* to take twenty-five companies into public ownership. This proposal, as we have seen, reflected the widespread distrust among party members of the leadership's commitment to the more radical policies that the party conference had adopted in the early 1970s. The activists who founded the CLPD did so because they 'felt the need to counter the moves which would merely ensure the repetition of the sorry tale of 1964–70'.[1]

Their decision to concentrate exclusively on issues of intra-party democracy throughout the 1970s was partly a pragmatic one. By sticking to 'a strictly formal democratic platform' the CLPD hoped that 'party members and trade unionists holding very different views on policy issues could unite in support of this vital democratic reform.'[2] But the CLPD's resolute abstention from campaigning on issues of policy during the 1970s should not obscure (and certainly did not, in the eyes of most observers) the fact that the CLPD's founders and activists were committed socialists like so many others in the party, motivated by the turn to the left that produced the party's 1973 Programme, and especially by the provisions in it that involved public ownership and controls over capital. When in 1986 the CLPD finally produced its first major policy pamphlet it was entitled 'The Case for Public Ownership',[3] and was aimed at resisting the policy reversals initiated by Neil Kinnock after he replaced Foot as leader in 1983. In the eyes of CLPD's founders, however, what distinguished it from other left groupings was that that the latter 'do not attempt to win the support of the majority, or, if they believe that this is what they are doing, the methods they choose to adopt to pursue their basic aims ensure they are not realized'.[4]

This perspective was very clearly outlined in a paper written in 1988 by Vladimir Derer, who ever since he became the CLPD's Secretary in 1974 remained the most important figure in the organisation. 'The basic problem of the Left', Derer argued, was 'its unwillingness and therefore inability to come to terms with the political environment of bourgeois democratic institutions which constitute the framework for political activity'. The institutions of parliamentary democracy, including the established political parties, had 'displayed a degree of stability quite unexpected by those who prophesied their inevitable collapse'. Their survival 'cannot be put down just to the "betrayal" of the leaders of mass working class parties ... the fact that the great majority of members of these parties as a rule chose to follow reformist leaders rather than "revolutionary" critics was not accidental'.[5] Derer contrasted the left inside the Labour Party with the left outside the party. The former assumed that socialist change could be initiated through democratic activities within the party, while the left outside the party

bases its politics on the assumption that political changes will come about as a result of mass movements, springing up spontaneously in places of employment and within working class communities. Such movements would create [their] own organs of political power, by-pass representative parliamentary institutions, come into conflict with them and ultimately replace them ... [I]n practice both conceptions ... share a failure to gain any significant political influence.

Derer's contention was that the Labour left was not wrong to take parliamentary democracy seriously, but its failure was due to the fact that there was never any serious attempt on the part of the Labour Left to make use of the opportunities available to it within the Labour Party in order to gain influence through winning its membership to a socialist programme. Such an effort would, of necessity, involve systematic activity to create a rank and file organisation opposed to the leadership but built on a programme that at any given time is acceptable to the mass of the Party's individual and affiliated members. In the absence of such activity the politics of the Labour Left parliamentarians is no different from that of the socialist sects outside the Labour Party. Both expect to be rescued from their chronic political impotence by spontaneously arising mass movements.

The CLPD's rank-and-file character did not rule out strategic or tactical cooperation with left-wing Labour MPs. Some MPs and national trade union officials were listed prominently on CLPD circulars as supporters (and even as honorary presidents and vice-presidents), but their role was mainly symbolic.[6] The organisation was run by unpaid activists, headed by an elected executive which over time increasingly involved newer party members (usually people with some higher education) in their twenties and thirties. Like the long-standing party activists who founded CLPD, they showed little desire to become career politicians – and remarkably few of them ever took that path. Operating with a budget that was still less than £5,000 a year in 1978–9 (rising to a high of £10,000–15,000 in the early 1980s), almost all CLPD's expenses went on printing, paper and secretarial assistance to feed the most important weapon in the CLPD arsenal – the gestetner in Vera and Vladimir Derer's house, the CLPD's only 'office'.

The campaign itself involved building support through affiliations by constituency parties and trade union branches as well as through enlisting individual supporters; sending out model resolutions and convincing CLPs (each of which had the right to forward only one resolution to the party's annual conference) to use them; and organising among trade unions to have their delegates mandated to support reforms to the party's constitution. Throughout the year, regional coordinators would be contacted (the priorities usually being set at executive meetings in London) and told they needed this or that resolution to be advanced or supported in CLPs or unions by working through the established structures of these bodies, which the CLPD was always exceedingly careful to respect. All this entailed a lot of work but it proved remarkably easy to get results due to the political vacuum that by then existed at the base of the party. Much additional work was done in the immediate run-up to the annual party conference and at the conference itself, not only in mobilising support for key resolutions (especially among union delegations), but also in educating delegates at fringe meetings on how the conference really worked, how the agenda was set and by what procedures it could be challenged. Whereas most fringe meetings at the conference, and especially the mass Tribune meetings, were political rallies addressed by a leading parliamentary or movement figures, the CLPD meetings were more like workshops where strategy was debated (or at least explained), the tactics of challenges to the platform or agenda outlined, and delegates guided on how to vote – all on the basis of detailed information on the conference timetable and policy agenda. A crucial victory for the CLPD was when one of its most active members, Peter Willsman, was elected to the party's Conference Arrangements Committee. His reports to the CLPD fringe meetings on how resolutions were composited were like reports by meat inspectors about what went into the sausages.

The key to 'the iron law of oligarchy' in mass socialist parties had always been the leadership's control over the party administration and conference agenda on the one hand, and disorganisation and deference among the active membership on the other.[7] It was this pattern that the CLPD was challenging. The typical leading figure in the Labour Party more and more resembled a 'notable' – an MP who had cut his (rarely her) teeth politically in the Oxford Union – rather than a labour movement 'organiser'. The number of full-time agents working for the party (who could hardly ever have been designated as leading figures in the party, and who often acted more as gatekeepers than as organisers) had declined from 296 in 1951 to only 77 by 1978.[8] The CLPD activist, stepping into this vacuum, resembled in some ways the classic 'organiser'. But it was an organising role turned inwards on the party as a collective organisation: the mobilisation of active party members to challenge the policy autonomy of the 'notables' rather than organising 'workers into a class'.

The Struggle for Reselection

The CLPD's initial Statement of Aims of June 1973 undertook to ensure that conference decisions were binding on the Parliamentary Party by focusing mainly on the role of the NEC, calling on it to carry out fully its responsibility as the custodian of conference decisions, to take 'firm action' to ensure that election manifestos accurately reflected these, and to be responsive to rank-and-file opinion between conferences by making its meetings open to CLP representatives, sending out quarterly written reports, and extending the process of consultation with CLPs.[9] This focus on the NEC was soon dropped, however. Instead, the 150–200 constituency activists who attended the CLPD's first public meeting at the 1973 conference demonstrated an overwhelming interest in automatic reselection conferences in Labour-held parliamentary seats (nine of those in attendance were fresh from the battle to deselect Dick Taverne as their MP in Lincoln). The CLPD responded to this by deciding to concentrate on mandatory reselection as 'the immediately most appropriate means' of realising the CLPD's 'basic aim – the translation of Labour Party programmes into Labour Government policies'. This shift in focus was partly adopted for the highly pragmatic reason that 'reselection alone ... appeared capable of commanding wide support'.[10] After the PLP elected Callaghan as leader in 1976, the CLPD added the election of leader by the party conference as its second objective for constitutional reform.

The forces identified with the status quo did not remain passive or merely defensive in face of the growing strength of the CLPD activists. Despite the NEC's adoption of the Alternative Economic

Strategy (AES), on the issues of intra-party democracy the NEC 'operated less as an initiator of reform than an arena of struggle'.[11] In fact the 'counterinsurgency' on the issues of party democracy began not in 1981 (when the constitutional changes were eventually secured), as most accounts have claimed, but five years earlier, in the fateful year of 1976; and it was conducted in terms of pure power politics.

In fact, the very same speech in which Callaghan pronounced the death of Keynesianism also launched the counterinsurgency against the new left. Callaghan concluded his address by making it clear that he, unlike Wilson, would not be content with merely reasserting that the government was only 'accountable in a parliamentary democracy to Parliament', and that MPs could not 'suspend their judgements in favour of extra-parliamentary bodies'. 'I do not want to retreat behind the stock defence that "the Government must govern", if that becomes a polite way of telling the Party to go to hell.' Far from being embarrassed by having been dubbed a machine politician by the media, Callaghan told the delegates that he accepted the desig-nation of 'Party man' as an 'accolade'.[12] Contrasting the cooperative relationship that had 'grown up between the TUC and the Government in the past two and half years' with the critical stance of the party, he made it clear that his goal was to re-establish the domi-nance of the parliamentary leadership over the NEC, and to restore the social-democratic centralism of the party apparatus. To this end, he suggested that the NEC might need to be restructured, perhaps by including local government and regional council representatives. And he insisted that the NEC launch a formal investigation of 'those elements who misuse the word "socialism" and who seek to infiltrate our party and use it for their own ends . . . not because I am on a witch hunt but because I want the Government and the Party to work closely together'.[13]

This determination to use the issue of alleged infiltration as a means of bringing the party into line with the government meant that throughout the autumn of 1976 – when, amid the trauma of the IMF crisis, party members were going through the agony of watching their

86

government abandon the policy bedrock of social democracy – the public's attention was diverted to the issue of 'Marxist' infiltration of the Labour Party. What Stuart Hall called 'the conspiracy of the Red Scare' now became the prism through which Labour's parliamentary leadership and the mainstream media conveyed to the British public the meaning of the struggle taking place in the Labour Party. This was how the 'crisis' came finally to be appropriated – by governments in office, the repressive apparatus of the state, the media, and some articulate sectors of public opinion – as an interlocking set of planned or organised *conspiracies*. British society became little short of fixated: the idea of a conspiracy against 'the British way of life . . . The tighter the rope along which the British economy is driven, the finer the balance between compliance with and overthrow of the "social contract", the greater the power the conspiratorial metaphor has exerted over political discourse'.[14]

Particularly important for the eventual success of the counter-insurgency against the left – and an important indicator that opposition to the social contract did not necessarily mean a shift to the left – was the election in 1978 of Terry Duffy and John Boyd, two classically anti-communist leaders, as president and general secretary, respectively, of the Amalgamated Engineering Union (AEU). Although it was Terry Duffy who moved the resolution at the 1978 party conference rejecting wage guidelines 'until prices, profits and investment are planned within the framework of a socialist economy' (a resolution which was overwhelmingly passed), his use of such phrases was purely cynical. On the very next day, enough union votes were available, including those of the AEU, to ensure the sound defeat of a resolution to amend the constitution so as to take the election of the leader out of the exclusive hands of the parliamentary party – and it was Duffy who leaned particularly heavily on Scanlon to ensure that the Engineers' vote was cast against reselection of MPs, in defiance of the wishes of their conference delegation.

In light of Scanlon's behaviour at the 1978 conference, Benn interpreted the 'abuse of the block vote by the trade union leaders [as] a very important development because it will in the long run lead to a clean-up'.[15] But this assumed that the balance of forces would in the long run redound to the advantage of the left. At this conference the left had apparently been strengthened by the election of Dennis Skinner and Neil Kinnock to the NEC's constituency section. But little noted at the time was the simultaneous election to the NEC's trade-union section of John Golding, a right-wing machine politician from the West Midlands, a 'committee room Napoleon: a tough shrewd street-fighter'.[16] At a PLP meeting to discuss the reselection issue in March 1978, Golding had described how he had personally packed many constituency General Management Committee selection conferences with union delegates, and vowed that, if reselection went ahead, 'it will be a traumatic experience because we shall start packing GMCs to see that our people get in'. Golding was a key player in the formation of the hardline right-wing St Ermin's Group of union leaders who were determined not to compromise in the counterinsurgency against the new left. He was to play the leading role in challenging and eventually defeating Benn and Heffer's leadership of the NEC.

These developments within the unions enabled Shirley Williams, who would soon leave Labour to form the Social Democratic Party, to assure the Foreign Press Association in a speech as late as February 1979 that, as a social democrat within the Labour Party, she was far from politically 'dead': 'Many people have failed to notice the extent to which there has been a considerable shift of power in respect of our major unions . . . They are clearly moving back to the centre. It is only a small handful now which represent the far Left.'[17] It was true that, with the shift to the right in the AEU, the leaderships of four of the six largest unions, accounting for two-thirds of the vote at the party conference, were now unambiguously on the side of the leadership and against the new left. The leaders of the remaining two had joined Trade Unions for a Labour Victory (TULV), formed in 1978, whose priority was to protect the parliamentary leadership from intra-party democratic pressures from below before the next election. Even when the 1978–79

'Winter of Discontent' arrived, moreover, the union leadership made no common cause with the NEC on policy. They were as embarrassed by their inability to control their membership, and by the damage the strikes were doing to the government, as they were angry with Callaghan for not having listened to their warnings that their members would not stand for another year of wage restraint. Indeed, it was the explicitly corporatist 'concordat' that the government and TUC reached in February 1979 that allowed Callaghan to reject with impunity the election manifesto the NEC had been so painstakingly preparing for three years.

Yet Shirley Williams spoke too soon; or, at least, she relied too much on the power of union leaders to keep their activists in line on the issue of intra-party democracy in a conjuncture when they could not even keep them in line on wage restraint. The push for democracy in the party, together with alienation from the government, had not left the unions entirely untouched; and it was further encouraged by the CLPD's campaign among union activists through its remarkable mobilisation of support in virtually every institution and region of the labour movement between the 1978 and 1979 conferences (during the course of which, union branch affiliations to the CLPD went up from forty-seven to eighty-five). This thwarted the full exercise of the repressive role of the 'union bosses' upon which the counter-insurgency against the new left so heavily depended. While the adherence of NUPE and the TGWU's more left-wing leadership to TULV no doubt looked very promising to the parliamentary leadership, by 1979 these two unions' very sizable block votes (NUPE's affiliation to the Labour Party grew six-fold over the decade, to 600,000 members) were mandated to support reselection.[18] When the NEC resisted a behind-the-scenes attempt by the TULV leaders after the 1979 election to postpone once again consideration of the constitutional reforms, it did so knowing that the union leaders would not be able to hold back their delegations on the issue of reselection. At the 1979 party conference, mandatory reselection was finally passed by 4 million to 3 million votes. But it was a victory that would not last.

The Limits of Constitutional Reform

It had taken five long and arduous years of dedicated organising to win just the first of the CLPD's constitutional reforms, entailing a change which, as one student of comparative political parties would observe, was 'long-accepted as normal in most European social democratic parties [and] extremely difficult to refute by any standards of democracy'.[19] In light of the determined opposition the CLPD faced in confronting the deeply entrenched elitist aspects of the parliamentarist mode of representation in Britain, not to speak of the challenge reselection posed to the traditional arrangements between the industrial and political leaders in the Labour Party, it was certainly a remarkable victory for the Labour new left. But if it took this long to secure this one modest internal party reform, how long would it take to turn the Labour Party into an adequate vehicle for socialist advance?

The vesting of control of the party manifesto in the NEC and the issue of open and accountable decision-making in the PLP were also taken up immediately after the 1979 election. Other key issues of internal party democracy – the way delegates to GMCs were themselves selected in the constituencies; the role of the general, non-active party membership; the pattern of elections to the NEC; the trade-union block vote at the party conference – were all at least implicitly, even if not explicitly, put into question by the CLPD's achievement in making the mode of representation the immediate object of struggle. The CLPD was surely correct in thinking that mandatory reselection would never have been won, even after five years of campaigning, if all these issues had been allowed to come into play at once. Yet this made the CLPD vulnerable to the charge that it was prepared to tolerate and work within a broader constitutional framework that was hard to defend in democratic terms.

But it must be said that although, from year to year, the CLPD did broaden the range of democratic reforms it placed on the agenda, its determination to play by the existing rules (which was in fact the condition of its success on reselection) could easily be made to look like uncritical constitutionalism. There was some justice in Michael Rustin's criticism of the Labour new left in 1980 to the effect that 'constitutionalism within the Party is the equivalent of parliamentarism within the State, in its inhibiting effects on political understanding and action'.[20] The development of an understanding among active party and union members about how the conference really worked as a political institution, and about how the power of the 'platform' to control the agenda might be challenged effectively, marked an enormous advance over past practice. Yet there was an element within the CLPD whose world was contained by what transpired at annual party conferences, and for whom rules and procedures could be as fascinating – and imprisoning – as parliaments can be for MPs. There was also an element within the CLPD that actually was narrowly parliamentarist, in the sense that it was thought that if a Labour government would only implement the party programme, this would generate mass support just by virtue of the benefits it brought the majority of people – or, at least, that if and when undemocratic forces tried to stop the government from doing so, the people would rush to the defence of parliamentary sovereignty. To frame the issue this way, as the CLPD only too often did, was seriously to underrate the necessity and difficulty of generating broad popular support for socialist policies, as opposed to just getting people to vote for a Labour government.

But to dismiss the CLPD for its parliamentarism in this sense is to ignore the fact that it generated such 'hysterical overreaction' (as Derer not unreasonably called it),[21] precisely because it presented the most powerful practical challenge that had ever been mounted to the most central characteristic of parliamentarism: 'the complete separation and non-participation of the masses in the work of parliament'.[22] There could be no denying that this was the fundamental factor in the fateful 1979 election that brought Mrs Thatcher to power. The rot that had developed in Labour's electoral base during the term of the 1966 government had continued during Labour's term of government in the 1970s. At the core of this was Labour's declining support even among manual workers.

Notably, the number of manual workers who spontaneously identified themselves as working class actually increased from 34 per cent in 1970 to 39 per cent in 1979 (having stood at 44 per cent in 1964); but this yielded no more of a stable base for the Labour leadership's electoralism than for its continuing commitment to corporatism. On the contrary, despite this increase in class identification, there was a further fraying of traditional party identification among voters in Labour's main working-class electoral base – precisely when it was most needed to sustain Labour's support through a period of crisis. The renewed fall in Labour's vote among manual workers in 1979, which had been temporarily arrested in 1974, left the party with only 50 per cent of the manual workers' vote.[23]

Shortly after the 1979 election, Lewis Minkin and Patrick Seyd (who were then devoted academic partisans of the CLPD) clearly expressed the perspective that guided much of the Labour new left's thinking at the time. They did not ignore the evidence of a decline in support for social expenditure and public ownership, even among traditional Labour supporters, but they rejected the conclusion reached by 'many in the parliamentary party, and many outside commentators . . . that Labour would be better off accommodating' itself to this. They pointed to the evidence that showed that

> the drop in support for the party's values took place in two stages – 1964–70, and after February 1974. Between 1970 [and 1974] there was a *recovery*, when Labour was in opposition and its policies moved to the left. The important point is that parties help to structure public opinion. The actions and speeches of Labour leaders prepare the ground for future appeals.

The leadership's 'obsession with the role of mass media', however, had devalued the party's own communication role and neglected the essential role of activists, who 'paid close attention to the political messages, and would, *if sufficiently stimulated*, spread them further among others' in the immediate environments of workplace, association and neighbourhood. Far from becoming obsolete, Minkin and Seyd insisted, organisational capacities at this level were acquiring a new importance, in a context where the relationships between class and party were becoming less habitual. It was precisely this that made the struggle for internal party democracy so crucial:

> Democracy, accountability, and the health of Labour's grassroots are now inextricably linked. The membership is increasingly assertive and demanding a greater say in policy-making. This democracy encourages membership and raises morale. Conversely, making the party leadership accountable forces it to take an interest in the number, activity and elan of the activists ... For the first time in fifteen years there is now an emerging consensus that the party activists are significant, and that it is in nobody's interest for the party's roots to shrivel.[24]

The expectation of an emerging consensus within the Labour Party on these terms was, however, a delusion – albeit one shared by a good many Labour intellectuals at the time. Stuart Hall's fear that the struggle to transform the institutions of the British left might prove 'too traumatic', and that the forces representing the status quo within the left would prove 'too rigid, deeply entrenched, historically binding to be overcome', was to prove far more realistic.[25] It took almost a whole decade for the Labour new left finally to win the first of its constitutional reforms to enhance internal party democracy. Yet all such reforms could at best be only an organisational starting-point for a new mode of political representation whereby, to employ Seyd and Minkin's formulation, a socialist political leadership concerned to 'structure public opinion' would also seek to 'stimulate' party activists to spread the political message directly in their communities and workplaces. Far from generating any such strategic consensus within the party, the modest constitutional changes that were achieved provoked such a violent reaction from those who were attached to the old mode of representation that the Labour Party was plunged into the sharpest internal polarisation in its history.

The Crisis of Representation: 1979–81

According to the prevailing myth, the new left in the Labour Party swept all before it following the 1979 election. An 'unstoppable' impetus for change is said to have built up inside the party, emanating from an 'elite' of far-left local activists ('Stalinists, 57 varieties of Trotskyists, Tribunites, the emerging "soft left", the old utopian socialists and peaceniks').[26] Operating under the umbrella of the CLPD, and in alliance with an NEC dominated by Tony Benn, this elite is supposed to have 'wielded extraordinary power', culminating in the imposition on the party of 'that unbelievable document, Labour's 1983 Election Manifesto, which Gerald Kaufman memorably called the longest suicide note in history'.

The endurance of this myth reflects the continued strength of the parliamentary elite in the party, and of their media friends. It is certainly true that, after the 1979 election, the new left engaged with the forces of the status quo in the party in a major confrontation over party structure, strategy and leadership. The intensity of the confrontation, however, was not because the challenge came from the 'far left'. On the contrary, even by the turn of the decade most of the activists who were working to change the Labour Party from within were still regarded on the British left (and for the most part regarded themselves) as rather moderate and 'reformist'. When Robin Blackburn interviewed Tony Benn in September 1979, he asked: 'Aren't your remedies very modest considering the magnitude of the crisis?'[27] Benn agreed – and so would have most of the activists who belonged to the CLPD. This was even truer of most constituency activists, including even the one-third who defined themselves as left-wing towards the end of the 1970s.

There was a surge of membership in the CLPD – from 443 in 1979 to 807 in 1980 and 1,016 in 1981, before peaking at just over 1,200 in 1982 – while the number of CLPs affiliating to it doubled from 77 to 153 over the same period. The Labour Coordinating Committee also grew well beyond the small group close to Benn, which had set it up in 1978 to popularise the AES; by 1981, it had

94

800 members and over fifty affiliated organisations. The Rank and File Mobilising Committee, formed in 1980 as a coalition of left groups inside the party to advance the constitutional reforms, would become, with the CLPD's Jon Lansman as its secretary, the backbone of Benn's 1981 campaign for the deputy leadership. Of course, the activists in these groups remained a minority of all party activists.[28] In this sense, they could perhaps be called an 'elite', even if not a 'far left' elite; but they were clearly an elite of a very different kind from the parliamentary elite, which was resisting the campaign for democratic reform within the party. All political activity, including movements for the extension of democracy involves leadership; the important distinction to be drawn is between those who mobilise support for extending democracy and those who oppose it. What is certain is that, for a few years after the 1979 election, it was the new left activists who had the ear of the party membership. But it was far less any commitment to doctrine, and far more the 'persistent and, sometimes, contemptuous disregard of the voice of the majority, as articulated by conference pronouncements ... the rejection by the leadership of traditional majoritarian democracy', as Eric Shaw put it, that called into question the leadership's right to rule in the eyes of so many party members:

> After two instalments of Labour Governments had failed to satisfy even their most moderate aspirations, a deep disenchantment with those who ran the Party set in. After 1979, this became so ubiquitous, so palpable that it expanded from antagonism to particular leaders to an alienation from the very structure of authority within the Party ... Loyalism and the 'veneration of leadership' virtually vanished to be replaced, amongst much of the rank and file, by a radically different collective syndrome: a psychology of mistrust, defiance, even of betrayal.[29]

It was in this context that the Labour Party finally had the great debate on democracy that Benn had called for almost a decade earlier. The Labour new left posed the question, more sharply than ever before, about whether a social-democratic party might yet be adapted into a political force for radical democratic change. Yet in the confrontation that followed, neither the overall balance of power nor the greatest determination to win at all costs belonged to the new left. The deep aversion of the bulk of the parliamentary leadership even to having the debate, let alone seriously trying to refashion Labour's conventional interpretation of parliamentarism, was strongly supported by establishment opinion and virtually all of the British media.[30] Those who resisted change were also helped by the old Labour left (epitomised by Michael Foot's brief tenure as leader) and the union leadership (who still yearned for a better corporatist partnership). Moreover, the old characteristics of diffidence and deference on the part of most party members, while diminished, were by no means wholly eradicated. The result was that, although the new left won a few battles between 1979 and the beginning of 1981, well before that year was over it had lost the war. Indeed, before the ink was even dry on Labour's constitutional changes, the counter-insurgency against the new left had become a counter-revolution. The balance of forces in the party had temporarily shifted enough to allow the new left finally to carry through two modest constitutional reforms – reforms that had first been proposed when Labour had gone into opposition a decade earlier. But it had not shifted anything like far enough to enable the new left to resist the counter-revolution when it came.

All of the themes that had emerged out of the new left's turn to community politics in the early 1970s strongly informed its agenda at the end of the decade. When Benn defined the key task after the 1979 election as that of restoring 'the legitimacy in the public mind of democratic socialism', he first of all thought in terms of making 'the Labour Party reintegrate with other activists with whom we sympathised, such as the women's movement and the Friends of the Earth';[31] and he recognised, too, that this had to mean broadening out beyond traditional conceptions of the constituency for socialism. As he put it in the preface to the collection of speeches he published during the 1981 deputy leadership campaign: 'Inequality in Britain is not by any means confined to the class relations deriving from the ownership of capital.' Although this remained 'a central obstacle which must be overcome if any real progress is to be made', it was 'a pity that the nature of the argument for socialism should have been so narrowly conceived ... If democracy is based on a moral claim to equality, the issues opened up are as wide as life itself' – including women's inequality and discrimination against ethnic and racial minorities, and gays.[32] Benn expressed this in generous, not reproachful or recriminatory tones; his aim was to allow people 'to draw new energy ... to take up the struggle with renewed faith and commitment'.[33]

Given the impact of feminist and black activists on community-level politics through the 1970s, it was hardly surprising that the struggle for women's and black sections within the party became one of the defining elements of the Labour new left's agenda.[34] Ken Livingstone went so far as to credit Benn with 'being the first to highlight the need for a wider Labour movement actively encouraging the involvement of women and black people alongside the traditional white male trade unionists'.[35] It is certainly the case that the later charge that Benn was too narrowly tied to a defence of traditional trade unionism simply ignores what he was actually saying. It was in fact large sections of the Tribunite left associated with Foot (and later Kinnock), not to mention Trotskyists and elements of the old CP broad left, who were more likely to be suspicious of the vision of the Labour Party as a federation of social movement groups articulated by Benn and the LCC and CLPD activists. And while the others would sometimes actively play on working-class parochialism, Benn was often prepared to challenge it directly, particularly by strongly encouraging trade-union involvement in 'the evolution of sensible strategies of development upon which communities depend for their lives and amenities', and arguing that this depended on forging strong links with activists engaged in anti-nuclear, ethnic, pensioners' and women's issues.[36]

In advancing this argument, Benn was in fact making the most pointed criticism of the trade-union leadership's embrace of corporatism offered by any leading European politician on the left. Not only rank-and-file workers, he argued, but even capitalists and bureaucrats had become disillusioned with the constraints of corporatism, leaving many trade-union leaders alone in defensively clinging to this 'sterile partnership':

> If the trade union movement is seeking to offer an alternative industrial, social and political perspective for the future of Britain, it will be called upon to provide a far more positive and constructive leadership than its critics believe is possible ... If the sights of the trade unions are lifted above the defensive battles on the industrial front to a bolder perspective, the alliance with the Labour Party will need to be strengthened at every level. But if the lessons of the past are learned, democratic socialism will be seen to be quite different from the consensus corporatism that marked the evolution of labour power in the post-war years.[37]

But, in rejecting corporatism, Benn was in no way invoking the old dichotomy between reform and revolution. At the 1979 party conference, recommending on behalf of the NEC that Conference reject a Militant-inspired resolution calling for the nationalisation of the 200 leading corporations, Benn described himself as 'a Clause IV socialist, becoming more so as the years go by'; but he insisted that if the conference expected the PLP to take its resolutions seriously, then it had also to take the Labour Party seriously, as 'a Party of democratic, socialist reform. I know that for some people "Reform" is a term of abuse. That is not so. All our great successes have been the product of reform.' Taking reform seriously, however, meant coming to terms with

> the usual problem of the reformer; we have to run the economic system to protect our people who are now locked into it while we change the system. And if you run it without seeking to change it then you are locked in the decay of the system, but if you simply pass resolutions to change it without consulting those who are

locked in the system that is decaying, then you become irrelevant to the people you seek to represent . . . We cannot content ourselves with speaking only to ourselves; we must raise these issues publicly and involve the community groups because we champion what they stand for. We must win the argument, broaden the base of membership, not only to win the election but to generate the public support to carry the policies through.[38]

This remarkably clear-sighted and thoughtful argument was ignored by the entire mainstream media, including the *Guardian*. Scarcely anyone who did not attend Labour Party conferences, including most of the left, would have known he had made it. They would have heard it, however, if they were among the capacity crowd of 2,600 at Central Hall, Westminster, who came to hear Benn and Stuart Holland debate with Paul Foot and Hilary Wainwright in March 1980, at the 'Debate of the Decade' between the left inside and outside the Labour Party. The revolutionary socialist groups, Benn insisted, confused real reform with revolution. Their talk of revolution

implies, and nobody believes it, that there is a short cut to the transfer of power in this country . . . What the socialist groups really do is to analyse, to support struggle, to criticise the Labour Party, to expand consciousness, to preach a better morality. These are all very desirable things to do. But they have very little to do with revolution.[39]

Revolutionary groups had to come to see that they too were part of the problem, and that the limits of their own practices, just like those of the left in the Labour Party, could also be measured in the simple fact that 'we do not have a majority of support outside for any of our solutions'. It had to be recognised, moreover, that even those among 'the rank and file' who were acutely aware of the inadequacies of the Labour leadership's policies, and were sympathetic to socialist solutions, were not prepared to agitate for them at critical moments:

The reality is that the rank and file of the labour movement do not want to put at risk the survival of a Labour government. We must be prepared to face the fact that the problem of the balance between agitation and loyalty has got to be solved. Unless we can deal with that problem we are going to continue to be radical in opposition and somewhat conservative in office.[40]

This was indeed the Labour new left's central dilemma, made all the more pressing by the fact that the contradiction between agitation and loyalty existed not only when Labour was in office. An agenda for change as extensive as that which was being advanced after 1979 was obviously going to be fought tooth and nail, and the divisions this would engender would have to be at least concealed from public view in good time before the next election if Labour was to have a chance of winning it. Benn recognised this, but hoped that after fifteen months of controversy, during which the new left would 'lay the foundations' of its agenda for change, the party would reunite to 'campaign together' for the 1983 election.[41] But this scenario assumed that the centre-right parliamentarians would be as loyal to the party as the long-suffering rank-and-file activists. This was very soon shown to be a serious miscalculation.

Those social democrats who stayed in the party evinced a very different mix of loyalty and agitation – and their agitation, unlike that of the rank-and-file activists, had the national media as its amplifier. Their claim that it was impossible to win elections with radical socialist policies was initially dented by the Mitterand victory under the Programme Commune in France. And despite the socialist policies adopted at party conferences, Labour actually ran well ahead in the opinion polls all through 1980 and most of 1981. But the social democrats' persistent denigration of the left through the media eventually took its toll on the party's popularity. The problem faced by the Labour new left in this context was captured by 'the usual problem of the reformer', just as Benn had identified it at the 1979 conference. Those who set out to reform the party were concerned with keeping it electorally viable in order to protect all those who looked to it for the protection of their immediate political interests; yet if they refrained from trying to change it, they would be locked into the decay of the system.

It was the most intractable of dilemmas. That Benn was so acutely aware of it, and yet refused to give up, reflected not only the strength of his commitment but also the depth of his understanding that accommodating oneself to this 'decaying system' (as he saw it, in moral as much as in material terms) was itself no long-term answer. This approach was made all the more poignant by his recognition – even on the optimistic scenario that the foundation for changing the Labour Party might be laid in as short a time as fifteen months – that the larger democratic-socialist agenda could only be realised on the basis of a very protracted and long-term struggle. As he wrote in his diary on the eve of the 1979 conference: 'I think we are going to be engaged in the most bitter struggle over the next ten years, and if this [new right] philosophy gains hold in the public mind then not only might we not win the next Election but socialism could be in retreat in Britain until absolutely vigorous campaigns for democracy are mounted again.'[42]

The battle for the Labour Party in the years after 1979 was really about the role it would play in relation to that long-term struggle. It was because it sensed this that the new left fought the battle with such determination. At the 1980 conference, the approval in principle of an electoral college for the election of the leader and deputy leader, as well as the reconfirmation of reselection, appeared at the time to be a major victory for the Labour new left. But the victory was a highly qualified one. Even before the vote on the leadership election was taken, the decision of the 1979 conference on control of the party manifesto being vested in the NEC rather than the PLP leadership was reversed (albeit by a margin of only 100,000 out of over 7 million votes).

The implications of this for the struggle over the democratic accountability of the shadow cabinet were enormous. But it also exposed the cynical practice of those 'moderate' union leaders who covered their flanks by supporting radical resolutions at conferences while in fact joining the counterinsurgency against the new left. On the two issues to which both senior PLP figures like Foot and Shore, and up-and-coming ones like Robin Cook and Jack Straw, gave highest priority – withdrawal from the Common Market and unilateral nuclear disarmament – the union block votes were there to pass overwhelmingly resolutions which supported both of these. And in the name of the General and Municipal Workers' Union David Basnett moved the main economic strategy resolution as the first item on the agenda at the 1980 party conference. It ostensibly committed the party to the position that 'Britain's economic and social problems can only be solved by socialist planning', including specifically restrictions on the export of capital, selected import controls, a wealth tax, and the reflation of public-sector spending.[43] Benn was not unjustified in pointing out to the delegates that every one of these economic policies had been advanced by the NEC before the 1979 election, and yet had been ruled out of inclusion in the election manifesto by Callaghan. He publicly challenged Basnett to justify how he could put them forward as the centrepiece of economic strategy in 1980 while at the same time voting against the NEC's position on the issue of whether the shadow cabinet would be expected to include them in the next manifesto.[44]

Perhaps even more ominous, at least in terms of prolonging and deepening the trauma, was that after endorsing in principle (again by a narrow margin of 100,000 votes) a broader franchise for the election of the leader through an electoral college consisting of the PLP, the unions and constituency delegates, the conference went on to defeat all the proposals on the specific distribution of the votes among these, leaving the reform completely in limbo. Basnett moved an emergency resolution that a special rules revision conference be called in January 1981 to settle this. With the prospect on everyone's mind that Callaghan might resign before then, to allow the PLP alone to choose his successor under the existing rules, Callaghan came to the rostrum, and after teasing the delegates about what he would do, offered this pledge:

I think the proper course of action ... is for the PLP to elect the Leader in the traditional way in November, on the understanding and in the knowledge that the Conference, in light of whatever amendments are put forward at the Special Conference in January, may want to reach different conclusions. I would hope that is clearly expressed, clearly understood without any bad faith at all, but with the intention of carrying on the business of the Party in the best possible way.

Eric Heffer, speaking for the NEC to close the debate, immediately followed this by expressing his understanding that what Callaghan had said guaranteed that 'there would be no elections of new leaders ... Jim has made an important statement; let us take it on the basis of what he said, that the PLP must take into consideration the Conference decision on the question of the future leader.'[45] In the event, of course, these assurances were ignored. Callaghan did resign within weeks of the conference, and, despite a sixteen-to-seven vote by the NEC that the PLP suspend its standing orders to allow an electoral college vote after the January conference, the PLP went on in November to elect Michael Foot as leader over Denis Healey by a narrow margin. Foot immediately designated Healey as his deputy, and this was followed in December by a secret agreement between Foot and the TULV leaders that, whatever the outcome of the special Wembley conference to be held in January on the method of electing the leader, the union leadership would support no challenge to Foot and Healey.[46] Thus, despite the disastrous effects of the 1974–79 government, the Foot–Healey axis which had been its foundation was now installed in the leadership of the party.

5

Disempowering Activism:
The Path to New Labour

Virtually the whole of the British left were elated by Michael Foot's election as leader in succession to Jim Callaghan in November 1980.[1] The Labour new left, for the most part, shared this feeling and enthusiastically celebrated his victory, even though Foot had opposed their project since the early 1970s. His concern was not just unity within the parliamentary and union elite; he also genuinely opposed the new left's project, believing that its conception of democratic reform, 'carried to its logical conclusion, would destroy Parliament'.[2] The Labour new left's confused attitudes towards Foot made it hard for activists and the general public to understand why it continued to pursue its project against his wishes.

A Foot–Healey leadership team certainly had greater capacity to stifle the Labour new left than a Healey–Foot team. But whether the gains in terms of 'party unity' justified putting the ineffectual Foot rather than the pugnacious Healey in the role of Thatcher's main opponent was doubtful. Either way, as Raymond Williams wrote at the time, 'The current position of what is called the leadership – "don't rock the boat, let's unite to get Thatcher out" – is not only an opportunist negativism; it is complacent in its assumption that it is bound to be the beneficiary, and that if it is it will know what to do (except go on being the leadership)'.[3]

Yet Foot's election did entail some real costs in policy terms for the centre-right MPs, costs which those who left to form the SDP were not prepared to sustain – above all because having Foot as leader guaranteed that the Labour Party would finally adopt a non-nuclear defence policy. But the party's continuing commitment to NATO, together with the fact that the centre-right continued to dominate shadow cabinet elections, left considerable space for manoeuvre for the great majority of social-democratic parliamentarians who opted to stay. Their staying was, however, conditional upon Foot and later Kinnock proving that the changes in the party's constitution that had been adopted could be contained and rendered innocuous in terms of their implications for the autonomy of the parliamentary party – and that the Labour new left would be defeated and marginalised.

A Special Conference was held in Wembley in 1981 to decide on the party's constitutional changes. At the conference, the CLPD's tactical brilliance and the efforts of the Rank and File Mobilising Committee (as the new umbrella organisation for left activists was called) prevented the adoption of an electoral college for the election of the leader that would still have been dominated by the PLP. This ultimately ensured a victory for the CLPD's preferred electoral college method. One other option on offer to party members at the Special Conference, championed by David Owen – Callaghan's foreign secretary and future founding member of the SDP – proposed that every individual party member should have the right to vote for the leader, but with the PLP alone determining who the candidates should be. This received only 400,000 votes out of nearly 7 million. The insincerity of the social democrats was a factor here – just as with reselection, they advanced 'one member, one vote' (OMOV) only after their steadfast opposition to any broadening of the franchise had been defeated. But what really told against OMOV was that it meant entirely bypassing the unions. This was, at the time, a complete non-starter in every section of the party. Although there were elements within the Rank and File Mobilising Committee coalition who supported OMOV, most of the Labour new left preferred an electoral college in which one-third of the votes would be cast by the PLP, one-third by CLP delegates, and one-third by the unions.

The CLPD's careful monitoring of what the various union delegations had been mandated to vote for led to a tactical decision to organise support for an option slightly weighted towards the unions

(30-30-40) as the only way of defeating alternative options which were designed to leave the PLP with 50 per cent or more of the vote.[4] Although the Wembley conference decision to leave the unions controlling 40 per cent of the vote in the electoral college was a massive reduction from their 90 per cent of votes on motions at the party conference, it was immediately presented by the social democrats and the media as a vote for the domination of the party by 'union bosses', and against the ostensibly more democratic OMOV method. This completely drowned out the Labour new left's actual aim, which was to make MPs accountable to an informed and active local party membership, and to politicise and democratise the unions' role in the party, not jettison it.

The defeat suffered by the right of the party at the Wembley Special Conference was one of the reasons given for the issuing of the Limehouse Declaration by the 'Gang of Four' (Roy Jenkins, Shirley Williams, David Owen and Bill Rodgers) at the end of January 1981. The split occasioned by the declaration, and the subsequent formation of the Social Democratic Party, was bound to affect the balance of forces in the Labour Party. But it did not tilt the balance in favour of the new left, which turned out to be weaker than it had appeared to be in 1980. A sober assessment in February 1981 by the brilliant young CLPD activist, Jon Lansman, recognised that the work of the Labour new left through 1980 had been done by 'too few people', and that their concentration on the 1980 conference and Wembley had demonstrated 'a lack of clear long term aims'. The victory at Wembley was, Lansman argued, 'narrow and probably unrepeatable':

One of the major sources of our weakness at Wembley was dissatisfaction with and even hostility towards the trade unions' influence in the party which is rife even amongst the Left in the CLPs. We need to defend trade union participation at all levels ... whilst not condoning any undemocratic use of block votes (i.e. decision-making by too few). The most immediate application of this principle is the defence of the Wembley decision, but we also need to play a wider educative role to counteract the hypocritical attacks of the Right.[5]

It is in this light that the purpose – and eventual outcome – of Benn's fateful decision to stand against Healey for the deputy leadership needs to be understood. Lansman thought there would 'almost certainly' be such a contest, and that the Rank and File Mobilising Committee would have to involve itself in it, not by running 'a "Tony Benn for No. 10" campaign', but by supporting 'a candidate committed to conference policies'. This would entail defending the central role of the unions in setting policies and choosing leaders 'while not necessarily accepting existing levels of democracy within the trade unions'.[6] The key point of Benn's campaign was, as Lansman put it, to 'actually save the [Wembley] decision' by testing the electoral college and forcing Healey into a debate on policy: 'The right would be far more interested in stopping Benn than changing the proportions in a college. It is a big job to get people interested in constitutional changes; it is a much bigger job for the right than the left because the right don't have the activists on the ground, they don't have the active support.'[7]

Indeed, Michael Foot had told the shadow cabinet: 'the Wembley decision will not be allowed to stand'.[8] Benn had by this point already privately decided that he would stand for the deputy leadership under a new electoral college – though he did not, then, or at any time later, expect to succeed. To contest Healey was, of course, also to challenge Foot and the trade union general secretaries. They were not only fearful that Benn might win, and that this would force more of the social democrats out of the parliamentary party; they were also 'sick to death of all this argument about Party democracy'.[9] Foot pleaded with Benn to desist, but Benn did not find this 'typical' Foot stance – 'where everything you want to do will always lose us the next election' – to be at all convincing: 'Well, as we followed his advice rigorously for the last five years of the last Labour Government and we did lose the Election in May 1979, I can't say I found it very credible.' Benn's own rationale for standing for the deputy leadership was to force people to make choices. That's what's called polarisation, divisiveness, and all the rest, but ... you can't go on forever pretending you're a socialist party when you're not, pretending you'll do something when you won't, confining yourself to attacks on the Tories when that's not enough. People want to know what the Labour Party will do and I think this process is long overdue; the Labour Party are having a Turkish bath, and the sweat and the heat and the discomfort are very unpleasant.[10]

The Counter-revolution

In the final ballot for deputy leader in September 1981, Healey defeated Benn by the narrowest of margins – 50.4 per cent to 49.6 per cent. The fact that Benn secured over 80 per cent of the constituency party votes on both ballots, and almost 40 per cent of the trade union votes (and even one-third of the PLP votes) on the second ballot, could be seen as a remarkable victory, given the strength and determination of the forces marshalled against his candidacy, and the fact that many Tribune MPs either abstained or voted for Healey rather than Benn on the last ballot. In reality, far more important for the defeat of the Labour new left was another set of votes for the National Executive, taken in the traditional manner.

At the 1981 conference, left-wing representatives were removed from the trade-union section of the NEC, as increasingly right-wing union leaderships finally fulfilled their promises after the 1979 election to produce right-wing delegations at the conference. Yet, it wasn't only from the trade union section that left-wing representatives were being removed. They were also being removed from the women's section – and there was a particular irony in this. Women's representation in the Labour Party had always been the most indefensibly undemocratic aspect of its structure. The Women's Action Committee of the CLPD had been campaigning for reforms but, in a pattern reminiscent of the 1970s, the Conference Arrangements Committee had kept their proposals off the conference agenda. The 1981 conference opened, however, in the glare of massive international as well as national television and press coverage, not with the deputy leadership ballot but with a protest staged at the podium by women delegates. The horror on the faces of the union and parliamentary leaders at this feminist lack of deference showed very clearly that it was not the Labour new left who represented old-fashioned 'white male' traditional socialist politics.

Although it took until the 1982 conference for all those targeted in the purge to be removed from the NEC, the success of the right-wing union machine at the 1981 conference considerably enhanced the influence of some of the least democratic and most ruthless elements in the labour movement. If the significance of their increased power was not immediately apparent, this was for two reasons. First, the successes of the new left in the party and the energising effect of the deputy leadership campaign had attracted many activists from social movements and pressure groups. For the first time in many years the Labour Party was where the action was for young left-wing activists. This was especially reflected in the launch of *New Socialist*, a lively discussion journal, explicitly 'Bennite' in orientation, which gave the party a new intellectual presence among left activists.

Second, at the local level the rise and fall of the Labour new left followed a different tempo. Labour did well in the May 1981 local council elections in both the north and the south of the country, and this created new opportunities for new left activists to try to put some of their ideas into practice. In particular, the Greater London Council (GLC) under Ken Livingstone's leadership became the focus of national and international attention. The history of that remarkable experiment has been well documented.[11] Its most creative and innovative practices, including opening 'its buildings, its funds, its research and – very much more selectively – its decision-making process to some of the most radical and most needy sections of the public' were at this stage still embryonic, and came to fruition only in the mid 1980s. In the meantime, as Wainwright admits, 'There was much about the GLC's work for insiders and outsiders that was very messy and frustrating, as well as exciting and hopeful.'[12] Yet the Labour new left's advances at the local level also provided a new front for the counter-insurgency – the main effects of which were felt initially at the national level of the party. Bitter right-wing Labour councillors, some of whom were about to defect to the SDP, fed the press minute details of every local political conflict (some of which involved cleaning up the rotten machine politics of the old Labour councils). And the press, centred in London, made a sensational national issue out of every unconventional statement or practice (personal or political) by young and often inexperienced new left activists in every London borough and constituency party, as well as in the GLC. At the Palace of Westminster, in-jokes with lobby journalists about the 'loony' local left became a handy means for Labour MPs to offer proof that they were 'sound'. Well before the 1981 conference, such headlines had already appeared as: 'Worried Labour Men Plot to Oust "Rent-a-Quote" Livingstone'.[13] Livingstone later lamented: 'It would be nice to think that as the press attacks mounted we could have looked to the Parliamentary Labour Party for support. The more we were attacked the more the PLP dissociated itself.'[14]

The Labour new left had long understood that only a long-term campaign of mobilisation and education could securely restore Labour's electoral base. But they had also expected that this might still be accomplished by scraping back into office, as Labour had done in 1974 – and was still doing at the local level even after the 1983 election – and using the resources of the state to help empower popular forces. When it became clear that Thatcherism might not be a temporary interregnum, it was also apparent that the Labour new left's attempted balancing act – of seeking to change the party fundamentally while relying in the meantime on an anti-government vote to sustain the party's electoral viability – was no longer possible. After 1981, the choice between a long-term campaign and immediate electoral success became a stark one.

The dilemma became more acute in the mid 1980s, as the effects of a new international economic crisis, and the commitment of Western governments to give priority to defeating inflation through pushing up unemployment, began to make themselves felt. The attempt to change the Labour Party now ran up against the most intractable problem: trying to change any party as fundamentally as the Labour new left proposed involves a long period of conflict within it; and even if it is the defenders of the status quo who do the worst damage, the fact remains that a visibly disunited party cannot win elections. This was no small consideration when winning elections appeared ever more important in the face of Thatcherism and world-wide recession.

This logic was already dominant in the Labour Party well before the 1983 election campaign. But Labour's parliamentary team failed to restore Labour's electoral fortunes. They were unable to dispel the image of a party at war with itself. The blame that was subsequently heaped on the Labour new left was not justified, however. The 1983 manifesto was in some respects less radical than its 1974 counterpart. The so-called 'longest suicide note in history' was not only considerably shorter than the Tory manifesto; it contained little of the élan of *Labour's Programme 1982*, even though it often referred back to that document and retained much of its policy package. The terms in which the campaign itself was conducted were, of course, less radical still, as the shadow cabinet took centre stage. In fact, the internal strife that Labour exhibited during the 1983 election campaign itself was entirely within the Foot–Healey camp, as old conflicts resurfaced, now that the new left enemy had been neutralised. While the new left showed remarkable discipline in keeping a low profile, the tactics of the old Labour right wrought enormous damage, in a manner that carried an ominous message for the future.

By the time the campaign began, nothing could have defeated Thatcher. Tory support stayed between 45 and 47 per cent right through the campaign, before registering 43 per cent on the night of the election. But, as W. L. Miller has shown, the drop in Labour support from 33 per cent at the beginning of the campaign to 28 per cent at the end – entirely to the benefit of the Liberal–Social Democratic Alliance, which moved up from 18 to 26 per cent – took place about halfway into the campaign.[15] The reason for this seems clear. Towards the end of May, the national press featured an alleged ultimatum by Healey that he would withdraw from the campaign if

Foot interpreted the manifesto as saying that Labour was in favour of unilateral nuclear disarmament. This was followed a day later by a calculated move by Callaghan, who, with the authority of a former Labour prime minister who had 'been there', made a highly publicised attack on Labour's defence policy. From the moment Healey and Callaghan took this stand, election coverage was dominated by the obvious discomfort of Foot as he tried to bridge the gulf between himself and the right on defence policy – a gulf that had indeed been only thinly obscured by a form of words in the manifesto, designed to exploit popular support for getting rid of Cruise and Polaris missiles, while at the same time minimising the impact of the unpopular expression 'unilateral disarmament'.

It was thus ultimately an election campaign in which the radical democratic issues raised by the new left hardly surfaced, and in which voters did not find Labour very much more credible than the Tories on the issue of reducing unemployment. Above all, however, as Miller concluded, it was

> dissension at the top rather than spontaneous desertion at the bottom [that] was the cause of Labour's very poor performance in 1983. That does not mean policies are irrelevant. If Labour leaders cannot agree policies amongst themselves on what they define as the central issues in politics then they will not succeed in convincing the electorate ... If they can agree on policies, however, they may well be able to turn public opinion in their favour or divert public attention to issues on which they do have public support. In particular the left must either convince the right or compromise with it, not because left wing policies in themselves preclude electoral success, but because they need the support or acquiescence of all wings of the party before they can present a credible alternative.[16]

The Fracturing of the Labour New Left

The right wing of the party, however, would not accept left-wing policies. This was clear from the whole previous decade. As Mark

Wickham-Jones puts it in his comprehensive study of economic policy within the Labour party during the period 1970–83, 'one central theme emerges: the degree to which right wingers within Labour remained opposed to what was official party policy'.[17] Given the collapse of Keynesianism, the party had to move to the left or drift to the right. When Neil Kinnock, whose position on unilateralism and defence of the welfare state made him acceptable to many on the left, succeeded Foot as leader after the 1983 election, this was not yet clear – even to Kinnock himself. He took the position that the problem was not policy, but disunity.

This was always the Tribune left's position, and it was what Kinnock now argued in every speech he made at the 1983 party conference. He stood for all the left's policies. His overwhelming defeat of Eric Heffer in the leadership election reflected this (Benn, having lost his seat, ruled himself out of the race). It was also related to the general sense, felt very strongly by Labour new left activists, that the election campaign had shown that there was, as newly elected Labour MP Jeremy Corbyn put it, 'great incompetence in the party machine'.[18] Heffer, who had chaired the NEC's Organisation Committee for many years, astonishingly obtained only 7 per cent of the CLP vote – compared with Benn's 83 per cent in 1981. What was involved here was more than Kinnock's impassioned assertion that winning the next election had to be a 'total precondition' of all strategic and policy decisions. He offered 'unity plus', the 'plus' being a youthful leader offering a modernised party apparatus better able to campaign for left policies. At fringe meetings at the conference, he even quoted Lenin and Gramsci to underline his left credentials.

Yet the support for Kinnock also reflected a change of orientation among activists. Important signs of this began to appear even before the 1983 election. For instance, there were strong differences over whether to abide by the party's new list of proscribed organisations: Vladimir Derer, Lansman and the CLPD felt that conference decisions had to be adhered to, while others, including Benn and much of the leadership of the Labour Coordinating Committee (LCC), thought the reimposition of 'social-democratic centralism' had to be opposed on civil libertarian as well as strategic grounds. Meanwhile, the leading Communist historian Eric Hobsbawm's interventions were influential in providing an intellectual underpinning for Foot and Kinnock's position.[19] On the basis of an acute analysis of declining proletarian culture, Hobsbawm called for the broadest political unity to oppose Thatcherism while, like Foot and Kinnock, remaining silent about the issues raised in the debate on internal party democracy and policy, as well as about the role played by the centre-right in the course of it.

Until the 1983 election, the possibility of developing a new kind of socialist practice that would attract rather than lose votes had by no means yet been effaced in the party, or more broadly on the British left. In the immediate aftermath of Labour's crushing defeat, however, many of those who had supported the Labour new left became as fixated on the appeal for unity as they had been on the demand for change after the 1979 election. There was also a desire to take account of the limits of the Labour new left itself, the contradictions of relying on the unions' votes while not being able to democratise them, and the need to give even more weight to gender and racial issues. Especially among those who had been connected with the Labour Coordinating Committee – where the leading activists were more often intellectuals, some of whom were interested in a career in parliament – there was a move towards the idea that some sort of 'Bennism without Benn' might be achieved under Kinnock's leadership.[20] In a March 1984 pamphlet, the LCC criticised the left for having concentrated too much on democratic change in the party during the 1970s and early 1980s. What was needed now, they said, was to popularise socialist ideas while also accepting Kinnock's leadership, thereby avoiding destructive conflict. In return, the LCC – revealing either astonishing naivety or wishful thinking – expected from Kinnock a 'committed attack on the nature of capitalist society itself'.[21]

Intellectual grounds for this were provided by a current within the widely read 'Euro-Communist' magazine *Marxism Today*, which suggested that a Kinnock leadership would be open to GLC-style 'social movement' political activism, and would distance itself from the old Labourist class politics. Ken Livingstone himself, as GLC leader, had no such illusions.[22] He knew very well how much the parliamentary leadership actively disliked – or at least feared being embarrassed by, in the eyes of the press – black and/or feminist activists like those who took over the podium at the 1981 conference. But the influence of *Marxism Today* helped to create a climate which undermined the kind of enthusiasm that supporters of the LCC had once had (and which *Marxism Today* had once encouraged) for internal party democracy and for the Alternative Economic Strategy. The trouble was that the kind of thinking *Marxism Today* represented was incapable of producing (any more than Hobsbawm could, with his more sober 'popular front' line) any *other* kind of socialist strategy. As Donald Sassoon, who still saw the 'iconoclasm' of *Marxism Today* as having been 'indispensable', acknowledged: 'once the ground was cleared of old-fashioned leftism, the journal and its followers remained unable to go beyond it . . . In the manner of modern gurus they noted a trend (post-Fordism, flexible specialization or charity events for Third World Countries), called it progress, and projected it into the future. By the time the journal folded in the 1990s, it had nothing left to say.'[23]

A core group of the Labour new left, including the Socialist Campaign Group of Labour MPs that had recently formed around Benn and Heffer, did not share the illusions of the LCC and *Marxism Today*. Their support of extra-parliamentary struggles and the links they formed with the independent socialist left – from the Socialist Society, established in 1982, to the Socialist Conferences held in Chesterfield later in the decade – pointed towards a creative politics beyond Labourist parliamentarism. But having lost the initiative within the party, this residue of the Labour new left, continually fighting a series of losing battles against the party's drift to the right, lost such creativity as it had previously displayed. Benn himself, re-elected as MP for Chesterfield in March 1984, remained the left's 'prominent voice', and continued to focus on the need to democratise the state at every level. But this was not echoed by many members of the Campaign Group, and both it and the various socialist groups outside parliament became more politically marginal.

Most of the Labour new left's activists – especially those mobilised by the CLPD – were much more realistic about what Kinnock represented than they had been in relation to Foot. They were not impressed when Hobsbawm introduced Kinnock with fulsome praise at Fabian Society conference fringe meetings. Even when Kinnock promised them that unity would be based on retaining left policies, the party activists who voted for him did so with some sense of discomfort. At any meetings where Kinnock and Benn shared the platform, there could be no doubt about who was closer to the CLP activists politically – and this was revealed year after year in Benn's remarkably high vote in the balloting for the constituency section of the NEC. The CLP activists' support for Kinnock was quite pragmatic – on his past record he seemed to offer a chance to retain left policies and still win the next election. They could not know how far he would go in accommodating the counter-revolution, and that on Kinnock's watch 'unity' would in fact mean what Healey had bluntly told the NEC immediately after the election in July 1983: 'We want more tolerance of the Shadow Cabinet by the Party and the NEC must accept the former's leadership role.'[24] They felt they had no option but to 'let Neil get on with it' in the name of unity – and to hope for the best in terms of left policies being retained.

Once the Labour new left's unity of purpose was removed, its heterogeneous make-up worked to fragment it into what became simplistically – and misleadingly – known as the 'soft' and 'hard' left. A number of its leading figures, including David Blunkett, Tom Sawyer, Michael Meacher and Peter Hain, gradually parted from Benn and realigned themselves with Kinnock. In doing so, they hoped to 'push him to the left', but instead soon found themselves moving with him steadily to the right. Eric Shaw summed up this trend as follows:

Members of the soft left joined the front bench in the hope of influencing party policy as well as to further their careers but, for

some at least, it was *their* views that were more often altered ...
Perhaps most important of all, many former Bennites changed
their minds, because of the conclusions they had drawn after
their experience of the strife of the early 1980s, in response to
electoral defeats or because they no longer believed that the policies they had earlier espoused were workable, politically viable or
electorally acceptable ... By damaging – probably beyond repair –
the unity of the left, the effect of realignment was the isolation of
the hard left who, by the end of the 1980s, were left as the only
organised yet largely impotent focus of resistance to Kinnock's
modernisation project.[25]

The massive vote for the Kinnock–Hattersley 'dream ticket' in the
leadership election at the 1983 conference, and for the expulsion of
Militant members; the marginalisation of Tony Benn and the
absorption of a number of his erstwhile supporters into the Kinnock
'team'; the election of a shadow cabinet with many new faces, but
still dominated numerically by the centre-right of the parliamentary
party – for those who had tried to change the Labour Party, these
were all severe defeats. By 1984 the number of individual members
of the CLPD had already fallen to half its 1982 level, as had the
number of CLP and trade-union branch affiliations.[26] The initiative
had passed to those elements, by no means any longer confined to
the traditional centre-right, who attributed most of the blame for
the election defeat to the process of change having gone 'too far',
and who looked to policy 'moderation' as the basis for unity and
electoral success.

The trouble with this strategy, however, at least initially, was that
unity on these terms was unable to respond to the deep social polarisation that the Thatcher government was by then generating in
Britain. Its own 'counter-revolution' against the Keynesian welfare
state had produced such mass unemployment, destitution, alienation
and conflict that the maintenance of public order came to depend
not on a smaller state, but on a stronger, more coercive one. Moreover,
the fact that the Labour new left had been so clearly weakened lent

support to the arguments of those who held that the battles had to be fought in the streets.

Kinnock's Response: The Organisational Reaction

Thanks especially to the division of the opposition vote caused by the SDP split, Thatcher easily won the general election of 1983, as well as the following election in 1987; but intense popular resistance generated by her policies in one area after another finally brought her down. This activism was a direct descendant of that of the late 1960s and early 1970s. The Labour new left had wanted to build a bridge between the party and that activism, to inflect it in a socialist political direction and infuse the party with it. That project had now been defeated; the activism continued, but could now only take the form of a series of defensive actions. This was a measure of the huge political cost of the Labour new left's defeat. It had not only failed to democratise and transform the party, but this in turn meant that it had been unable to politicise the great industrial militancy of the time, or to 'nationalise' the myriad creative forms of community politics and local socialism.

This is not the place to retell the story of the great miners' strike of 1984–85, or the struggles over local democracy which continued through the abolition of the GLC and the other metropolitan counties in 1986, or the poll tax revolt of 1989–90 and beyond. But the scale and intensity of these struggles can hardly be overstated. The miners' strike, above all, focused the attention of the country – indeed, of the wider world – on the nature of the Thatcherite project in a way that the Labour leadership singularly failed to do. As Raymond Williams observed at the time: 'In a period of very powerful multinational capital, moving its millions under various flags of convenience, and in a period also of rapid and often arbitrary takeover and merger by financial groups of all kinds, virtually everyone is exposed or will be exposed to what the miners have suffered.'[27]

Kinnock's equivocations in relation to the miners' strike – once Thatcher and the full resources of the security apparatus, the police, the judicial system and the media had done their work – contrasted painfully with his bravado at the 1985 conference.[28] Kinnock's celebrated assaults on the leadership of the National Union of Mineworkers (NUM) and Militant leaders of Liverpool Council at that conference represented – and were intended to represent – far more than a distancing of the party from what he called 'the generals of gesture' and 'the tendency tacticians' of the 'hard left'. His speech was, above all, a full re-declaration of independence from the sovereign authority that the Labour new left had claimed for the conference, and for the extraparliamentary party more generally, with respect to the Parliamentary Labour Party. As Labour leaders had done so often in the past – but with far greater effect, given recent party history – Kinnock spoke as much over the heads of the delegates as he spoke to them. He was effectively saying to the media, to the Tories and the Liberal–SDP Alliance, and not least to the right-wing social democrats who still dominated the PLP: you may say that the Party is beholden to the unions, you may say the constituencies are dominated by extremists, but you can't pin that on me.

The great majority of the delegates gave Kinnock a prolonged standing ovation, and this was more than a matter of playing their allotted role before the television cameras. Many of the same 1,800 people who attended a *Labour Herald* rally the night before to hear and cheer Benn and the NUM leader Arthur Scargill were the next morning on their feet applauding Kinnock. This political schizophrenia was due to the fact that Kinnock, like Foot before him, retained a substantial base among the rank and file of the party of a kind that right-wing parliamentarians had never had. And however much the delegates might have preferred, and indeed continued to vote for, left-wing resolutions and NEC candidates, they also badly wanted to win the next election, to get Thatcher out at all costs.

The trouble with this was that it closed off the possibility of constructing out of the crisis anything resembling a socialist alternative to Thatcherism. Moreover, the media's adulation did not last. They sensed that the strength and depth of the previous socialist mobilisation in the party had been such that Kinnock's social-democratic rhetoric would not be enough to enable the party to present a unified face to the electorate. The exorcism of the left could not be a one-off event. Despite Kinnock's attack on Militant and the mineworkers, *The Times* immediately turned its attention to women and black activists:

> The face of the Labour Party has not stabilised. What is offered to the voters in Brent, Haringey or Hackney is not Mr Kinnock's emollience but Miss Abbott's rhetoric of class struggle and skin-colour consciousness and the insurrectionary talk of Mr Bernie Grant. In a party with no boundaries, in a church with no cate-chism beyond the nullity of Clause Four, they have as good a claim to speak for 'socialism' as he does. Exit (perhaps) Mr Mulhearn, Mr Hatton and sundry other followers of the Fourth International; enter – with no one to bar their way – class and race warriors in thrall to the same Marxist doctrine.[29]

This was red-baiting of the crudest kind. It is very improbable that more than a handful of Labour new left activists, male or female, white or black, were ever 'Marxists' of any description. But *The Times*'s crudity stemmed from a passionate wish to see off the threat of 'socialism' in Britain, and this passion was not much less strong among those in the parliamentary party who also longed for an end to Thatcherism. There was work still to do in making the Labour Party a safe alternative government for the British establishment.

This work Kinnock now began. He set in motion an organis-ational transformation that would culminate ten years later in the emergence of a new kind of party, increasingly detached from what was left of the labour movement. The trade unions would lose much of their influence inside the party, and would be told to expect no special favours from a future Labour government. Party membership would be expanded, but the influence of active members diluted and curbed. Control would be ever more frankly concentrated in the hands of a leadership elite of professional politicians – and above all in the hands of the leader himself.

The central theme of all the changes was to allow the leader to determine party policy with only the formal approval of the party outside parliament – both its trade union wing and its constituency activists – and to be seen by the media to be doing so. The Labour new left was to play very little part in this story. Some of its principal figures, as we have seen, aligned themselves with Kinnock. The 'soft' left supported him when he conspicuously dissociated himself from the mineworkers, closed the *New Socialist* magazine, and drastically reduced the influence of the NEC's policy committees. Those MPs who remained with Benn in the Socialist Campaign Group through the 1980s were increasingly marginalised in the PLP as they continued to articulate the new left's analysis and vision of the future, which still had resonance in the labour movement and in a wide variety of social movements; and they strongly supported activist resistance to Thatcherism, whether by the miners or the 'poll tax' resisters.

In addition to keeping tight control over policy formation in the short run, Kinnock also pursued two linked strategies designed to reduce the long-term influence of both the unions and active party members. First, in the name of 'one member, one vote' ('OMOV'), he proposed that all individual party members should be able to vote in elections for the party leader, in the selection of candidates for parliament and delegates to annual conferences; and the balloting would be done by post, not at meetings that only activists attended. Kinnock and his advisers assumed that less active members would be less left-wing. He also argued that this would make more people want to be members; he envisaged a doubling of the membership from its then level of about 250,000 (at one time he rashly set a target of 1 million). Second, as individual membership rose, Kinnock proposed that the weight of the trade-union block vote at annual conferences should be reduced.

These proposals addressed real problems. Party activists were indeed unrepresentative of Labour voters, although Kinnock had been happy to rely on the activists' support while he still championed unilateral nuclear disarmament. On the other hand, the trade-union leaders' block votes were no less unrepresentative; they were casting millions of votes for members who were less and less politically involved – and, moreover, they often did so with little prior consultation with these members, and with no weight given to minority views among them. Now that this means of curbing the power of activists had itself become unreliable, it was declared to be indefensible. Kinnock's 'soft leftism' did not extend to wanting to democratise the trade unions and get their members more actively involved in politics, as the Labour new left had wished. Instead, he sought a new source of *in*activist (and hence 'moderate') support for the leadership in the shape of a wider membership who could be directly consulted through postal votes.

Of course, enlarging the party's individual membership was certainly desirable. But dropping the need for members to attend any meetings in order to vote on policies, combined with the leadership's espousal of policies beamed at 'middle England', gave the change a specific political meaning. Kinnock and his general secretary Larry Whitty maintained that they wanted not only to increase the number of members but also to 'increase activism within the party'.[30] In fact, between 1984 and 1988, 60,000 members left the party, and individual membership fell to its lowest level for forty years; and by 1991, when membership had very slightly recovered, a survey by Seyd and Whiteley revealed that 'four in every ten members felt themselves to be *less* active . . . than they were five years [earlier]'.[31] What the changes really portended was a North American–style party of professional politicians, supported by a membership that was treated as consisting of donors and election helpers, not participants in party policy formation, or mobilisers of local opinion.

Kinnock met too much resistance from both left and right, however, to be able to do more than initiate this transformation of the party. He was able to get the 1987 conference to agree to a new system for selecting parliamentary candidates, which compromised between the principle of OMOV and the traditional weight accorded to the unions. All individual members in the constituency would be balloted, but the final selection would be made, following the ballot, by a local 'electoral college' in which locally affiliated trade unions might have up to 40 per cent of the votes. Kinnock also got the unions to agree that, in 1993, the weight of the trade-union block vote at the annual conference would be reduced from 90 to 70 per cent, and that, when individual party membership surpassed 300,000, consideration would be given to reducing this still further, to 50 per cent. But this was as far as he could go. He was obliged to leave it to his successors to complete the party's transformation from one that still saw itself as the political wing of a social movement into a an elite-run electoral machine with a membership comprising a broad cross-section of the electorate.

Labour's fourth consecutive general election defeat, in April 1992, when its share of the vote still barely surpassed 35 per cent, not only forced Kinnock to resign, but also reopened the issue of the power of the trade unions in the party, which the Conservative press continued to treat as fundamentally disqualifying it from office. Both the front-running candidates for the leadership, John Smith and Bryan Gould, called for the principle of OMOV to be extended, and Smith, having won the race, took up the question again. He established a Union Links Review Group which, urged on by Tony Blair in particular, eventually adopted OMOV for candidate selection, with only a slight concession to a continuing special role for the unions. It also approved a revised formula for leadership elections in which union members affiliated to the Labour Party, voting as individuals, would have a third of the electoral college votes (the other two-thirds being cast by MPs, MEPs and constituency party members, respectively). These changes were adopted by a narrow majority at the 1993 party conference (at which, in line with the previous agreement, the weight of the unions' block vote had already been reduced to 70 per cent).[32]

'New Labour': The Modernisation Project of Tony Blair

On 12 May 1994, John Smith died. On 1 June Gordon Brown decided not to run for the leadership, and on 21 July Tony Blair was elected leader with 57 per cent of the total votes. Rightly or wrongly, both Smith and Brown had been seen as sympathetic to the party's traditional 'labourist' ethos. The power to set policy was now placed in the hands of a leader who, for the first time in the party's history, was almost completely free of that ethos – from the mix of values and practices, evolved over some 150 years of collective political effort, which had hitherto shaped party policy. Not everything in this ethos was admirable – it contained a great deal that was archaic, formalistic and anti-intellectual;but it also comprised some of the most egalitarian, humanistic, internationalist and brave elements in British culture.[33] Previous party leaders had been influenced by this ethos to different degrees: none was as untouched by it as Tony Blair, either before he became leader in July 1994 or afterwards.[34] In the Leader's Office, and in his most intimate political circle, he operated in a milieu with a different ethos – that of professional politics based on higher education, management skills, and the culture of the communications industry. Some of the chief exponents of this ethos more or less openly despised that of the old labour movement. In particular, they rejected the idea that capitalism might one day be replaced by a superior social and economic system. For them, the task was only to manage it; socialism – a word most of them avoided – meant at most a set of values that should govern this task. For Blair, this meant, first and foremost, completing the process of taking power away from the party's activists, nearly all of whom thought capitalism should either be replaced, or at least radically modified.[35]

And the new membership strategy began to show results. Tom Sawyer, who replaced Larry Whitty as general secretary of the party when Blair assumed the leadership in 1994, launched a sustained membership drive inspired by the 'Sedgefield model' developed by Blair in his own constituency, and by American-style management thinking. Blair had secured the NEC's permission for the Sedgefield constituency party to recruit members by accepting whatever they were willing to pay by way of subscriptions, and making up the difference between this and the national membership subscription rate through local fundraising. The effect was to increase Sedgefield's membership to 2,000 by 1995, compared with an average of 470 members per constituency for the country as a whole. If, as critics complained, the price was that time had to be spent 'organising barbecues instead of meetings', the benefit was a broadly based membership, attached to the party as much by social as by political ties – as members of the Conservative Party traditionally were – and run by Blair and his core of loyal supporters, not by activists with political ideas and agendas of their own. As for the management approach to membership, it was reflected in constant advertising for members in the national press, and in a revealing interview given by Tom Sawyer in which he said he 'favoured management consultants [he mentioned the Cranfield Institute of Management] to help inject new thinking into the party's targeting of new members, including judgements on whether members are best recruited in marginals or heartlands, to raise funds or to be active. Different marketing techniques will be used for different goals'.[36]

By the middle of 1995, Sawyer reported that 113,000 new members had joined since Blair had become leader; total membership had reached 350,000. On the other hand, in the same period 38,000 members had left. This was a serious exodus, but a price the leadership was not unwilling to pay. The new members do not seem to have been very different in their attitudes from members of longer standing. A survey in May 1995 found that 57 per cent were in favour of Labour setting a rate for a minimum wage before the next election (an indicator of sympathy for trade-union demands, since Blair was resisting making such a commitment), while only 40 per cent said they 'agreed with the direction the party was going under Blair' (23 per cent disagreed, and – perhaps most significantly – 37 per cent didn't know).[37] But the new members' role in supporting Blair's successful campaign to rewrite Clause IV of the party constitution was to prove crucially important.

Clause IV famously stated that the party's central object was 'to secure for the workers by hand or brain the full fruits of their industry and the most equitable distribution thereof that may be possible upon the basis of the common ownership of the means of production, distribution and exchange'. Gaitskell had tried unsuccessfully to change it in 1960; ever since it had continued to be treated, as Harold Wilson had cynically remarked, like Genesis, as part of the Bible (and 'you can't take Genesis out of the Bible'). Soon after Blair's election as leader in July 1994 he resolved to return to this battle – indicating as much, in slightly veiled language, at the party conference in October that year. The NEC somewhat reluctantly agreed, and called a special conference for April 1995. A campaign of opposition to any change was begun by twenty Labour MEPs in an advertisement in the *Guardian* in January 1995, and taken up by the Socialist Campaign Group of Labour MPs and others outside parliament. Blair responded by undertaking a unique series of thirty-five highly publicised meetings throughout the country, attended by a total of some 30,000 party members. At these meetings, he argued that Clause IV no longer represented the range of values that the party stood for in the 1990s, while on the other hand it committed it to something – public ownership – that people no longer believed in: 'I don't think anyone now believes that vast chunks of industry should be taken over by a Labour government.'[38]

The latter argument was distinctly tendentious. The polls showed that a majority of the electorate still favoured public ownership of energy, water and railways, and the fact that the modernisers used the same implausible rhetoric as the Conservative press suggested they were unwilling to discuss the issue on its merits. Peter Mandelson, for example, in a debate with Arthur Scargill on the new Clause IV in May 1995, after its adoption, said: 'The old Clause IV threatened the end of private corner shops, newsagents, markets. That would mean buying our chips at the Common Ownership Fryers.'[39] But it worked. At the special conference on 29 April 1995, 90 per cent of the constituency delegates voted for the change, in contrast with the much narrower majority (54.6 per cent) cast in favour of it by the unions – a striking inversion of the old pattern, in which right-wing union leaders could be relied on to back the leadership against the left-wing activists in the constituency parties.[40] The old Clause IV was replaced by a portmanteau commitment to a range of other values (a dynamic economy, a just society, an open democracy and a healthy environment). These included – crucially for the media – an endorsement of 'the enterprise of the market and the rigour of competition', and 'a thriving private sector' – even if, as Hugo Young noted, no one at the special conference that finally endorsed the new wording displayed any notable enthusiasm for any of these priorities.[41]

Blair's authority was enhanced by this decisive victory, enabling him to contemplate further changes. One was to pursue the further reduction in the weight of the unions' block vote at party conferences to 50 per cent, already agreed in principle once the total individual membership of the party exceeded 300,000, which it now had.[42] This change came into operation in 1996. Another was to put pressure on the unions to ballot their members on issues to be decided at party conferences: 'There will have to be discussions to ensure that from now there is a much greater consistency of view between what ordinary members think and the votes cast by their leaders.'[43]

Blair also moved to end trade-union sponsorship of MPs – the system whereby, in over 150 constituencies, unions undertook to pay some of the expenses of the local party organisation. The sums involved generally amounted to around £600 a year, and between £2,000 and 3,000 at a general election. Although sponsored MPs received no financial benefits for themselves, they were expected to represent the interests of the union concerned in parliament, even though most sponsored MPs claimed that they were never asked to do so in any specific case. Blair, himself sponsored by the TGWU, saw sponsorship as an unnecessary hostage to the Conservative press, which always treated it as evidence that Labour was in thrall to the unions. By February 1996 he had secured the unions' agreement to switch from sponsoring individual candidates and MPs to giving financial support to local party organisations in marginal seats.

Blair secured three more major changes before the 1997 election. One was to build on his success in going directly to the membership over Clause IV by getting the NEC to agree that the entire party membership should be asked to endorse a 'pre-manifesto programme'.

The document containing this manifesto was finalised by a joint meeting of the shadow cabinet and the NEC, and submitted to the annual conference, which – not surprisingly, since the document had to be accepted or rejected as a whole – endorsed it unanimously. It was then sent out to the whole membership in a 'yes-or-no' postal ballot. Although presented as a way of consulting the membership more widely, the primary aim, commentators agreed, was 'to bind the rank and file into [Blair's'] vision of New Labour';[44] or, in the words of the document itself, *The Road to the Manifesto* (described by Blair as 'his contract with Britain'): 'There must be no doubt whatever at the end of this process that the party and its constituent parts accept and agree this programme.' In a postal ballot in October 1996, 61 per cent of party members responded, 95 per cent voting in favour.[45] Although this process was ostensibly grafted onto the existing policymaking authority of the party conference, its thrust was clearly to institutionalise a new plebiscitary relationship between the leader and party members, in relation to which the party conference would eventually become less important.

A second change was directed at Blair's critics in the parliamentary party. New rules of conduct were drawn up for MPs, which created the open-ended new offence of 'bringing the party into disrepute'. Strong hints were also given that, in future, local constituency Labour parties might be expected to select parliamentary candidates only from a central list compiled by the National Executive.[46] The third change, launched publicly on the eve of the 1997 election, concerned the composition and policymaking roles of the National Executive and of the annual conference. This was the dénouement of a review begun almost two years earlier on the initiative of the general secretary, Tom Sawyer. The essence of the changes proposed in his document, *Labour into Power: A Framework for Partnership*, and endorsed by the NEC in January 1997, was to make the extra-parliamentary party an auxiliary to the parliamentary party, rather than the other way round. Instead of being a potential alternative source of authority to a Labour government, the NEC should be its 'partner', committed to making the party support it. To this end, the NEC should no longer consist of members elected by the annual conference, but rather of representatives directly elected by a range of party 'constituencies', including the unions, the cabinet, the PLP, the European PLP, local government, socialist societies, the Youth Section, and black and Asian members. In particular, Constituency Labour Parties should be represented by ordinary members chosen at the local level; in other words, not by people with high-enough national profiles to win broad-based support at annual conferences. The 'old left' Derbyshire MP Dennis Skinner – the only dissenting voice on the NEC when the report was adopted – noted that, after surviving 'off and on' as an NEC member 'for about 20 years by a democratic process', under the new proposals he would not 'even be allowed to stand'.[47] The activists' last bridgehead in the party's centre was thus marked down for elimination.

Labour into Power also proposed that the party's policymaking process should be permanently changed to something like the Policy Review of 1987–89. A Joint Policy Committee of the cabinet and the NEC – like the one established by Kinnock, but in future chaired by the leader or his deputy – would originate policy documents in a two-year 'rolling' review cycle, steering them through a consultative process in which the chief role would be played by the National Policy Forum, a hitherto informal body of a hundred members who were, *Labour into Power* noted, 'drawn' – that is, not elected – 'from all parts of the Party and country', and who met in private.[48] The revised documents would finally be submitted to the annual conference; but the leadership clearly did not envisage that they would be hotly debated there. Though the conference was the 'sovereign policy making and decision making body of the Party', it must become better adapted to the fact that it was also a 'hugely symbolic event' and a 'showpiece'. It must avoid 'gladiatorial conflicts and deeply divisive conflicts' which gave the press opportunities to emphasise 'the alleged power and influence of key individuals, unions or groups'. It should be more of an occasion to listen to the leaders, become educated on policy issues, and show support:

We believe there is room for the Party Conference to become a more valuable and rewarding experience for all who take part. It could provide a serious opportunity to set out and publicize Labour's achievements and plans, be the occasion of in-depth consideration of policy, contribute to mutual political understanding, offer opportunities to hear the views of experts or key figures from inside and outside of the Party and be a clear exemplification of partnership in practice.[49]

The bland corporate style of *Labour into Power* was evidently meant to soften the impact of what it proposed. But rather than conceal its real intentions, the document's laboured and often disingenuous language tended if anything to draw attention to them. Formally, the conference would remain 'sovereign'; in practice, policy would be set by the leadership, discussed (privately) in the Policy Forum, and presented to the conference in such a way that open disagreement would be minimised; and NEC members elected by CLPs would cease to be primarily high-profile figures representing important segments of party opinion.

All this was very much in line with what Callaghan had proposed in his 1976 conference speech, when he adopted monetarism at the height of the last Labour government's conflict with a Labour new left majority on the NEC. In doing so, he had relied on the help of the union leadership. But abandoning Keynesianism really implied a broader counter-revolution that would entail the ultimate disengagement of the party from the labour movement, and *Labour in Power* had now finally put this on the agenda. Already, at the TUC annual conference in October 1996, the party's industrial relations spokesman, Stephen Byers, had speculated to journalists that the party might ballot its members on severing the trade-union link.[50] While this was immediately denied, most commentators thought it was a serious possibility, particularly if the union leadership failed to agree on a 'code of conduct' to avoid strikes, including binding arbitration and second ballots, which the Labour leadership was said to be urging on them in private discussions. Meanwhile, 46 per cent of

Labour supporters said they favoured ending the trade unions' voting rights at Labour conferences.[51] Publicly, Blair declared: 'New Labour will, in government, as now in opposition, be respectful of the unions' part in our past, but will have relations with them relevant for today.'[52] In any event, Labour's days as the political wing of a broad-based social movement, seeking to educate public opinion and lead a popular drive for social transformation, clearly appeared to be numbered.

6

New Labour in Power:
The Dénouement of Modernisation

After Labour's landslide election victory in 1997, the modernisers – rebranded as 'New Labour' – had thirteen years in which to put their vision to the test, backed by large majorities in the Commons and sympathetic treatment from the media. By 2010 the project had failed comprehensively. It was clear that there was in fact no 'third way' for 'hard-working people and their families' to lead stable and satisfying lives within the dynamics of neoliberal globalised capital. Yet many MPs, particularly those who had been recruited by the modernisers, and a majority of party officials, remained opposed to any significant change of direction in party policy. For the great majority of the party's remaining members, however, and even more for the thousands who had left, the need for a radical change eventually become unquestionable. Although the Labour left survived, with difficulty, through the New Labour years, Jeremy Corbyn's seemingly abrupt elevation in 2015 from the party's margins to its leadership can only be understood in the context of the modernisers' project and its failure.

New Labour's Vision: Adapting to the 'New Reality'

By the time of the 1997 general election, the policy differences between Labour and the Conservatives had become extremely narrow. The Policy Review of 1987–89 had already abandoned three of the party's long-standing commitments: unilateral nuclear disarmament, the restoration of trade-union immunities, and the renationalisation of privatised industries. Immediately afterwards, when Kinnock and John Smith announced their support for British membership of the Exchange Rate Mechanism, Labour effectively abandoned whatever objections it still had to the primary aims of Economic and Monetary Union. This meant ceasing to treat full employment as an overriding aim, and so full employment disappeared, even as a long-term goal, from the NEC's 1990 policy statement *Looking to the Future*. It also meant that Labour's commitment to Keynesianism (the way socialism had effectively been redefined through the postwar era to mean a different way of managing the capitalist economy) was itself being set aside.

What then was left to distinguish Labour's political project? According to Peter Mandelson, the modernisers stood for 'a new type of politics', 'a new synthesis to which all of the centre and left can subscribe'. At one level, this meant revisiting the Gaitskellites' failure thirty years earlier to expunge the commitment to common ownership from the party's constitution. Indeed, for Mandelson the revision of Clause IV was 'the essence of what New Labour and Blair's leadership [was] about'. The defeat of the Labour new left had already ruled out any notion of using Clause IV as a guide to policy; its decisive revision showed the importance the modernisers attached to symbolic change. The new type of politics would not, Mandelson said, seek 'equality of outcome', but only equal opportunity; it would not favour more public consumption and investment, but only investment; it would not want 'top-down centralised rules administered by powerful bureaucracies', but 'diversity and decentralisation ... with public goals sometimes achieved by market means'. Labour should see its job as representing not the working class, but 'ordinary families who work hard and play by the rules', because people no longer thought of themselves as members of classes, but as individuals. To win elections, Labour must adapt to the 'new reality' of global capitalism, and not only give up the idea of transcending it, but demonstrably reject any such idea. The most that could be done was 'to strengthen the so-called supply side' – 'to enhance skills, promote investment, and enlarge our economic capacity'.[1]

This view rested on a correct perception that globalised capitalism was no longer the capitalism familiar from the postwar years, when a private sector was partly offset by a large public sector and constrained by the political power of an organised working class. Thatcher's decision in October 1979 to abolish government control over capital movements had led to huge capital outflows from the UK. By the end of the eighties Britain had become once again a rentier nation, with by far the largest stock of direct investment overseas, relative to GDP, of any OECD country, and was the most open of any OECD country to investment from abroad. Economic policy had become subject to the approval of international investors through the rate of interest they wanted for renewing the public debt. In conformity with market sentiment, the Thatcher and Major governments also made low inflation their chief aim, and control of the money supply (as opposed to fiscal policy) their only means of achieving it.

The decimation of manufacturing through the 1970s and 1980s had led to a steep decline in trade-union membership, from over 12 million in 1979 to less than 7 million by 1996, accelerated by a series of Conservative measures that stripped the unions of immunity from financial attack for pursuing industrial action, and of other legal rights on which their strength had previously rested. After the defeat of the miners in 1985, and the printers in 1986, strike action had dropped to insignificant levels. As the job mix deteriorated for those in employment, with fewer and fewer new jobs being full-time and permanent, the power of workers to constrain the behaviour of employers, let alone to have much effect on government policy, declined still further.

As the demand for workers had fallen, moreover, the proportion of households with no one in work had risen sharply; and with ever more children living in poverty, most of them in these workless households, a major new form of marginalisation had been created. What is more, a significant proportion of adults in these households were claiming sick pay, having become ill under the stress of anxiety about redundancy, increased work intensity, or deteriorating work conditions. In the meantime the Conservatives had also stripped local authorities of most of their powers, severely limiting their ability to cushion the shock. This was especially important in the newly de-industrialised regions where few alternative employment opportunities existed. Many local services, most notably social care, had been privatised, while local authority spending was tightly controlled and cut. Schools had been transferred from direct local authority management to management by boards of governors drawn from their local neighbourhoods, which tended to disadvantage schools in poor areas. Local authority housing was compulsorily sold to tenants who wished to buy, or was transferred to Housing Associations or Trusts. The Conservatives were defeated in most local council elections through the 1980s and 1990s, but in the long run all these changes cost Labour more dearly. By the late 1980s, the party's two traditional bastions of support, local government and the trade unions, had been seriously undermined.

Thatcherism – or neoliberalism, as it would later be understood – also 'colonised the life-world' during these years through a radical shift from non-market to market principles in every sphere. The privatisation of the big utilities, starting with British Telecom, was crucial in changing public perceptions. The publicly owned utilities had become inefficient and unpopular, largely because they had been systematically starved of funds, which fed through into low productivity, low morale and poor management. As private companies, they quickly became profitable (thanks to being sold cheap, cutting jobs, and being placed under 'light-touch' – i.e. generous – regulation), and this enabled them to invest. The government used the proceeds of privatisation to help cut taxes, while millions of people took advantage of the low prices at which the utilities were put up for sale to make some money by buying shares and selling them at a profit. While most of them disposed of their shares quickly, their involvement in the transaction made them less likely to endorse the general outrage at the huge salaries and share options enjoyed by the utility company directors, or the grotesque bonus payments given to dealers in the City following its 'Big Bang' deregulation in 1986.

Radical changes in the state dictated by neoliberal ideology had also been initiated before 1997. 'Operational responsibility' was increasingly devolved from government ministries to 'executive agencies', nominally independent of ministerial control and subject to quasi-market incentives, charging each other for their work, paying their managers by 'performance' and intensifying the 'throughput' their junior staff were expected to produce. Across the public services a huge new industry of 'auditing' had grown up, as the concept was stretched to cover the pseudo-technical monitoring of every sort of performance, giving rise to 'a distinct mentality of administrative control': 'many more individuals and organisations [were] coming to think of themselves as subjects of audits'.[2] The public were also trained to think of themselves not as users of collectively provided services such as patients, or passengers, but as 'customers' – a relationship between the state and the citizen, encapsulated in John Major's so-called Citizens' Charter of 1991, that was diametrically opposed to the model of democratic public engagement with the state advanced by the Labour new left in the 1970s.

The modernisers considered that all this was not only irreversible, but largely desirable. The party had to accept and adapt to it. This meant that all new policies had to satisfy three requirements. First, the next election must be won at all costs. This meant catering to voters' existing ideas, rather than seeking to build support for new ones. Moreover, the electorally crucial voters to cater to were those who must be won back from the Conservatives to Labour, not those who had suffered most under Conservative rule – most of whom, it was assumed, would vote Labour in any case. Second, it must be accepted that voters' preferences had been shaped not just by twenty years of neoliberal propaganda, but also by profound changes in the real world. On this view, people no longer identified themselves primarily in terms of social classes or as producers, the workforce was no longer predominantly male, jobs were no longer permanent or secure, the state was no longer regarded as benign. 'New Labour' policies must reflect these realities. Third, the aim must be to win at least two successive elections, so that longer-term education and training policies to promote competitiveness would have time to bear fruit. This required that Labour must win acceptance by 'business' as a suitable, and if possible a preferred, governing party, so that investment would be forthcoming to support the growth on which everything else depended. This meant being realistic about the constraints imposed by globalisation – especially the need to keep corporate taxation and regulatory standards as low as possible, and to keep British labour costs down.

Policies to realise these aims were not going to come, as in the past, from the researchers in party headquarters, the unions, or socialistically inclined academics. Instead there was a proliferation of think tanks, directed by close associates of the New Labour leadership. At the end of the 1990s, three main New Labour organisations were in business: the Institute for Public Policy Research (IPPR), established in 1988; Demos, established in 1993; and Nexus, formed in 1996. Of these, the most significant in terms of practical policy ideas was IPPR, which published a range of proposals on topics such as devolution, elected mayors, 'family-friendly working', 'asset-based welfare', and public-service reform. But the think tank most emblematic of New Labour was Demos, whose founder-director Geoff Mulgan was a former chief adviser to Gordon Brown, and later served as director of policy in the prime minister's office under Blair from 2002 to 2004. Mulgan's politics had several distinctive features. One was a lack of interest in political economy, which he regarded as a 'weak' field.[3] Another was a heavy emphasis on complexity, differentiation and pluralism. A third was fascination with novelty. Past socialist thought, he said, was out of touch with the 'pace of change'. The resulting blend of utopianism, eclecticism, and especially novelty, were marked features of Blair's rhetoric, too.[4] As for Nexus, it was characteristic of New Labour in a different way, being a network rather than an institution: in office, Blair had a strong preference for creating 'task forces' rather than permanent bodies which might come to hold independent views. Nexus hosted debates in search of usable meanings for ideas such as the 'third way', and answers to questions such as 'What version of equality does the left now espouse, if any?'[5]

But while the modernisers' project may have had shallow intellectual roots, they invested heavily in media management. They saw media 'spin' as an electoral necessity, which meant keeping tight control over all policy pronouncements. This was the special preoccupation of Peter Mandelson, who since the late 1980s had already tirelessly 'managed' news and cajoled or bullied journalists and editors to give favourable treatment to the Labour leadership. Because he had a close personal relationship with Blair, he came to play an especially powerful role in New Labour policymaking. He took it as given that globalisation imposed very severe constraints on all social and economic policies, so that the only policies worth promoting are those that capital – 'the market' – would accept.

Included in these constraints was the power of the increasingly globally owned media. Labour must therefore do whatever it took to secure less venomously hostile treatment than Kinnock had received in the national newspapers controlled by Rupert Murdoch, which accounted for one-third of circulation. So in July 1995 Blair travelled to Australia to speak at the annual meeting of Murdoch's News Corporation International. It paid off, inasmuch as Murdoch instructed the *Sun*, whose attacks on Kinnock were widely believed to have cost Labour the 1992 general election, to declare for Blair in 1997. But it was an act of supplication that many party members found it difficult to stomach.

From 1994 onwards the role of the party's spin-doctor was taken on by Blair's press secretary, Alastair Campbell. 'Spin' became a central feature of New Labour policymaking, and was used not just to outmanoeuvre the Tories and hostile journalists, but also to help overcome resistance to New Labour policies inside the party. In the long run a high price was paid for this. Resentment at the constant 'fixing' of decisions on behalf of the leader, and the way spin was used to thwart resistance to it, led to a growing sense of alienation among even loyal MPs and party members.

De-Democratising the Party: The 'Rolling Coup'

The significance of the changes that Kinnock and Smith had already made to Labour's internal power structure was well illustrated by the fact that when Blair became party leader in 1994, journalists took it for granted that if he disagreed with previous conference decisions, these could no longer be seriously considered to be party policy. Policy commitments abandoned or significantly modified under Blair's leadership featured regularly in the press, and hardly any of the changes resulted from debates at party conferences. They were often announced first in the media, which could then be relied upon to treat any critical reactions within the party as evidence of a 'split', raising the stakes of opposition.

As a result, policy change was driven forward by Blair and his closest colleagues, with only 'regular and ineffectual spasms of Old Labour discontent'.[6] The unions complained strongly about Blair's refusal to set a specific figure for the minimum wage, which the party was committed to introducing (as well they might, given that the party's commitment to a minimum wage had been a quid pro quo for accepting the leadership's earlier decision not to restore the unions' former legal immunities). The Campaign Group of MPs likewise protested against Blair's willingness to entertain the possibility of Britain joining the European Monetary Union without a prior democratisation of the EU's political structures. But all these remained, or became, 'New Labour' policies.

In the short run, dissent was subordinated to the overwhelming shared aim of winning an election. But given the fundamental nature of the change in Labour's politics that the modernisers were determined to bring about – transforming it from a party of the working class to another party of business – it was obvious that they would face serious internal resistance.[7] To overcome this, they sought control of a new kind, at every level of the party – from CLPs through the annual conference to the NEC and the PLP. This was the ultimate aim of the 'Labour into Power' project, described in the previous chapter. The promise was that party members would enjoy influence through a set of coordinating and deliberative processes, in which the National Policy Forum (NPF) would play a central role. In practice, these processes were managed by party officials to ensure that the leadership's views always prevailed.

The weight of the trade-union vote in the annual party conference had already been reduced to 50 per cent, and had to reflect the distribution of opinion within the unions through the balloting of members. Policy resolutions could no longer be submitted by CLPs directly to the party conference, but went to the NPF, which sifted and prioritised them. From 1998 onwards a covert countrywide network of 'loyalist' party members was run from the centre to ensure that people who opposed the leadership were not elected to the NPF.[8] Moreover, the package of proposals produced by the NPF and submitted to the annual conference via the NEC could not be amended, but had to be accepted or rejected as a whole. Trade-union resistance to the formal elimination of the conference's authority led to a concession that 'contemporary' (i.e. urgent) motions from CLPs and affiliated organisations could still be submitted to the conference; but only four could be debated, and in the run-up to the pre-conference ballot to decide which these would be, the leadership could ensure that motions they disliked were not chosen.

The 1996 'Road to the Manifesto' exercise described in Chapter 5 had in any case established a precedent for the leadership to pre-empt debate at the party conference, with the NEC having agreed that, once the document had been endorsed as a package on a yes-or-no vote by the membership, all policy deliberation and submission of resolutions should cease until the general election that was expected the following year. But this was a self-denying ordinance which Blair did not apply to himself, continuing to issue new policies, both before the election and on numerous occasions later, without further authorisation from any party organ. John Pilger called the 'Road to the Manifesto' exercise 'the sort of black joke that juntas play on nations'.[9]

Power was shifted to the leadership in other ways as well, especially by eroding the power of the NEC. MPs were no longer eligible to stand for election to any of the six places on the NEC reserved for representatives of CLPs, so that prominent party figures on the left, who had traditionally won most of these positions, were replaced by local figures who carried no national weight. And although the NEC continued to assert its right to set party policy in light of conference decisions, that power became largely usurped by the Joint Policy Committee (JPC), set up by Smith in 1993. With Labour in office after 1997, the JPC – with its ministerial representatives and their advisers, plus party officials, in attendance – came to be treated as 'the policy-making body', and was also in charge of arrangements at the NPF. In practice, it became 'a leadership-dominated management tool largely unaccountable to the NPF or to the NEC'.[10]

The PLP presented the leadership with less of a problem than the membership did, partly because the left wing was in such a small minority after the 1997 election landslide. Nevertheless, in 2001, without formal party approval, Blair created a new position of party chair, appointed by him, ostensibly to be the voice of the party in the cabinet, but in reality to supersede the authority of the existing elected chair of the PLP. Blair also sought and secured increased central control of the selection of parliamentary candidates. In the run-up to the 1997 election, a number of people personally supported by Blair had been 'parachuted' into safe Labour seats, but the scale of Labour's victory meant that many seats which the party had not considered winnable were won by unknown candidates, not all of whom subscribed to the New Labour project. To prevent this from recurring in the 2001 election, the NEC set up a National Parliamentary Panel to review all would-be Labour candidates. It rejected 205 of the 886 people (22 per cent) who applied nation-wide, among them any who were considered likely to disagree at all strongly with the leadership.[11] Conversely, rule changes adopted in 1998 protected sitting MPs who were supportive of the leadership from being deselected by their local parties. The result of all this was that hardly any new left-wing MPs were elected after 1997. Thereafter the Socialist Campaign Group of MPs in the PLP, which had already been reduced from some four dozen in the early 1980s to half that in 1997, was further reduced through retirements and deaths during the years when New Labour was in office. Consequently, by 2010, with few if any new left-wing candidates having been allowed to stand for election, only about a dozen were left.[12]

But for the modernisers even these measures were not enough. In their view, what they called 'serious politics' were also needed:

> Party management was regarded as a special activity operating in a specially degenerate realm and under pressure from specially ruthless enemies ... Although ideally it was helpful to win [internal disputes] by persuasion and consensus, 'serious politics' involved an acceptance that an at times brazen ruthlessness in pushing the boundaries of managerial conduct and seeking 'what we can get away with' was integral to the capability of being effective in playing to win.[13]

A small army of professional fixers was deployed to implement this approach. This was a significant change, as Minkin noted:

> In the past, party officials were from a working-class background. They had generally not been to university but were committed to the party from their youth. They started from the bottom often as constituency party agents and worked upwards on long-term contracts, normally staying in post as the regional organiser until retirement ... The national officials were then drawn from those working in the field after long experience of the Labour Party – and a deep education into its history and culture. [14]

This, of course, did not mean that they were interested in democratising the party, or sympathetic to the Labour left. On the contrary, they were often hostile to activists, as epitomised in Ron Hayward's portrait of 'Old Bill' cited in Chapter 2. But they had a commitment to the party's established procedures that tended to make them less ready to go along with the radical break with the party's past that the New Labour project involved. For this, a different kind of official was needed:

> The members of the Blair machine were markedly different ... those appointed under Blair were 20–30, and virtually all university-educated with limited other experience ... most, although highly motivated in the party employment, were people who came to see this job as a stepping stone which might take them to other fields and occupations ... they had limited knowledge of past problems, less life experience to draw on, less integration into the local community and shared less of a collective political memory.

These young party staffers, dedicated to ensuring that the outcome of every meeting was 'what Tony wants', became a ubiquitous and widely disliked feature of party life.[15] Their efforts were often counter-productive. For the 1999 election of members of the European parliament, 'serious politics' secured internal agreement to the replace-ment of the pre-existing first-past-the-post electoral system with a proportional system of representation based on centrally determined party lists, in which 'most left-wing critics were not allocated to winnable positions'.[16] The result succeeded in producing a New Labour–supporting group of MEPs, but – to the dismay of party members – with the loss of over half of the seats formerly held by Labour. Similar efforts to control candidate selection for the first Scottish parliament produced still greater resentment, while the imposition of Blair's choice to lead the Welsh Labour Party in the first election to the new National Assembly for Wales, over the far more popular left-wing candidate, Rhodri Morgan, backfired spec-tacularly, depriving Labour of a majority in the elections. In the most high-profile case of all, rule-rigging prevented 'Red Ken' Livingstone from becoming Labour's candidate in the first election for mayor of London, even though he was overwhelmingly the favourite among London party members. This exercise in 'serious politics' failed even more spectacularly: Livingstone ran as an independent and defeated both the Labour and Conservative candidates by a wide margin. But the new party managers more often than not got the result the leader wanted.

'Spin', 'control freakery', and scandals involving the leadership's acceptance of funding from businessmen in return for favours, began to sap the enthusiasm of members and even many MPs, when the government's record in its first term in office would have suggested the opposite.[17] It had passed a string of liberal 'modernising' measures: removing hereditary peers from the House of Lords; devolving powers to Scotland, Wales and Northern Ireland; creating a Greater London Assembly; securing the Good Friday Agreement, which ended violence in Northern Ireland; and passing a Human Rights Act and a Freedom of Information Act. These measures did not form a coherent whole, and were sometimes half-hearted; but they were not insignificant and were generally popular.

Moreover, in 2001 some of the most hard-to-swallow aspects of the New Labour project, from the standpoint of the left, were not yet salient. Blair's crusade to reshape public services on neoliberal principles – which would prove a sticking-point for many party members, as well as for a growing minority of MPs – had not yet really got under way; the destruction of the Twin Towers, and Blair's decision to join the invasion of Iraq, had yet to occur; and no one – least of all the 'Iron Chancellor', Gordon Brown – entertained the idea that neoliberal policies and 'light-touch' regulation might lead to a financial meltdown. Yet the party's membership was already in free-fall. From an official peak of 400,485 in 1996, by 2001 it had fallen by almost a third, to 272,000, and would continue to decline.[18] Many members who had joined more recently lost interest or became disillusioned (their views proved to be not as different from those of older members as the modernisers had hoped). And in spite of the introduction of direct elections using 'one member, one vote' (OMOV) for positions on the NEC and for the nomination of parliamentary candidates, which was presented as a democratic advance, long-standing left-wing members saw that their input was in fact unwelcome, and that the leadership saw them as a problem rather than an asset.

New Labour's second and third terms in office would see the membership continue to fall, though more slowly. But as the policy implications of the New Labour project, over which members were systematically denied the slightest influence, became steadily clearer, many long-standing members became disenchanted.

New Labour Economic Policy

The modernisers' diagnosis of the 'new reality' created by globalisation implied that it was impossible for the government of any one country to manage aggregate demand and determine the level of economic activity and employment. All that could be done was to make the country as attractive as possible to foreign investors by keeping corporate taxes and inflation low, regulation 'light', and labour 'flexible' (i.e. easy to dismiss). Accordingly, one of the first steps taken by Gordon Brown as chancellor was to hand over the making of monetary policy to the Bank of England, with a mandate only to keep inflation down, reassuring capitalists that their investments would be safe and leaving employment to the vagaries of market forces. He also undertook not to exceed the spending limits set for the next two years by the outgoing Conservative government, so that for the government's first two years little redistribution could occur.

Meanwhile, Blair made it clear that there would be no significant reversal of the anti-union legislation inherited from the Thatcher years. He thus reassured employers: 'The changes that we do propose would leave British law the most restrictive on trade unions in the Western world.'[19] Nor would there be any renationalisation of the country's infrastructure (oil, gas, electricity and water, ports, airports, railways and airline, and telecoms). On the contrary, New Labour oversaw further sales of assets that were still in public ownership, such as parts of the nuclear fuel industry and air-traffic control. It also extensively privatised the physical assets of public services (especially hospitals, schools, government premises and roads) through the Private Finance Initiative (PFI), under which private consortia raised capital to build new premises, which they then leased on twenty- to thirty-year contracts to the public service providers who still used the privatised infrastructure.

All this reflected the belief shared by Blair, Mandelson and Brown that competition ensures that private companies are always more efficient than public bodies. From 1999 onwards, they set about applying this to all public services. In a characteristic exercise of spin, Blair allowed the media to declare that the party's 2001 election manifesto had made a general commitment to involve private companies in providing public services. In what was presented as a reforming 'crusade' against self-interested resistance from the workforce, New Labour privatised the provision of many public services, from prisons and the Probation Service to weekend primary medical care, outsourcing it to private companies. It also tried to make public organisations such as the BBC and the National Health Service mimic private-sector behaviour by reconfiguring them as 'internal' markets or 'quasi-markets', in which one part of the organisation holds the budget and buys or 'commissions' services from the other parts. All NHS specialist services, from hospitals to ambulance services, were grouped into semi-independent, self-financing local 'trusts', to be run, like private companies, by boards of directors and increasingly paid per completed treatment for every patient admitted or seen. The commissioners could then lower the price per treatment (the 'tariff') year by year, with a view to forcing hospitals and other NHS service providers organised as 'trusts' to keep finding new 'efficiencies', in the way private companies are supposed to have to do in order to survive in the market.

New Labour's faith in the superiority of private enterprise and competition also determined its two flagship educational measures: the handing over of schools (re-labelled 'academies') to so-called independent 'trusts', mainly run by corporate school-management chains; and the introduction in 2006 of substantial university fees. Universities would now have to compete for students, most of whom would have to borrow the money for the fees. In a further important step towards making government policy business-friendly, the policy-making ranks of the civil service were increasingly filled with private-sector executives, usually on short-term contracts, and especially with people recruited from global consultancies such as KPMG and McKinsey. Over the five years from 2004 to 2008, a third of all senior civil service positions, and over half of the top 200 posts, were filled in this way.[20] At the same time, many senior civil servants left to take up senior positions in companies that did business with their former departments. The boundary between the public interest and private interests became blurred, sometimes to the point of invisibility. Indeed, the head of the civil service even declared in 2012 that it would be a 'perfectly legitimate challenge' for policymaking itself to be put out to tender.[21] The truth was that, in some fields (including policy on health, the second-largest area of government spending), this had already happened.[22] The results were invariably damaging and usually extremely costly – and a source of some of the most serious discontent inside the party, including the PLP.

There was, it must be said, one set of reforms that distinguished New Labour's policies from Thatcher's. Those who worked with Gordon Brown in the Treasury, including Ed Balls, Yvette Cooper and Ed Miliband, were committed to a range of anti-poverty targets: halving child poverty by 2010 and ending it by 2020; and ending poverty for pensioners. Even during New Labour's first two years in office, while the government was committed to staying within the Major government's spending plans, Brown initiated a series of fiscal changes that, by 2010, had cut the number of children in poverty by at least 800,000, and taken most pensioners out of poverty. He also funded 'Sure Start', a country-wide network of children's centres, to give children of poor families the support they needed in their early years in order to do well once they started school. But even with these reforms, New Labour's rejection of state planning and state enterprise and reliance on market forces meant taking no serious measures to tackle the causes of poverty. Instead, the focus – inherited from the Thatcher and Major years – was on making individuals more employable, partly through education, to increase their 'social capital', but also through incentivising people in receipt of support, and especially single parents, to find jobs – 'workfare' replacing welfare on the Bill Clinton model. The one notable exception to the strong pro-market theme running through New Labour's social policies was the introduction in 1999 of a national minimum wage – a long-standing party policy, and a 1997 manifesto pledge. Although initially set at a very low level, it proved to be one of the few mildly egalitarian measures passed by New Labour to survive the crash and the austerity that followed it.[23]

But the result of New Labour's refusal to use the state to tackle the determinants of poverty was not only that Brown's social amelioration measures fell far short of achieving their targets, but that they were also easily reversed. As David Coates observed, 'The ultimate tragedy for New Labour's anti-poverty ambitions was that the financial crisis of 2008 not only wiped away in one year all the gains of the previous eleven on employment, fuel poverty, and the number of children living in poverty homes';[24] it also eventually triggered the replacement of New Labour in 2010 by the Conservative–Liberal Democrat coalition government, whose austerity policies eradicated whatever other anti-poverty gains had accrued in the New Labour years.

The Effects of New Labour Economic Policy

After a brief recession following the dot.com 'bubble' at the end of the 1990s, the UK economy grew steadily from 2002 to 2008, allowing the government to reduce the public debt inherited from the Conservatives (from 44.4 per cent of GDP in 1997 to 34.4 per cent in 2001), while also embarking, from 1999 onwards, on a major public-sector spending programme.[25] A major beneficiary was the NHS. In 1999 Blair promised to bring NHS spending up to the EU15 average – the first major improvement in its finances since its creation in 1948. In return for this, senior NHS personnel agreed to further reorganisation on quasi-market lines, and the first ever provision of NHS-funded clinical work by private health companies.

Capital spending also expanded in education, along with the introduction of competition in the shape of school 'league tables' and the private management of state schools (the above-mentioned 'academies' policy).

But what did not happen under New Labour was a regeneration of the non-financial sectors of the economy. In spite of everything possible being done to attract foreign direct investment, the overall level of investment remained chronically below the average of other OECD countries; the balance-of-payments gap remained unclosed, and was only prevented from leading to drastic cuts in consumption by the foreign-exchange earnings of the City of London, whose interests therefore continued to rank high in government policy. Redistribution through progressive taxation was rejected, and the drastic shift of income to the rich begun under Thatcher was accentuated rather than reversed. Under Blair and Brown, the share of all income going to the top 10 per cent of income earners increased to 32 per cent, while the share of the bottom 10 per cent fell from 3 per cent to little over 1 per cent.[26] The economic divide widened between the midlands and the north, on one hand, and the rest of the country, on the other, leaving the ex-industrial towns without hope: to be born in one of them was 'to suffer an irreversible life-long defeat – a truncation of opportunity, of education, of access to power, of life expectancy'.[27] These towns had been Labour's 'heartlands'; now they were the scene of a major swing to the far right. Labour came third, after UKIP, in the 2009 elections to the European parliament – a portent of the gains that the xenophobic right would make in the 2015 general election, and then the paralysing shock that would be delivered in the referendum on EU membership in 2016.

Many of New Labour's distinctive economic initiatives were also failures. For example, the Private Finance Initiative, inherited from the Conservatives, was presented as getting better value for money from the superior efficiency of the private sector. But its true value to the government lay in an accounting trick that allowed PFI debt to be kept off the public accounts, so that public borrowing appeared to stay within the limits agreed in the Maastricht Treaty. False comparisons were made with publicly financed procurement to make PFI seem cheaper. In fact it proved to be 70 per cent more expensive, landing hospitals – the single most important public service involved – with major annual charges that had to come out of their budgets for essential services, and increasingly threatened their financial sustainability.[28] The scale of the damage done to the public sector by the use of PFI was large and ongoing.[29] As the effects began to be felt in the constituencies, especially those where the local hospital was struggling with a PFI contract, opposition to PFI from the unions (and not only those with left-wing leaders), as well as from the Campaign Group MPs who had actively opposed PFI, gathered fresh support, and even some New Labour MPs became restive.

Left-wing backbench rebellions were too small to threaten the government, even after the 2005 election had cut Labour's majority to sixty-six. But a range of other domestic issues prompted broader dissent among Labour MPs during the New Labour years. Most concerned welfare – cuts in support for single parents, cuts in pension entitlements and disability benefits – about which Alan Simpson MP, the secretary of the Campaign Group, said: 'In the same way that the Mafia asks you to destroy something precious to demonstrate loyalty, Labour MPs were asked to give a good kicking to some of the most vulnerable in society.'[30] But New Labour's market-oriented reforms of public services also alienated a wider range of Labour backbenchers. They saw university fees as threatening access for working-class students, the conversion of schools into academies as reintroducing selection, and the introduction of 'Foundation Hospitals' as creating a two-tier system of hospital quality.[31] And PLP rebellions against encroachments on civil liberties (anti-terrorism legislation, police powers, assaults on freedom of information and on asylum) were reminders of a residual dislike of the leadership's inclination towards authoritarianism, even among a significant minority of New Labour MPs.[32]

Iraq

New Labour's second term in office was dominated by the decision to go to war on Iraq, despite massive opposition from Labour Party members and voters. Two cabinet ministers resigned, and two-fifths of Labour's MPs (139 out of 355) voted against it in parliament, while many others were opposed to the war but supported Blair's decision in order to avoid a government defeat. It is tempting, for this reason, to regard it as an aberration from the New Labour project.

But the Iraq decision was inherent in New Labour's project of embracing globalised capitalism as the 'new reality' to which everything must be adapted. The 'special relationship' with the United States was a central – although itself very far from new – feature of this reality. The UK's nuclear weapons capacity was a component of the American informal empire, within which the UK also hosted a dozen active US Air Force bases, and was intimately involved in US intelligence-gathering through a web of secret agreements. Giving Bush an unconditional promise of support the morning after 9/11 was rash and arguably unnecessary – Bush attached no weight to the UK's military participation, as opposed to what its involvement could contribute to legitimising an attack on Iraq. But the New Labour project depended on having a leader who understood that the special relationship was crucial to it, and who also intuitively understood that the new Republican president's hawkish 'neoconservative' entourage would disregard any support that was not unconditional. Blair was ready to accept the consequences, unconstrained by any personal attachment to the party's anti-imperialist tradition, any more than to its social-democratic tradition.

Following the terrorist attacks on 9/11, and having told Bush, 'We stand with you', Blair soon learned that the true target of the 'war on terror' was not Afghanistan, where al-Qaeda was based, but Iraq, which was not implicated in the Twin Towers attack. The decision to attack Iraq was in fact taken in Washington the day after the Taliban had been forced out of Kabul in November 2001. Blair knew this. But in a series of phone conversations and meetings with Bush over the next fifteen months, he never attached any conditions to British involvement, instead devoting himself to a frantic but unsuccessful effort to secure international support, and especially support for a UN resolution authorising an invasion, which the Labour Party conference in September 2002 had wanted to make a condition of its approval.

In the absence of any connection between Iraq and 9/11, the justification given for attacking Iraq was that Saddam Hussein was secretly developing weapons of mass destruction. Blair was informed by the head of MI6 that the Americans were 'fixing' intelligence and 'facts' to justify the attack, and he did not scruple to do the same, claiming to have reliable evidence that Iraq had weapons of mass destruction capable of being deployed in forty-five minutes. When the evidence for this was later admitted not to exist, Blair's justification shifted to a wider claim that the 'international community' was justified in 'intervening' to change regimes that threatened their own citizens or the rest of the world. It required a special capacity on his part to argue this with conviction while knowing very well that the US neocons' aim was, in the later words of one of Bush's speech writers, 'to put America more wholly in charge of the region than any power since the Ottomans, or maybe the Romans'.[33]

The attack launched in March 2003 resulted in an estimated 600,000 excess deaths, some 100,000 violent deaths, 4.4 million people internally displaced, 2 million refugees fleeing abroad – in all a quarter of the country's 2003 population – and continuing sectarian political conflict and economic collapse. The revulsion felt in the UK was profound. More than anything else in New Labour's record, Blair's determination to involve the UK in the invasion accounted for the loss of a further 1.2 million Labour votes between the 2001 and 2005 elections, and led to the formation in 2001 of the Stop the War Coalition, which outlasted the war and would prove a key source of activist support for Corbyn's leadership campaign in 2015.

Blair's distinctive mix of charisma, messianism and the capacity to persuade himself as well as others of the rightness of a course of action that appealed to him, all played a crucial role in the decision to go to war on Iraq. But we need to remember that Gordon Brown, the only plausible New Labour alternative to Blair as leader, understood the reality of the special relationship quite as well as Blair, and fully supported the decision.

The Crash

The global financial crisis of 2007–08, which, along with the attack on Iraq, most decisively registered the failure of the New Labour project, is generally thought of as having originated in the US sub-prime mortgage market. But it makes as much sense, if not more, to see it as in good part caused by New Labour's embrace of the strategy of making the City of London the world's leading centre for financial services by undercutting the standards of regulation that existed in New York.[34]

When New Labour took office in 1997, the financial services sector was still 'self-regulated'. As chancellor, Gordon Brown inherited powers to regulate the sector, but they were delegated to a variety of industry-based bodies. In 2000, after several banking scandals had shown that the City was losing its reputation for honesty, Brown established an external regulator, the Financial Services Authority (FSA). But the City's foreign-exchange earnings were critical to keeping the country's balance-of-payments deficit from becoming unsustainable. Brown saw this as a huge success story, telling an audience of bankers in 2006:

Financial services are now 7 per cent of our economy. Financial and business services as much as 10 per cent. A larger share of our economy than they are in any other major economy, contributing £19 billion of net exports to our balance of payments, a success all the more remarkable because while New York and Tokyo rely for business on their large domestic base, London's international ranking is founded on a large and expanding global market ... London is the favoured location of choice for more international business than ever before, the world's leading banking centre with more foreign banks than in any other city, the location for 200 foreign law firms – including home for six of the world's largest ten.[35]

Brown was well aware, however, that London's attraction as a financial centre depended on having lower levels of regulation than those in New York and Chicago. He explicitly rejected following the Americans' example, in their response to the Enron and WorldCom scandals, of tightening controls and sanctions in the financial sector, and instead gave the FSA a remit which epitomised 'light-touch' regulation. The emphasis in the Financial Services and Markets Act was explicitly on doing as little as possible to hamper profitable activities, including many that were against the law in New York – a policy enthusiastically followed by the FSA's leadership.[36] This allowed the City of London's role as a dealer in 'offshore' dollars, which had begun under Harold Wilson in the 1960s (opposed by the new left at the time), to continue to expand rapidly.[37] By 2007 the City was by far the biggest foreign-exchange centre in the world, with 35 per cent of all trades (New York was second, with just 17 per cent).[38] And since Thatcher's opening up of the City to foreign banks in the 'Big Bang' of 1986 it had also become largely foreign-owned. By 2000, there were 250 foreign banks and branches in the City, including all the leading American and European investment banks, which had bought up most of the long-established British investment banks.

In reaction to this competition, Wall Street lobbied hard to follow the UK's example and reduce regulation in the United States. The separation of retail from investment banking was abolished, allowing US banks, like British banks, to speculate with the public's deposits. And in the United States, as in London, foreign banks were only obliged to obey the banking rules laid down in their home countries, not those of the overseas country where they were doing business. In effect, this 'excused the City of London and New York from responsibility for the onerous oversight of the hundreds of foreign banks that congregated in their precincts'.[39] Moreover, under the second Basel Accord of 2004, the level of capital reserves which all banks were required to hold in relation to their loans was watered down. The global banking crisis that eventually resulted, when the mass of unpayable debts based on derivatives of the US mortgage market finally imploded, engulfed the UK economy. Because the banking sector had grown so large, the cost of preventing its failure from bankrupting everything else was huge. Nationalising Northern Rock, Lloyds, and RBS, thereby saving them from collapse, cost the public about £1 trillion in guarantees and £133 billion in cash, and increased the national debt from 42 per cent of GDP in 2007 to 76 per cent in 2010.[40] And New Labour entertained no thought of using the banks acquired so painfully and expensively to start direct-ing investment to national reconstruction. On the contrary: to reassure the markets, the government quickly made it clear that the nationalised banks would 'still operate on a commercial basis at arm's length' from government direction or control, and be sold off as soon as possible.[41]

In the meantime, under the unseeing eye of the FSA, British banks had also engaged in what John Lanchester justly called 'barely believable' unethical and fraudulent behaviour.[42] They manipulated the London Inter-Bank lending rate (LIBOR), on which $350 trillion transactions a year were based world-wide, to make large profits for themselves. They had also sold payment-protection insur-ance (PPI) to tens of millions of customers who did not need it and in many cases were ineligible for it, at an 80 per cent average rate of profit. Two of them – HSBC and Standard Chartered – had laun-dered dirty money on a large scale. In the aftermath of the crash, they were made to pay fines worth several billion dollars for these and other offences, though more by the US regulators than the FSA; and in 2017 British banks and insurers were still settling claims for mis-sold PPI worth an expected total of some £40 billion. No bank chief executive or chairperson paid any price for this. A handful of traders were later prosecuted for rate-rigging; but the bonus culture that had incentivised their behaviour with obscenely large rewards survived intact.[43] In 2007 the City's bonus 'pot' was estimated at nearly £9 billion. In 2010, in the midst of recession, it still stood at £7 billion. In 2009 even the staff of RBS, whose jobs had just been saved by the public at a cost of £73 billion, making them employees of the state, demanded and received large bonuses.[44] Meanwhile, the economy was plunged into recession.

The End of New Labour

Public anger with the bankers was intense. But Gordon Brown, who had replaced Blair as Labour leader and prime minister just before the crash in June 2007, was not at first seen as personally responsible. Instead, he initially received credit for leading the rest of the world in committing public resources to resolving a crisis generally seen as the fault of the Americans. It was only after Labour lost the election in 2010, and austerity began to be imposed by the Coalition government, that New Labour's complicity in the crisis began to be more widely admitted inside the party.

What was more immediately expressed within the party, and among the wider public, was a rejection of the undemocratic style of party management perfected by Blair, of which both Iraq and the crash were consequences. In response to this, Brown promised a more open and inclusive style of leadership when he took over, but failed to deliver it. Party structures simply withered. An important-sounding White Paper called *Building Britain's Future* was issued in June 2009, and when the Joint Policy Committee, which linked the NEC to the cabinet, met in the following month it would obviously have been a major agenda item; but the meeting 'was only attended by one Minister for ten minutes'.[45] Membership continued to decline, fewer and fewer CLPs sent delegates to the annual conference, and the unions were increasingly unwilling to mobilise at elections. By 2010, when Brown finally went to the country, Labour received only 8.5 million votes, almost 5 million fewer than in 1997, out of a larger electorate.

The New Labour project had called for Labour to become a party of the American 'elite pluralist' kind – not even answerable to its MPs, let alone to its members. What Blair wanted, and what was needed if the party was to embrace capital instead of resisting it, was, in Minkin's words, 'a plebiscitarian party working with a plebiscitary government'. Thanks to Blair's rhetorical and persuasive skills, New Labour had been able to pursue, over three parliaments, policies that called for such a party without Labour fully becoming one. The membership and the unions were no longer willing to put up with being ignored; and, as Kinnock had found earlier, attachment to public ownership and hostility to market-driven inequality proved deep-seated among both the membership and a significant minority of Labour MPs, in spite of two rounds of centrally managed candidate selection. By 2006, the public no longer trusted or liked New Labour, and Blair himself had become acutely unpopular.

Besides Iraq, Blair's crusade to marketise and privatise public services especially offended long-standing Labour values. Labour members and MPs felt they had nothing left to defend. As early as November 2006 an unnamed Yorkshire MP told Chris Mullin, with remarkable prescience:

> I think we will lose the next election. The Tories will come to some sort of understanding with the Lib Dems and we'll find that we've opened the door to the market in health and education. And when we protest they will reply, 'But this is your policy; you started it.' We'll be vulnerable for years. Our benches will be full of ex-ministers who won't have the stomach for the fight.[46]

By 2009, Labour Party membership was down to 153,140, and in 2010 less than two-thirds of CLPs sent delegates to the party conference. Yet it is arguable that, contrary to Blair's earlier calls for a huge membership, the party's shrinking grassroots were actually becoming closer to providing the kind of base the New Labour project really needed:[47] a modest core of loyalists willing to help at elections, but with a very limited interest in policy. Over time, with both party agents and the covert network of local loyalists referred to above doing all they could to ensure that CLPs delivered 'what Tony needs', there was a tendency for compliance with plebiscitary leadership to become normalised and accepted. Even local parties with a tradition of electing left-wingers tended to fall in line.[48]

But for the party to become a plebiscitary organisation sustaining a set of professional representatives over the long term, two prerequisites were lacking. One was that businesses needed to be ready to fund Labour as well as the Conservatives. For the year 1999, for example, the party hoped to get 20 per cent of its funding from 'high-value' (rich) donors, 40 per cent from membership subscriptions and small donors, and only the balance from the unions (30 per cent) and commercial activities (10 per cent).[49] In practice, donations from wealthy individuals were never on the required scale, membership subscriptions fell, and direct donations from large companies were negligible. New Labour remained financially dependent on the unions, whose readiness to provide a blank cheque gradually declined.[50]

The other prerequisite of a stable conversion of the Labour Party into a plebiscitary party was sustained economic growth and a reduction in income inequality. But the UK economy contained no market-based mechanism tending to 'rebalance' it, as the 'endogenous growth theory' subscribed to by Gordon Brown had implied. The growth model on which New Labour depended rested on an ever-growing mountain of private debt based on rising house prices, while productivity stagnated. Brown had boasted that the business cycle was a thing of the past just as the economy was about to enter its worst recession since the 1930s.[51] The Queen famously asked a group of academic economists, 'Why did nobody notice it?' She could have put the question even more pertinently to Gordon Brown and the Treasury. The question was not entirely rhetorical: Her Majesty was feeling the pinch, having lost about £25 million in the crash, and was asking the government for additional funds and tax relief.[52] Labour's rank and file shared the Queen's sentiments, although their pain, as opposed to hers, would later be exacerbated through Conservative-imposed austerity. Outside the ranks of the Blairite members of the PLP and their erstwhile leaders, the cost of the crisis finally extinguished any remaining enthusiasm for the New Labour project.

7

The Left versus New Labour: In and Against the Party

As Gordon Brown's £37 billion bail-out plan was unrolled in October 2008, at the height of the global financial crisis, Tony Benn was moved to comment in his diary: 'When you advocated the nationalisation of the banks years ago people said you were absolutely bonkers and dangerous and irresponsible and out of touch with reality, and now, a right-wing government, because that's what it is, has decided that's what they've got to do.' Benn still hoped the government would give itself 'a voice in the rewards of top banking executives [and] in guiding where the money goes for investment', but the government quickly made it clear that any nationalised bank would operate at arm's length from the government, on a commercial basis. In any case, Benn had few illusions: 'Of course, they'll try and privatise it again later.'[1]

Benn had announced halfway through Blair's first term that he would not stand in the 2001 election: 'Having served for nearly half a century in the House of Commons, I now want more time to devote to politics and more freedom to do so.'[2] These famous words not only perfectly encapsulated Benn's disdain for New Labour's stifling brand of parliamentarism, but also displayed his sense of the possibility of reconnecting socialist politics to the new type of radical protest that exploded at the turn of the millennium with the anti-globalisation and anti-war movements.

The contradictions of trying to sustain a socialist orientation from inside the Parliamentary Labour Party had indeed become especially acute within the framework set by New Labour. Watching the party conference before the 1997 election turn into an imitation of a Democratic Party presidential nominating convention, Benn confided to his diary: 'a cold hand went round my chest'. And indeed Blair's daily pronouncements in the run-up to the 1997 election proved how correct Benn had been in insisting, as he often had at party meetings over the previous years, that Labour was 'a party that has adopted Tory policies'. Yet as the day of the election approached, Benn admitted: 'I desperately hope that we win and I desperately hope we have a big majority.' When that was achieved, the spectacle of 'The Red Flag' being sung after Benn's victory speech at Chesterfield Labour Club was filled with irony – all the more so as membership and attendance soon plummeted in his local party in reaction to the New Labour government's policies.[3] Observing that this was also going on in other CLPs, Benn sadly noted the passivity of constituency delegates – even after the invasion of Iraq – at the 2003 conference: 'Constituencies are no longer on the left, because all the decent socialists have left, so it's a Blairite romp. But Blair is in deep trouble with the public at large.'[4] It was a fair summary.

Jeremy Corbyn and the Campaign Group

By the time of the 1997 election, Jeremy Corbyn had become, next to Benn, the most prominent voice of the Socialist Campaign Group of MPs. Corbyn's steadfast practice as the PLP dissident most closely linked to radical extra-parliamentary campaigns had been nurtured through his close relationship with Benn, and the Blairite machine's attempts to stifle Corbyn had just as little effect on him.[5] While this mentorship was a credit to 'Benn's foresightedness and Corbyn's reputation', as a sympathetic biographer has put it, it did nothing to benefit Corbyn's oratorical style: 'His words come unvarnished and unpolished [with] fluffs and stumbles and mistimings and heedless remarks'.[6] This may have actually enhanced his credibility among the many activists fed up with the pre-packaged rhetoric of career politicians. But it no doubt reinforced Blair's confidence (as he had put it to a journalist in September 1996) that 'you really don't have to worry about Jeremy Corbyn suddenly taking over'.[7]

Twenty years later, shortly after Corbyn had taken over the leadership of the party, he was characteristically candid about how surprising this was: 'the difference between Tony [Benn] and me was that whereas he was one of those very unusual politicians who was actually very successful in a conventional career pattern, I have been monumentally unsuccessful in the conventional career pattern.'[8] Very much fitting the profile of the new-left activists at the local level in the 1970s, Corbyn's political career had begun with his election in 1974 to Haringey Council in London. His election to parliament for the London constituency of Islington North in 1983 came in the wake of the defeat of the Bennite left, and he immediately made the Socialist Campaign Group, which had earlier formed around Benn, his political home. As he later recalled,

> It was then a large organisation with 40 or 50 MPs. There were big discussions about economic policy, the miners' strike and foreign policy debates. In one hilarious meeting, the Greenham Women addressed us. They were trying to buy bolt-cutters to cut the fences at Greenham Common, but any time they turned up at a shop anywhere near they were denied the right to buy them. So each Campaign Group member agreed to buy one set of bolt-cutters and donate them to the Greenham Women. Which we duly did.[9]

Despite being the strongest opponents of privatisations, welfare cuts and assaults on trade unions under the Tory governments, by 1997 the Campaign Group only attracted some thirty MPs out of the 417 elected that year. Their number would fall significantly further over the following decade: the New Labour political machine at party headquarters, and Blair personally, were so obsessively concerned with every parliamentary selection that strong left candidates were excluded through underhand means while New Labour candidates, carefully vetted and coached, were 'parachuted in' to constituency selection meetings.[10] Nor, of course, would anyone associated with the Campaign Group be allowed to have any significant presence in the New Labour government, let alone of the kind Benn had had during the 1970s. A cartoon in *The Times* in December 1997 showed No. 10 Downing Street, with Mandelson's face visible through a window, as Benn, Livingstone and Skinner looked at a sign on the door saying 'Socialism Exclusion Unit'.[11]

Yet, since it had displaced the old Tribune Group as the natural home of the left, it was to the Campaign Group's fringe meetings that those disgruntled CLP and union delegates who were still coming to party conferences increasingly turned for guidance and inspiration.[12] Blair and Brown themselves actually saw the Campaign Group 'as the driving force of a limited opposition' to the new government.[13] Brown's widely reported response to the Campaign MPs leading the large PLP revolt over cuts to lone-parent benefits in December 1997 was: 'We'll get those bastards'; and Blair, fearing they might have similar resonance with the base as the Bennites once had, told the PLP: 'You will have to tell your activists to accept what we are doing. Things will get a lot rougher, as they did between 1976 and 1979.' This seemed borne out when the CLPD, although only a shadow of its former self, formed the centre-left Grassroots Alliance (GRA), which succeeded in getting the four most left-wing members of its NEC slate elected in 1998 – even though 'no NEC election campaign in history had been fought by party officials showing so little pretence of impartiality'.[14]

Yet the left on the NEC now had no impact whatsoever. The union representatives joined the party leadership clones in consistently outvoting them – even on policies their own unions supported – reflecting their 'long-held disdain for "impractical idealists" and "posturers" who they saw as aiming not to solve problems but to appeal to an outside audience . . . simply to embarrass the government'.[15] After the rules on CLP balloting for NEC representatives were arbitrarily changed in 1999, it took the better part of a decade before the GRA slate would again take the first four places; but by then only 20 per cent of the party's members bothered to participate in NEC elections. As the CLPD acknowledged, this not only had the 'effect over time of weakening the organised left wing current at the grassroots', but also of making 'an openly consistent left-wing identity less comfortable' for those remaining in the party.[16]

The Campaign Group itself was incapable of organising a struggle within the party to prevent this. Like the Tribune Group in its heyday, it had little capacity for broader political organisation; even within the party base, this was largely left to the CLPD. Moreover, whereas the NEC policymaking committees under Benn's influence in the early 1970s had provided a relatively clear and coherent radical programmatic focus for left activists, the Campaign Group lacked both the resources and the strategic capacity to replicate anything like this.[17] That said, it was given a more coherent sense of direction when it was joined after the 1997 election by John McDonnell, who immediately became 'the most rebellious' of the 1997 intake of MPs.[18] He also brought with him a quite sophisticated 'in and against the state' strategic orientation – one honed in practice as the GLC's deputy leader and chair of finance in the early 1980s.[19] McDonnell was also more oriented than others in the Campaign Group towards effecting a broader reorganisation of the British left by linking up those inside and outside the party. As chair of the Campaign Group, McDonnell's summary of its political orientation in 2007 may be taken as authoritative. In addition to advancing policies 'overwhelmingly backed by Labour party conference', such as rail renationalisation,

> members of the Campaign Group have been the first to be at the forefront of mass campaigns on trade union rights, private equity, council housing, public services and against the war. We consistently raise uncomfortable issues and support campaigns that no other parliamentarians will touch, on issues like asylum, deportations, international trade union and human rights, campaigns for those killed or injured at work, safety of vulnerable workers, including sex workers, cuts in legal aid and English for speakers of other languages funding ... we campaign within parliament so that the campaigns which are excluded by the Westminster elite and the media get a voice and some recognition.[20]

However little impact all this had on the government, it still had considerable resonance among those party members, and increasingly ex-members, disappointed – indeed often disgusted – by the New Labour government. They had mostly turned their skills and energies to a wide range of non-party organisations and campaigns, some with long histories, others new, but all of which formed a pool of political commitment and experience that New Labour disdained and alienated. This explains why the main political focus of so many of the key players in Corbyn's leadership team after 2015 had previously been organisations such as the Stop the War Coalition, War on Want, Greenpeace, the Civil Service Union, the Communications Workers Union, the East London Mosque, and campaigns for social housing and public transport.

There was also a new generation of 'millennial' activists for whom party politics held no attraction whatsoever, but who were still politicised, as earlier generations had been, by hearing Benn speaking at meetings and protests, and now also by hearing Corbyn, who 'commanded near-universal respect among grassroots campaigners', as McDonnell put it. When very few others in the PLP 'had any time for any of the social movements whatsoever Jeremy was touring round the country', and he would come back to Westminster saying, 'Oh I met so-and-so, we met him 10 years ago when we were involved in that occupation', or, 'We did the Chile campaign together.' Indeed, if it often seemed, McDonnell joked, that one of their 'primary roles in political life [was] booking rooms at the House of Commons for all these different organisations', what really mattered was the recognition that 'these people are talking our politics, they've worked alongside us, we need to support them'.[21]

Despite the persistence of the Campaign Group MPs, it certainly appeared that New Labour in power was finally dispelling once and for all the 'most crippling of illusions to which British socialists have been prone', as Ralph Miliband had put it in the early 1970s – namely, that this party could ever be transformed into 'an instrument of socialist policies'.[22] Ironically enough, as those disenchanted with New Labour became active at the community level, they were often more directly engaged with Labour municipal councillors than they had previously been.[23] Certainly, few of them were attracted by any electoral alternative to Labour on the left. Livingstone's victory as an independent in the election for London Mayor in 2000, after the Blair machine grotesquely manipulated the London local party electoral college in order to deny him the right to run under the Labour banner, was an important exception to this, but it proved to be a very special case.

The Socialist Labour Party, created by Arthur Scargill the year before the 1997 election in the wake of Blair's removal of the party's lingering lip-service to socialism from Clause IV of the party's constitution, had gained no traction whatsoever, in spite of Labour voters' obvious disappointment with New Labour's first term in office.[24] Instead, the main effect of the wide disappointment with New Labour in power was a sharp decline in working-class turnout at the 2001 general election, leaving a PLP 'packed to the gills with so-called career politicians', with fewer than ever from working-class backgrounds.[25] The Respect Party, formed in 2003 in alliance with the Muslim Association of Britain and the Socialist Workers Party (Britain's largest Trotskyist formation), had a much broader left provenance than Scargill's SLP, but by 2007 Respect was already running out of steam amid splits in its unwieldy coalition of forces.[26] Apart from their own shortcomings, a crucial factor in the failure of these new parties was, of course, Britain's democratically restrictive 'first-past-the-post' electoral system. The greater electoral success of new socialist parties in other European countries was directly related to their proportional electoral systems. Had PR been introduced for UK general elections, it is conceivable that some Campaign MPs might have joined attempts to reconfigure the British left electorally around the turn of the millennium, and Corbyn would never have been elected leader of the Labour Party fifteen years later.

Indeed, the same outcome might have resulted from the expulsion of the Campaign Group MPs for their rebellions – which was by no means out of the question after the 1997 election, given the government's very large parliamentary majority, coupled with the Blair machine's intolerance and ruthlessness. They were not expelled, as one of the Campaign Group MPs, Alan Simpson, later explained, only because Blair's 'managerialist' obsessions were so blatant that MPs, whips, and others backed away, knowing that 'Blair would get the blame ... And since protecting the leader had already displaced promoting the party as the overriding duty, the hounds always got called off.'[27]

The Campaign Group's own lack of organisational reach outside parliament figured in this as well. Although they were often the most prominent spokespeople at the big anti-globalisation and anti-war rallies, it was the experienced political cadres of the Socialist Workers Party (SWP) who played the leading role in organising them. Marvelling that no less than 1,300 people attended an anti-globalisation conference in London in early 2001, Benn admitted: 'The more I think of the SWP, the more I realise how important that element is in any successful political movement.'[28] This was confirmed soon afterwards when the SWP, anticipating the US imperial response to 9/11, moved swiftly to organise a public protest meeting of some two thousand people, with Corbyn as one of the main speakers. Out of this emerged the Stop the War Coalition, which established branches all around the country. The many impressive anti-war protests under its auspices included the estimated 2 million people who marched and demonstrated on 15 February 2003 – often said, very likely accurately, to have been the largest demonstration in British history.

Notably, it was just at this time that 'the Trotskyist movement was reaching the end of a long period of disintegration, splits and decline [and] even the creation of the SWP-led Stop the War Coalition in 2001 was unable to halt these trends'.[29] The unprecedented degree of cooperation the Stop the War Coalition encouraged across the left was to prove the most positive legacy of this political cadre. Benn was the Coalition's president from 2001 until his death in 2014, and Andrew Murray was Stop the War's very active chair until 2011, when he was succeeded by Corbyn. The fifty or so Stop the War branches still in existence in 2015 were important launching pads for activist mobilisation behind Corbyn's leadership campaign. Even more importantly, Stop the War helped lay the foundations of union support for Corbyn. Benn's acute political antennae had registered the broader political significance of the Stop the War Coalition at a large meeting chaired by Andrew Murray during the 2005 Trade Union Congress, where Tony Woodley, the recently elected left-wing General Secretary of the TGWU, made an impassioned speech against the Iraq war. In his own speech, Benn remarked 'how lovely it was to come to a Labour-movement conference where you weren't searched for socialist literature on your way in'.[30]

'Watch the unions, that's my tip': Round 2

As we saw in Chapter 2, in 1965 that veteran of the old Labour left, Ian Mikardo, signalled with the above words the upheaval that would shake the party to its foundations by the mid 1970s. If there was any similarly perceptive signal of what would take place in the party by 2015, it came from Andrew Murray, the long-time *Morning Star* journalist and TGWU staffer. He had stayed well away from *Marxism Today*'s superficial flirtations with capitalist modernisation and class mobility, sustaining the long-standing practical orientation of Communist Party activists in Britain who worked within the trade unions to encourage 'the strengthening of the left trends within the Labour Party'.[31] His 2005 book, *A New Labour Nightmare*, argued that for all of the reversals suffered in the previous two decades, the trade unions – 'still the largest and deepest-rooted single social movement in the country' – were just then in the process of revealing 'the greatest potential to be the real opposition to New Labour, at the heart of a broader alliance of all those discontented with the present government but aghast at the thought of any Tory return to office':

> That is what politics needs. It is apparent that it is also what trade union members themselves want. The last two years have seen an almost unbroken run of victories in union elections for leaders

who offer, to some degree or other, just that alternative. The care-fully-cultivated 'moderation' of 1990s trade unionism is being rejected. Instead, overt opponents of Tony Blair and the whole thrust of his governing project are being elected. As one very senior union leader remarked a few months ago 'you can't be elected in a union as a Blair supporter today'.[32]

A shift to the left in the union leadership was initially signalled in 2000 by the election of Mark Serwotka (whose *Socialist Organiser* affiliations had led to his expulsion from the Labour Party a decade earlier) to lead the civil service union, PCS, followed in 2001 by the election of Bill Hayes to lead the postal workers' union, CWU. And in 2002, the year before Woodley's election to lead the TGWU, the amalgamated engineers and electricians union, Amicus, elected Derek Simpson, a largely 'unknown left-winger and ex-Communist, who (at that time) saw Tony Benn as an inspirational figure', over the old standard-bearer of the union right, Sir Ken Jackson, who had once called on the TUC to 'scrap its annual conferences and unite with the CBI to end the "us and them mentality".'[33] Unite, Britain's largest union, would emerge a few years later out of the merger of the TGWU and Amicus, Woodley and Simpson acting initially as joint general secretaries. Len McCluskey, elected to succeed them in 2010, would appoint Andrew Murray as his chief of staff; two Unite officials with close ties to McCluskey, Karie Murphy and Jennie Formby, would respectively become the chief of staff in the leader of the opposition's office and general secretary of the Labour Party under Corbyn.

The mood of the rank and file was registered in the number of days lost to industrial action in 2002 – the most in well over a decade. The municipal workers' strike, the largest by women work-ers in British history, which had attracted, as Murray noted, 'a very high degree of initial public support', was followed by a firefighters' strike that ran right through the first half of 2003. This was a response to a report initiating massive structural changes oriented to making the fire service more 'flexible', the long-term reverberations of which would be felt fifteen years later in the 2017 Grenfell Tower disaster. But, in tones that recalled the 'Winter of Discontent' a quarter-century earlier, the Fire Brigades Union was vilified in the media, so much so that when 'other union leaders expressed support for the FBU in the midst of the dispute, the *Sun* declared: "It's a Class War."' All this was stoked by Downing Street's spin machine, which had earlier branded the union's leaders as 'Scargillites' who had to be 'crushed'.[34] This caused the FBU to disaffiliate from the Labour Party in 2004; and this was followed by the party's expulsion of the RMT, Britain's largest rail union, after its radical socialist leader, Bob Crow, threw the union's support behind the Scottish Socialist Party.

It was in this context that in 2004 John McDonnell took the initiative to create the Labour Representation Committee (LRC). Taking the name of the broad union forum out of which the Labour Party had emerged a century earlier, this was the first real organisational initiative, since Benn and Corbyn's engagement with the Chesterfield Socialist Conferences in the mid 1980s, to link the Campaign Group in parliament with socialists outside the party. The FBU and RMT affiliated with the LRC; but among the unions still affiliated to the Labour Party, only the bakers and postal workers did so. That most of the new union leaders discreetly kept their distance recalled Jack Jones's famous line in 1968 about the union leaders' attitude to their tortured relationship with the party: 'murder often, divorce never'. Indeed, still actively leading pensioners' demonstrations against the Blair government, Jones now reaffirmed, almost word for word, what he had argued during the Wilson government, telling Andrew Murray:

> The trade union movement would be very foolish to allow a break, although it may satisfy Blair. For the working class to have any possibility of political influence it must be on a major political party, and we should exercise it as strongly as we can. It's just that some of the people we send to Labour committees don't do it . . . They should be more assertive – my feeling is that the trade union leaders should be more socialistically inclined, as we were

in the past ... Union education has become divorced from the political angle.[35]

This recognition that the Labour Party could not be changed in a socialist direction unless the unions laid the ground for this through the political education of their members echoed the strategic perspectives of the Labour new left in the early 1970s. As we saw in Chapter 3, Benn in particular made this an important theme of his speeches to union conferences. But we also saw that the left union leadership did not even then take this very far, and that eventually even Jones himself deferred to the position taken by the union representatives on the party committees in lining up against the Bennite left in the early 1980s. In fact, Jones's call for the unions to reassert their influence in the party was to say the least quixotic, given the consistency with which the union representatives on the party's committees were still sustaining New Labour's control. Thus, even though the new union leaders delivered many well-publicised rebukes to the government over PFI and foundation hospitals at the 2002 and 2003 conferences, these same conferences were manipulated – with the crucial assistance of the union representatives on the party committees – so as to avoid entirely the burning issue of the invasion of Iraq.[36] When Murray claimed that the shift to the left among the union leadership showed that 'the era of "social partnership" and "New Labour" [was] drawing to a close, albeit painfully and fitfully', it was these last words that really needed stressing.[37]

The new union leaders concentrated on reasserting their influence in the party, and securing a more united front in the Trade Union and Labour Party Liaison Organisation (TULO). For their part, Blair, Brown and the whole New Labour machine were well aware – for all their disdain for what they and their media friends derided as the 'awkward squad' – of how dependent they remained on union funding. This led to the so-called 'Warwick Agreement' of December 2004. The big concession by the New Labour leadership was holding off the privatisation of the Post Office, even while still insisting on opening up postal markets. A good many of the other items in the

Warwick Agreement, to do with labour rights and 'narrowing inequalities' at work, found their way into the 2005 election manifesto. Yet, as Minkin noted, the Warwick agreement had 'many uncertainties of specificity and commitment', not least because 'no attempt was made to renovate the old "rules" and "protocols" of the union–party relationship'.[38]

This allowed the party machine to reassert New Labour's purpose and control after the 2005 election, when the party's regional organisers manipulated the selection of constituency delegates to National Policy Forums, so that those most sympathetic to seeing the Warwick policy commitments implemented were 'squeezed out'.[39] Efforts were redoubled to secure greater autonomy from the unions by soliciting more financial contributions from business. After the 'cash for honours' scandal which this triggered in 2006 (Blair was interviewed by the police about allegations that he had offered appointments to the House of Lords in exchange for loans to the party), the government commissioned a retired civil servant to look into state funding for political parties, which was duly recommended, to be supplemented only by individual private donations. To donate to the Labour Party, trade unions would be required to have each of their members 'opt in' by signing a form declaring that a specific portion of their dues could be allocated to this purpose.[40] Although New Labour could not achieve the cross-party consensus needed to implement this policy, it would continue to hold considerable attraction for the PLP.

The cash-for-honours scandal played out in the PLP in a manner that McDonnell compared to 'an episode of the Sopranos', with Brown supporters smelling blood. Tom Watson, first elected in 2001, a former Treasury whip and now junior defence minister, turned the knife by resigning from the government after signing a letter calling on Blair to go.[41] Many of the new union leaders also suffered from the delusion that Brown, who was more comfortable speaking in their idiom, was inclined to take the party in a somewhat different direction – a view shared even by a good many activists who had left the party. Yet, as one of Brown's closest advisers put it privately at the time, the fact of the matter was that 'you could not fit a piece of paper between the two of them ideologically'.

As early as mid 2006, John McDonnell had told a Campaign Group meeting that he wanted to run against Brown for the leadership if he could get the requisite number of MPs and MEPs (12 per cent) to sign his nomination papers. He was well aware that few of the new union leaders would back him: even though his 'programme read like a wish list of union demands', he was 'unpopular in the highest echelons of the union movement, often because he had supported grassroots trade unionists in internal disputes or elections'.[42] This reinforced the new union leaders' alliance with the other union leaders in TULO, as did their reluctance to back a candidate with little chance of winning. Yet McDonnell knew, on the basis of the meetings he had held all over the country since launching the LRC in 2004, that his candidacy would secure sufficient support from party members in the constituencies, as well as from union activists, to become a much-needed showcase for a democratic-socialist alternative to the reproduction of New Labour under Gordon Brown. In the event, Michael Meacher, expecting that he would be better able than McDonnell to get enough MPs to sign his nomination papers, also tried to run – until 'Brown, desperate to inherit the leadership unopposed, unleashed a formidable operation that quickly cowed most of the "soft left" MPs Meacher was targeting', with the result that Meacher withdrew.[43]

With McDonnell unable to get the requisite number of nominations, there was much derision in the media over how isolated the two dozen or so MPs in the Campaign Group were in their opposition to New Labour. A more viable challenge to New Labour from inside the PLP was detected in the bid that John Cruddas (closely associated with those in the PLP whom the Blairites derided as the 'soft left') made for the deputy leadership, with the Campaign Group MP Jon Trickett (a former student of Ralph Miliband at Leeds University) acting as his campaign manager. Cruddas was a key figure among the self-described 'left of centre' commentators and academics who, in 2003, had issued the *Compass Manifesto* critique of New Labour in power.[44] This had challenged both how far the New Labour government had travelled in a neoliberal direction and how far the Progress group, which supported Blair in particular, had gone in cementing its control over the party. But by nevertheless accepting much of New Labour's 'modernisation' discourse and practices in both the party and the state, those who identified with Compass were always careful to distinguish themselves from all those they, like the Blairites, lumped together as 'Old Labour'. This term was misleadingly used to encompass not only the 'Labour First' group of parliamentarians, who harked back to the good old days of the Cold War, the welfare state and reliable right-wing industrial union leaders, but also those on the Bennite new left whose project of democratising and radicalising the Labour Party those very parliamentarians had fought tooth-and-nail to defeat in the 1970s and 1980s. When Cruddas came first among the six candidates in the first deputy leadership ballot, despite ending up third on the final ballot, this seemed to suggest new possibilities for a 'centre-left' alternative to New Labour.

Indeed, when in 2007 Labour suffered its worst local election defeat in forty years, Benn wrote in one of his last diary entries that this 'terrible, terrible day for the Labour Party is happily, I think, the death blow of New Labour'.[45] It was no doubt with the goal of putting another nail in New Labour's coffin that Meacher decided at this time to launch his explicitly 'Bennite' *Left Futures* blog, which would become quite widely read among activists within and outside the Labour Party in the years before 2015. Meacher now hired Jon Lansman, officially as his parliamentary assistant, tasking him with devoting his time and energy to testing whether conditions were indeed ripe at the base of the party for a renewal of the Bennite project. After serving as campaign manager for Benn's deputy leadership campaign while still in his early twenties, Lansman had stayed active in the CLPD until the mid 1990s when – partly for personal reasons, but also because he saw how far the balance had tilted under New Labour – he stepped back from his CLPD activities. He had even stopped attending the annual party conferences, seeing them as 'a waste of time'.[46] But after aiding McDonnell in his attempt to run for the leadership, and then being hired by Meacher, he was soon active again on the executive committees of both the CLPD and LRC, deploying his unrivalled knowledge of party rules and procedures, as well as his acute sense of how to use them to help shift the balance of forces inside the party.

The 2008 crisis having proved that the economic model on which New Labour depended was unsustainable, a revolt finally took place at the 2009 party conference. Even if Brown was less personally directive over the party machine than Blair had been, party officials nevertheless still behaved as they had been trained to do before. So it was very significant that a constitutional amendment, coming from the South Islington CLP with strong CLPD support, calling for the introduction of one member, one vote (OMOV) for CLP elections to the National Policy Forum, received almost 80 per cent support from the unions. Their decision finally to stand up against 'the most corrupted part of the implementation of Partnership in Power under Blair and then Brown', as Minkin calls it, was a major shock: 'what had appeared to be a deepening atmosphere of demoralised disengagement within the party proved to be a revolt awaiting an opportune moment and an appropriate issue ... the biggest defeat for the General Secretary and the managerial regime under New Labour.'[47]

This revolt would lay the foundations for Ed Miliband to become leader of the party on the basis of his campaign promise to break with New Labour's legacy. Of course, no one could then have imagined that a still further extension of OMOV under his leadership would pave the way for Corbyn to be elected leader in 2015. But Lansman did foresee at the time that the loosening of top-down policy control, and the return to resolution-based party conferences signalled by the revolt at the 2009 conference, opened the way to a possible further shift in the balance of forces in the party: 'With better policies we will attract new members and are likely to get more people joining from the broader left. All we need is the ability to argue our policies in a democratic forum. If we get that we will win some arguments and even if Ed delivers little, we will make some gains.'[48]

8

Beyond New Labour:
The Revival of the Labour New Left

After Labour's crushing defeat in the 2010 election (its 29 per cent share of the vote was almost the lowest in the party's history), Ed Miliband – who had overseen the production of the election manifesto – emerged as the party's new leader. As he put it in the opening speech of his leadership election campaign, while he was 'proud of our record in government over thirteen years', it was 'time to move on from the era of Blair and Brown'. Not having been compromised by the disastrous illegal Iraq invasion already distinguished him from the two heirs apparent, David Miliband and Ed Balls, but even more so did his insistence – while peppering his speeches with 'words that had been banned from the New Labour lexicon such as socialism and equality' – that the fundamental reason he was standing was to change the party so as to win elections, 'not despite our values but because of them'.[1]

Alongside Peter Hain, Sadiq Kahn and Hilary Benn, who led the centre-left minority in the PLP in backing his candidacy, Ed Miliband also drew support from long-time Bennites associated with the Campaign Group, like Michael Meacher and John Trickett, as well as from prominent figures of the old parliamentarist guard, like Roy Hattersley and Neil Kinnock, who had played key roles in the defeat of the Bennite project in the early 1980s. With not much more than a dozen MPs in the new PLP now affiliated with the Campaign Group,[2] it was hardly surprising that John McDonnell was again unable to secure the thirty-three nominations needed from MPs in order to be able to stand. Dianne Abbott was able to, but 'only because a number of Labour MPs who shared little or nothing with her politically had nominated her in order to ensure the leadership race would not be fought by four, 30–40 something, white men'.[3] In the event, only seven MPs actually voted for her. The fact that she did not even win much support in her own CLP, and that Ed Miliband himself came a distant second in the constituency section of the electoral college, testified to the lingering effects at the base of the party of the earlier defeat of the left. The only thing that countered this in 2010 was the overwhelming support the union section of the electoral college gave to Ed Miliband. Not only the more radical leaders of Unite and CWU, but even the normally more cautious leaders of the GMB and Unison actively mobilised their members to vote for him.

From 'Red Ed' to 'One Nation'

The experience of the Wilson governments of the 1960s goes a long way in explaining the political trajectory of Jeremy Corbyn; the experience of the Thatcher governments in the 1980s does the same for the political trajectory of Ed Miliband. When he became involved in politics it was getting Thatcher out that mattered. To this end, the utility of his careful calculation, as a twenty-four-year-old, demonstrating that the tax burden for most people was no lower than it had been before Thatcher was elected, led him to be recruited by Gordon Brown into his shadow Treasury team. Despite his warm relationship with Benn ever since working as a teenager in Benn's home office, his disdain for the 'third way' as an economic strategy, and his disagreement with the Iraq invasion, he never considered afiliating to the Campaign Group after he was offered and elected to a safe working-class seat in the 2005 election. In November 2005 his decision not to join the forty-nine Labour MPs who rebelled against the government's change in the law to allow police to hold terrorism suspects for ninety days without charge was directly related to his knowledge that doing so would have ended his prospects of being brought into the cabinet. Yet he relished appealing to the radical sentiments of CLP and union delegates at party conferences. Against Brown's advice, in his first speech from the platform, in

2008, he even went so far as to recall his father's speech at the 1953 Labour Party conference calling for the social ownership of the means of production, distribution and exchange. His appointment by Brown as minister of the newly created Department of Energy and Climate Change in October 2008 gave him the opportunity to develop 'a politics of climate change that speaks to people's idealism as well as their wallets'.[4] For young activists whose experience of New Labour in government was of a regime that showed nothing but disdain for idealism, this was at least refreshing.

The promise of moving the party well beyond 'New Labour's comfort zone' attracted almost 50,000 new members – the first signs of growth in a decade – bringing total membership back to some 200,000. The media moniker of 'Red Ed' for the new leader did the party no harm in this respect; nor did his oft-heard condemnation of 'predatory capitalism', which he condemned as unable 'to generate stable prosperity for the many, at the same time as it created spectacular rewards for the few'.[5] Policies he advanced for a higher minimum wage, curtailing precarious ('zero-hour') work arrangements, a 50 per cent tax on the highest incomes, and a freeze on energy price rises, were all of a piece with this. But nothing more clearly symbolised Ed Miliband's attempted break with his predecessors than two steadfast anti-imperialist stands. The first was against Rupert Murdoch's News Corp media empire in the wake of the 2011 *News of the World* phone-hacking scandal – 'an act of absolute courage', in John McDonnell's words. The second was his refusal, under enormous pressure, to allow parliament to endorse the US empire's bombing of Syria in 2013, as requested by President Obama before he put it to Congress, and in the absence of which he did not proceed.

Yet what would matter most in terms of a real break with the New Labour regime was a change in the relationship with the party outside parliament – and, as Miliband often put it, changing the party itself into a movement. This was the purpose of the 'Refounding Labour' exercise he launched shortly after becoming leader, as he explained to the National Policy Forum:

Let's be honest, the leadership believed its role was to protect the public from the party. It never really believed the party could provide the connection to the British people. And we didn't build a genuine movement. By the end, it was our party members that were trying to tell the leadership what the public wanted it to hear ... Old Labour forgot about the public. New Labour forgot about the party. And, by the time we left office, we had lost touch with both.[6]

Despite all this, Ed Miliband's tenure as Labour leader would ultimately reveal the severe limitations of trying to renew social democracy from within the Parliamentary Labour Party.

Nothing of substance came of the Refounding Labour exercise, although the initial consultation document which Peter Hain was tasked with preparing identified the problems well enough, describing a party that 'looks inward rather than outward, is stuck in its structures, and is not engaged with local communities or national civil society'.[7] Yet, if the consultation exercise that was thereby launched was quite impressive, yielding some 3,500 submissions, the report that followed scarcely made any mention of them. The only outcome was a proposal brought to the 2011 conference whereby a new category of 'registered supporters' would be allowed to vote in leadership elections in yet a fourth electoral college. A much more radical proposal, advanced collectively by the unions through TULO, was to consider abolishing the electoral college altogether, and have the leader elected by one member, one vote (OMOV). Of all the issues raised about the party's internal processes, the union submission argued,

Possibly the most serious is the electoral college, which contains a clear hierarchy of membership. During the 2010 leadership election, the vote of an MP was worth the equivalent of 450 Party members and worth nearly 1000 trade unionists. Such a hierarchy is at odds with our passionate belief in equality. The hallmark of the modern Labour Party is OMOV, and it is time to give fresh thought to how that principle could be applied in our leadership elections. A simple OMOV election for the leader comprising all individual & affiliated members would level participation in the process.[8]

The TULO brief was scarcely noted at the time, but it would prove prophetic. Its revival at the height of Ed Miliband's conflict with the unions would pave the way for Jeremy Corbyn's election as leader.

Meanwhile, expectations of a radical shift in policy, encouraged by the new leader's announcement at the 2010 Policy Forum that twenty-two new working groups were to be formed, looked less likely to be fulfilled when Liam Byrne was appointed to coordinate the policy review process. Byrne was identified with the Blairites in the previous government, and was now carrying much of the responsibility in the shadow cabinet for adapting Labour's welfare policy so as to offer an 'austerity-light' alternative to the new government's harsher approach. His replacement in 2012 by John Cruddas was much more in line with what might have been expected from a 'left-centre' leader who called for replacing 'predatory capitalism' with 'responsible capitalism'. Cruddas was closely identified with Compass's complaints regarding New Labour's lack of 'understanding of the role of the state in reforming and constraining global capital'.

Yet such complaints had always sat uncomfortably beside Compass's support for New Labour's drive for 'modernisation' and 'economic efficiency'. This ignored the state's active role in the making of global capitalism; that it also ignored its role in the making of the global financial crisis soon became all too clear. By the time Cruddas took over the task of policy renewal in the party, it had also become apparent how deeply embedded the 'modernised' state was in the reproduction of global capitalism in the wake of the crisis. The bankers and investors whom the state had saved from the worst consequences of the crisis were now insisting that a 'responsible capitalism' depended above all on the state's adoption of fiscal austerity.

While the massive fiscal stimulus of 2009–10 coordinated by the G7 and G20 prevented another Great Depression, the UK then took the lead in the internationally coordinated policy of fiscal austerity that soon followed. Both Ed Miliband and his shadow chancellor of the exchequer, Ed Balls, initially contended, in response to this, that 'the best way to get the deficit down' was to develop 'a plan that puts growth and jobs first'.[9] But whatever wind might have been in the sails of this proposed renewal of social democracy was stilled when, at the beginning of 2012, Balls affirmed that, even if the cuts undertaken by George Osborne at the Treasury went too far, too fast, the next Labour government would 'keep all these cuts'. And if that was not enough, he added that it was now 'inevitable that public sector pay restraint will have to continue'. Those in the trade-union movement and the party who thought that Labour in opposition would oppose pay restraint would have to accept 'that's something we cannot do, should not do, and will not do'.[10]

The negative reaction this produced from the unions was only to be expected, but the sharpness of it went well beyond what New Labour had been used to experiencing. Unite's Len McCluskey warned Miliband against being 'drawn back into the swamp of bond market orthodoxy', and urged those who wanted a real alternative 'to get organised in parliament and outside'. Unison's Dave Prentis said the hope and reason his members needed to be given to vote Labour had been 'snatched away'. Even the GMB, the hitherto always reliable union backbone of the party machine, warned that it might disaffiliate from the party. The decision Miliband made to prove his leadership mettle by refusing to soften Balls's policy position 'in the face of threats' – despite having criticised New Labour just two months earlier for seeing its role as 'protecting the public from the party' – was a fateful one. 'Of course, there are some people in the party who don't like it but I'm afraid that's tough', he said. The leader's priority 'must be to show that Labour can be trusted with the nation's finances'.[11]

Although this stand partly reflected an obsession with fiscal rectitude that all those in Gordon Brown's Treasury team shared, underlying it was a more fundamental political socialisation – one at the very root of Labour's brand of parliamentary socialism. Unlike those Blairites who would have liked nothing more than to be rid of Labour's class image, Ed Miliband had often spoken in terms of once again making Labour into a working-class party; indeed, one of the first tasks he gave John Trickett as his shadow Cabinet Office minister was to address how to get more working-class parliamentary candidates. It was seen as very significant that Ed Miliband was not only breaking with over two decades of previous party leaders' practice by speaking at the annual Durham Miner's Gala union rally, but even showed up to speak to the massive anti-austerity demonstration organised by the TUC in London in March 2011. Yet it was also very significant that his message to the 2011 TUC conference was that 'strikes are always the consequence of failure. Failure we cannot afford as a nation. Instead your real role is as partners in the new economy.'[12]

The aversion to class struggle this expressed was a message designed to be heard by the media, and by the bankers, managers and investors, as well as by the PLP. But that it reflected something more fundamental could be seen in Ed Miliband's embrace of the so-called 'Blue Labour' academics who proposed overcoming the party's identity crisis by replenishing its historic roots in the 'reciprocity', 'trust' and 'mutuality' of those traditional elements of the labour movement that were most entangled, as Maurice Glasman put it, in those institutions of Britain's 'ancient constitution' that promoted a 'common good' across class divisions.[13] This was, of course, closely bound up with the question of the best tactical way to respond to the appeal to working-class voters of the UK Independence Party, to which the Blue Labour answer was to proudly stress Labour's traditional identification with the 'patriotism of the British people'.[14]

Ed Miliband's own new 'big idea' – his 'One Nation' theme, launched with much fanfare at the 2012 party conference – was a product of this, although it also followed logically from the notion of 'responsible capitalism'. Even if the Tories were the party of 'predatory capitalism', New Labour had been 'too silent about the responsibilities of those at the top and too timid about the account-ability of those with power'. This kind of accommodation to predatory capitalism, he contended, could only be countered by a party that explicitly stood for class harmony in the 'national interest', rather than class struggle from below. One Nation meant: 'we can't go back to Old Labour. We must be the party of the private sector as well as the public sector ... There is no future for this party as the party of one sectional interest of our country.'

Yet this is what Old Labour, understood in terms of what guided those at the helm of the party throughout the twentieth century, had always been about. As Ralph Miliband had put it in his *Parliamentary Socialism* (published eight years before Ed Miliband's birth), the leadership's general aversion to class struggle was embedded in a 'whole philosophy of politics' wherein MPs saw themselves as the agents of the 'national interest'. The party's leaders 'have always sought to escape from the implications of its class character by pursuing what they deemed to be "national" policies: these policies have regularly turned out to the detriment of the working classes and to the advantage of Conservatism. Nor can it be otherwise in a society whose essential characteristic remains class division.'[15]

Anti-Austerity Class Struggle Inside the Party

It was precisely the sharp expression of class divisions in the form of mass movements against austerity that opened the way for Jeremy Corbyn – who personally embodied the Labour new left's challenge to both New Labour and Old Labour – to become leader of the Labour Party. To be sure, as Andrew Murray put it, the politics of protest these movements represented was 'generally more class-focused than class-rooted. While it places issues of social inequality and global economic power front and centre, it neither emerges from the organic institutions of the class-in-itself nor advances the social-ist perspective of the class-for-itself'.[16] Yet if the economic and political weakening of the unions over the previous decades meant that class struggle could no longer take the form of long-sustained mass strikes, like those of the 1970s, it did find expression in short bursts of strike action (including a series of large public-sector strikes against pension cuts), as well as in new forms of political conflict between the unions and the PLP over the Labour Party's endorsement of austerity. This involved, as Murray added, 'synthesizing what remain[ed] of the traditional labor movement with the new movements of the last twenty years, channelling the mobilizing strengths, and many of the people, associated with twenty-first century "movement" politics through the embedded structures of the country's traditional left'.

The formation of UK Uncut in October 2010, just a month after Miliband became leader of the Labour Party, was the first signal of what was to come. Explicitly organised to 'make it clear that the cuts are a political choice, not a necessity', it was, Hilary Wainwright noted, an initiative of

> a group of mainly young people, many of whom had already had the experience of challenging and influencing the dominant political agenda, with considerable success, on climate change, through targeted and media-savvy direct action ... They wanted to organise action that engaged people in a way that the habitual demonstrations of the 'traditional left' failed to do. They decided to focus on corporate tax avoidance and occupy Vodafone and Topshop, the shopfronts of companies avoiding billions of pounds of tax ... The impact of their action and their ability to spread their arguments through social media was dramatic.[17]

The formation in the same month of Disabled People Against the Cuts (which would later join UK Uncut in blocking streets in central London) was another significant political development. Corbyn and McDonnell were both 'heavily involved' in creating this 'first radical disability movement in the country', as they also were in supporting the students who were sent to prison after the 'raucous protests' of November–December 2010 against the tripling of tuition fees.[18] All this took place a year before Occupy Wall Street, whose 'we are the

99 per cent' class-struggle logo inspired an encampment in the City of London outside St Paul's Cathedral (which McDonnell attended on the first night).

The direct-action style, inherited from the previous decade's anti-globalisation protests, was in deliberate contrast with stage-managed and police-escorted traditional union marches. Yet it was symptomatic of the limits of direct action that it was not Occupy but rather the TUC-organised 'March for the Alternative' six months earlier that really knitted the anti-austerity protesters together, including the many union, community and direct-action activists jointly involved in organising anti-cuts groups at the local level across the country. With attendance estimated as high as half a million, the March for the Alternative through London on 26 March 2011 was not only the largest demonstration since Stop the War's in 2003, but the largest labour movement march since the Second World War. After the waves of protest waned in 2012 in Britain, as elsewhere, it was again the left union leadership who were primarily behind the call, issued near the beginning of 2013, for a People's Assembly Against Austerity 'to bring together campaigns against cuts and privatisation with trade unionists in a movement for social justice' and to 'provide a national forum for anti-austerity views which, while increasingly popular, are barely represented in parliament'.[19]

Expectations that this signalled a major political realignment in Britain, of the kind that accompanied the shift from protest to politics around this time in Greece and Spain, appeared to be reinforced a month later when two of the signatories to the call for the Assembly – the filmmaker, Ken Loach, and the head of CND, Kate Hudson – initiated another call for exactly this. The time had come, they argued, 'to fill the left space' which Labour's 'embrace of neoliberal economic policies' alongside its social-democratic 'sister parties across Europe' had opened up for a new party of the left offering 'an alternative political, social and economic vision'.[20] But the space for this was actually far less than appeared. This was not only due to the familiar limitations imposed by the first-past-the-post electoral system, or the Trotskyist provenance of the Left Unity party founded, on Ken Loach's initiative, later that year.[21] It was also due to two important developments inside the Labour Party.

One of these was the emergence in 2011 of Red Labour, a small but 'cheeky and assertive digital Bennite social media project' that quickly became 'the biggest Labour-related page on Facebook bar the party's official one', with some 20,000 followers. In Alex Nunns's account, the name Red Labour was adopted in response to 'what passed for debate at this time . . . a remote argument between party elites over what was the best colour . . . Blue Labour duked it out with Purple Labour (Progress' favourite hue) and even In The Black Labour – "all attempts to discuss the Labour Party as though we were shopping for paint", quips activist James Doran'. The Red Labour activists were highly attuned to the irreverent radical discourse that infused the horizontal communications of the direct-protest movements; but they were at the same time explicitly dedicated to using this as a means of reviving the democratising project of the Labour new left. One of Red Labour's founders, Ben Sellers, saw it as an important new 'serious intervention into the party, but we weren't prepared to play by the rules which seem to have been set on the left and right of us. It wasn't quite so earnest either – it was explicitly populist and accessible.' Sellers was a veteran of the Labour Representation Committee, which had by now run out of steam amid the arcane conflicts all too familiar in small political groups, but for the most part Red Labour was animated by a new generation of activists. Max Shanly, having drifted into the Labour Party in 2011 after becoming active in his union while working in his first job, saw Red Labour as 'a popular education project' which would gain traction by going 'on the offensive' against the right in the party in order to 'explain that what they are saying is rubbish'.[22] In search of ballast for this, Shanly took to the library and found Ralph Miliband's *Parliamentary Socialism*. Soon in close touch with Lansman and McDonnell, he not only came to understand the project as Bennite, but provided support to Benn in the last year of his life.

The other development, far more weighty inside the party in both the short and the long run, was Unite's political strategy for shifting the balance of forces in the Parliamentary Labour Party. It was this, rather than organising the disparate anti-austerity forces into an electoral alternative to Labour, which was the overriding priority for Unite under McCluskey's leadership.[23] Developed by the union executive with considerable debate and planning through the course of 2011, it primarily involved identifying and mentoring as prospective parliamentary candidates people with experience of organising in workplaces, and shifting CLP selection contests in their favour by encouraging shop stewards and activists to join the party as individual members. It also encouraged their fellow workers to do so, by taking advantage of a scheme set up under Tony Blair to have their subscriptions initially paid by the union. As explained by Dan Quayle, the chair of Unite's National Political Committee, when the strategy was endorsed at the union conference in July 2012:

We want to shift the balance in the party away from middle-class academics and professionals towards people who've actually represented workers and fought the boss . . . If we want working-class political representation we need to change the way the relationship works. It's about class politics . . . Obviously there'll be a need to work to make sure any candidates who are selected remain politically accountable, but that's an ongoing process. We want a firmly class-based and left-wing general election campaign in 2015. We've got to say that Labour is the party of and for workers, not for neo-liberals, bankers, and the free market. That might alienate some people, but that's tough. Labour has to be a working-class party – a party for workers, pensioners, unemployed workers, single parents, the whole class.[24]

Trade-union sponsorship of MPs was of course a long-standing practice in the Labour Party. The GMB especially had always put a lot of effort and resources into this, and was indeed also stressing the importance of doing so at this time in response to austerity. Yet it was a different matter when it was advanced as an explicit political strategy by the radical socialist leadership of Unite with a view to changing the balance of forces in the PLP. This was exactly what the Blairites' Progress organisation had itself often done with ruthless discipline during the New Labour years, but now that Unite was taking a similar initiative it was not only inevitable that it would produce conflict with the Blairites, but also that it would be presented in the media as involving an illegitimate take-over of the party by 'union bosses'.

As Unite's strategy began to be implemented in the first months of 2013, the class war that ensued inside the Labour Party was intensified by the fact that it took place just when support for UKIP was increasing dramatically. David Cameron committed the Tories to a future EU referendum, while introducing anti-immigrant legislation and making a further assault on universal social benefits. But in the face of polls showing that a majority of voters blamed Labour for the welfare bill being too high, Labour MPs were instructed to abstain on a government bill cutting the unemployment benefits of those deemed not to be actively seeking work – against which forty-four Labour MPs revolted. Blair weighed in to warn Miliband against giving in 'to the interests that will passionately and often justly oppose what the government is doing . . . the exercise of political will lies not in going there, but in resisting the temptation to go there'. McCluskey responded by urging Miliband 'to take no notice of the siren voices from the boardrooms of JP Morgan or wherever else [Blair] is at the moment', nor to be 'seduced' by the Blairites in his shadow cabinet 'into offering the British electorate an austerity-lite programme, that won't capture their imagination'. If he was 'brave enough to go for something radical, he would be the next Prime Minister, but if not he'll be defeated, and he'll be cast into the dustbin of history'.[25]

Thus was the stage set for the infamous confrontation, triggered by the resignation of a right-wing Labour MP in Scotland, between the Blairites and Unite in the Falkirk West CLP over the selection of a candidate to replace him.[26] What had happened in the confrontation over Dick Taverne's deselection by the Lincoln CLP in the early 1970s (as we saw in Chapter 2) was repeated in Falkirk in 2013. The Blairites charged Unite with corruption for using the very provision they themselves had invented, and indeed were also using in this instance, to induce the subscription of new members. In comparison with the national coverage of the tiny Falkirk CLP, the media largely ignored the many meetings and rallies across the country just then taking place in the lead-up to the People's Assembly Against Austerity at Westminster Hall in London. While the 4,000 people who attended were no doubt prompted to do so by speeches both Balls and Miliband had made that month calling for fiscal discipline, including a cap on overall benefits, it was still the Falkirk scandal that 'set off a chain reaction of political explosions', capturing all the attention. Party headquarters put the Falkirk CLP into 'special measures', and not only imposed a shortlist but temporarily suspended the Unite candidate, Karie Murphy, as well as Stevie Deans, the chair of both Unite in Scotland and Falkirk CLP. Ed Miliband announced he would scrap the 'union join' scheme which Unite had 'frankly abused', and even invited the police to look into the alleged 'corruption'. [27]

The Blairites raised the stakes still further by calling for a commission to look into severing the link between the unions and the party, to which Miliband responded by making it clear his own goal was to 'mend the relationship, not end it'. He proposed to do this by appointing the party's former general secretary, Ray Collins, to undertake a review, with the unions, on how to effect a fundamental change in the basis on which trade unionists became members of the party. 'Trade unions', Miliband said, 'should have political funds for all kinds of campaigns and activities as they choose':

> But I do not want any individual to be paying money to the Labour Party in affiliation fees unless they have deliberately chosen to do so. I believe we need people to be able to make a more active, individual, choice on whether they affiliate to the Labour Party . . . So we need to set a new direction in our relationship with trade union members in which they choose to join Labour through the

affiliation fee: they would actively choose to be individually affiliated members of the Labour Party and they would no longer be automatically affiliated ... I believe this idea has huge potential for our Party and our politics. It could grow our membership from 200,000 to a far higher number, genuinely rooting us in the life of more people of our country.[28]

It had in fact long been Miliband's view that it would be much better to have 300,000 active trade unionists in the party than 3 million inactive affiliated ones. That opting out of the Labour Party involved a deliberate decision, while being a member of it did not, was indeed always highly problematic, in terms of what it said about the political commitment of Labour's affiliated membership. The passivity of the affiliated membership underpinned not only what Miliband now claimed Falkirk had revealed about the 'politics of the machine', but also the way the block vote had traditionally been used at party conferences and elections to sustain the control of decision-making and the party apparatus through arrangements between union leaders and parliamentary elites. This had usually operated to the detriment of the left in the past, and certainly contributed much to deadening democratic initiatives and capacity-building at the CLP level.

Many on the left saw Miliband's proposal as an expression of Blairite disdain for the working class, and as a cynical cover for reviving New Labour's aim of securing state funding for political parties. But this ignored his genuine interest in rebuilding Labour's working-class base. The trouble was that Miliband's 'One Nation' approach, which he now invoked again to contrast it with 'the politics of the machine', was at the same time explicitly designed to eschew class struggle. Seeing strikes as always a failure, standing up to the left union leaders, making the case for responsible capitalism through fiscal discipline and austerity, was the least effective way imaginable to enthuse trade-union activists to become active in the party. A distaste for the machine politics of the union bureaucracy was one thing; a suspicion that all forms of collective organisation

were unrepresentative, and that collective action through class struggle was always a failure, was quite another. What Ed Miliband failed
to articulate was what TULO's response to the Refounding Labour
consultation document had expressed so well:

> We find it odd that the document talks about improving the
> relationship between Labour MPs, councillors, and candidates
> with trade union *members*. Like those political representatives,
> the trade unions have shop stewards who represent their members
> and are able to provide leadership for their members. The key
> to improving the relationship between the two wings of our
> movement is to facilitate the re-engagement between union repre-
> sentatives and party representatives. Through this model, trade
> unions are able to mobilise their members in support of a mutual
> political agenda.[29]

But the TULO document recognised that bringing this about required
not only addressing the party's relationship with the unions and their
members, but also addressing the loss of collective power *inside* the
unions and the party:

> It is true that local trade union engagement has declined. This is
> partly due to the loss of 65% of union stewards since 1980,
> compared to a loss of 50% of members; simply put, there are less
> union activists, and those remaining have less time to devote to
> political matters. For many union activists, the apparent deafness
> of former Party leaders to union issues proved a disincentive to
> participate. The commitment to retain the majority of legislation
> that restricted trade unions in the workplace was the most obvious
> example of this – we should not expect volunteers to work hard
> for a party that opposes their aspirations.
>
> These issues were exacerbated by the decline in local power
> structures, leaving trade union activists unable to influence the
> political discourse in the Party. Attendance was unproductive, and
> therefore not a good use of personal time.

This was exacerbated by an apparently hostile atmosphere within the Party to collective forms of organisation, which viewed such organisation as unrepresentative and out of touch.[30]

It is one of the greatest ironies of the way the class struggle unfolded inside the Labour Party, from the Falkirk crisis to the Collins Review, that it was not this aspect of the TULO document that informed Collins's recommendations, but its proposal to use OMOV for the election of the leader. Most of the union leadership, including most of those on the left, were furious over the mandate Ed Miliband had given Collins, which they saw as endangering the organic party–union link. While Tom Watson took this as an opportunity to resign once again from the Labour front bench, on the grounds that Miliband had not consulted with the unions before setting up the Collins Review, Blair immediately praised Miliband for this 'defining moment': 'It's bold and it's strong. It's real leadership, this. I think it's important not only in its own terms, because he's carrying through a process of reform in the Labour party that is long overdue and, frankly, probably I should have done it when I was leader.'[31] It was all the more remarkable, therefore, that McCluskey, at first virtually alone on the left, embraced what Miliband was proposing, recognising that he was not challenging the unions' political levy in general, nor, necessarily, the funds that could thereby continue to be passed on to the party by affiliated unions:

What he's talking about is those of our members who pay the political levy, he wants them to have a second option, as it were, to see whether they want to opt in to becoming associate members of the Labour party. And it would be on that basis that unions would pay the affiliation ... The principle of what he's saying, about making certain that individual trade unionists actually take a conscious decision to opt in to being active in the Labour party, is something that I would welcome ... The vision that [Miliband] has set forward, that this would attract literally tens of thousands of trade unionists into active participation in the Labour party is something that I would 100% support . . . I thought it was very brave, very positive, and it's that I am absolutely committed to engaging in.[32]

Few shared McCluskey's enthusiasm. The GMB leadership, traditionally the closest to the party leader, declared that it would reduce its annual affiliation fee from over £1 million to the tiny sum it would get from the few members it expected to opt in. Most of the left associated with the Campaign Group, the CLPD, the Labour Representation Committee (LRC) and Red Labour feared that McCluskey was playing into the hands of the Blairites, and even Tony Benn tried to get McCluskey to change his mind. In the event, after a lot of deft negotiation on the part of Collins, well-seasoned for this by his long experience in the TGWU, it was agreed that the unions would initiate a process, to be completed within five years, whereby only those members who explicitly agreed that part of their political levy should be paid to the party would be affiliated to it. But when a Special Conference was called in March 2014 to deal with the Collins review, the most important alteration in the party rules put to that conference actually had to do with how the change in union affiliations affected the procedure for election of the party leader – the very procedure established at that other Special Conference of January 1981, which had created the electoral college system. It was in this context that the OMOV proposal that TULO had advanced in its 'Refounding Labour' submission was revived, alongside the one concrete reform endorsed by the party conference at that time, which allowed 'registered supporters' to vote in leadership elections.

The notion that an MP's vote for the leader should carry no more weight than that of any other party member was a proposal that cut to the heart of Labour's traditional parliamentarism – which, it was by now all too clear, the constitutional reforms of 1981 had not undone. And even TULO's proposal in 2011 drew back from going too far in the direction of downgrading 'the role of our parliamentarians in a leadership election' by endorsing the continuation of 'the exclusive right of parliamentarians to nominate candidates'. This special and powerful privilege of sitting MPs was unknown in most other social-democratic parties, but its retention in the Labour Party was still not open for debate. Indeed, to 'compensate' the PLP for the shift to OMOV, the threshold for the number of nominations a prospective candidate for the leadership would have to get was raised from 12.5 per cent to 15 per cent. Since this was seen to leave control over who would run for leader in the hands of MPs, no one imagined, when the rule changes were passed as a package at the Special Conference by a delegate vote of 86 to 14 per cent, that the procedural way had just been cleared for a Campaign Group MP to become leader of the Labour Party. Indeed, the conclusion that most of the left drew from the rule change for electing the leader was that the Blairites had regained control.

Notably, however, while having strongly opposed the Collins Review himself, at least Lansman was not convinced that the Blairites had 'tightened their grip', as he put it in his response to comments on a moving essay he had penned in *Left Futures* entitled 'I am still a Bennite', to mark Tony Benn's death just two weeks after the Special Conference. While recognising that the Blairite forces in the party remained 'strong in organisation and within the PLP . . . with a well-oiled machine for providing assistance to young careerists up the greasy pole to the PLP', he discerned they were 'weak in CLPs . . . and especially in the trade unions', and that even in the party's bureau-cracy 'their corrupting influence has weakened considerably'.[33] He noted with satisfaction, moreover, that no Blairite candidates were now winning election to the NEC, and that in 2012 the left slate had won 47 per cent of the vote (in the September 2014 election the left slate would win 55 per cent, its best result since the 1980s). He might have added that the effect of Red Labour could also by now be felt in the thirty or so local groups that had formed themselves under its banner; and that in 2013, even if more by luck than any strategic planning, six of their supporters were elected to Young Labour's national committee. But in considering 'what the Bennites have to do', it was still a distinctly long-term agenda that Lansman set out in March 2014: 'create an effective alliance of the CLP Left with trade union activists; campaign in the party from constituency level upwards for democratic reforms in the party and progressive policies; give backing to those in Young Labour battling to liberate it from Progress clutches and create a healthy campaigning youth section'.[34] Electing a Bennite as leader of the party was notably missing from this list.

Corbyn's Election to the Leadership

Yet in just over a year, after Labour's defeat in the 2015 election, Lansman would be at the epicentre of Corbyn's campaign for leader. And he would go on to help found Momentum, building on the massive enthusiasm that Corbyn's campaign generated among young people who had previously embraced protest rather than politics. Long before the day of the election, it was clear that Labour would not be able to win an outright majority, thanks to the predictable loss of Labour's Scottish seats to the Scottish National Party. The massive defection of Labour's working-class base in Scotland was directly the result of the identification of the Labour Party with Westminster-imposed austerity. It was also the price Ed Miliband paid for having gone along with the Blairites in joining the Tories in the 'Better Together' campaign in the Scottish independence referendum.[35] Labour's adoption of the language of patriotism in the One Nation slogan helped fuel not just UKIP's but also the Tories' appeal to English nationalism during the 2015 election, invoking the threat of a Labour government dependent on the votes of the SNP. But it was not the switch of working-class Labour voters to UKIP that determined the unexpected extent of Labour's defeat in the 2015 election – UKIP's sharp rise to 12.6 per cent of the total vote drew far more from the Tories.[36] The greatest determining factor, as Labour's own post mortem showed, was the low turnout among those who had indicated in pre-election polls they were more inclined towards Labour than any other party, but proved not to be enthused enough to come out to vote – thereby repeating a consistent pattern in every election since New Labour's initial victory in 1997.[37]

It was scarcely surprising that as soon as Ed Miliband resigned the leadership, Blair and Mandelson jumped up to proclaim that the election was lost because he had 'discarded New Labour', nor that their anointed candidate to succeed him, Liz Kendall, started her campaign in exactly this vein.[38] Rather more surprising was that the leadership candidates who came from Brown's camp, as Ed Miliband had, echoed Kendall's call for individual 'aspirational' values over collective egalitarian ones. Yvette Cooper set out her wares not only by granting the case for corporate tax cuts, but also by wrapping this in the tired old call to 'move beyond the old labels of left and right'. Andy Burnham, widely expected to be favoured by the unions as the least objectionable alternative, not only averred that Labour governments 'didn't prioritise deficit reduction enough', but also declared Miliband's break with New Labour to be a 'mistake'.[39] In short, in the leadership campaign the 'soft left' in the PLP had been neutered by the Blairites.

In this context, it seemed that whatever democratic significance might have been attached to the Collins OMOV reform was in fact about to be entirely discounted. The power of Labour MPs to choose who could stand for the leadership had been reinforced through the increase in the required nomination threshold to 15 per cent. The chances of anyone from the tiny Socialist Campaign Group, whose numbers were further depleted by retirements and defeats in the 2015 election, getting enough nominations to stand against the re-emerging New Labour hegemony in the PLP were slimmer than ever. McDonnell and Abbott both forswore another candidacy in the face of this, as did Meacher and Trickett, despite overtures from Lansman and Peter Wilsman, the chair of the CLPD. It looked as if the allegedly greatest democratic party reform in the party's history, finally vesting the election of the leader in the hands of the party's members and supporters, was about to be inaugurated with less real choice than ever between the PLP's candidates. In an article for the LRC's *Labour Briefing*, McDonnell – noting that the fact that 'the candidates for the Labour leadership so far have failed to mount the slightest challenge to capital shows the abject state of near surrender of the Labour Party' – pronounced it 'the darkest hour that socialists in Britain have faced since the Attlee government fell in 1951'.[40]

A first sign that the balance of forces inside the party had at least changed sufficiently for this not to be readily accepted came from ten newly elected Labour MPs in the form of a letter to the *Guardian* whose central message was: 'We need a new leader who looks forward and will challenge an agenda of cuts, take on big business and will set out an alternative to austerity – not one which will draw back to the New Labour creed of the past.'[41] But while this suggested that the Campaign Group's numbers might be replenished, and partially validated Unite's strategy of electing more working-class socialist MPs, it did little to improve the chances of getting the thirty-five MPs needed to nominate such a candidate in a parliamentary party that was, as Lansman noted, not significantly to the left of its predecessor. Yet just as the idea was being mooted that the left might have to run a 'Not the Labour Leadership' speaking tour, there appeared, quite out of the blue, an online petition calling for 'an anti-austerity candidate to stand'. Inspired by the new MPs' letter, it was launched by two working-class women who were long-standing members of the party in the south-east. With the help of Red Labour's nationwide social-media network, the petition immediately attracted 5,000 signatures. Lansman, sensed that this sort of pressure from below might influence enough other MPs to show they were at least prepared to allow the anti-austerity case to be made by signing the nomination paper for someone in the Campaign Group who would not stir their ire too much. He consulted with Byron Taylor, the national officer for TULO since 2002, and came away thinking: 'It's got to be Jeremy Corbyn.' At the Campaign Group meeting the next day, it was Corbyn who, having heretofore been overlooked in the desperate search for a candidate, 'tentatively, raised a suggestion: "What about if I stand?"'[42]

The story of what transpired over the summer of 2015 to get Jeremy Corbyn elected leader of the Labour Party, and in the process to bring in hundreds of thousands of new members, turning Labour into Europe's largest political party, has been told in rich detail in Alex Nunns's *The Candidate*. Suffice it here to underline Nunns's emphasis on the 'three nerve centres' that would now 'coalesce in the Corbyn campaign, their distinct cultures shaping distinct parts of the operation. The campaign machine would be infused with CLPD organising skill; its political centre of gravity would owe much to the LRC; and Red Labour would effectively become the "Corbyn for Labour" social media team.' Comprising at most a couple of hundred people, this was the core of the campaign that went into action at the beginning of June 2015, first to put enough pressure on MPs to get the necessary thirty-five signatures; then, over the summer, to win the unions' support (nine unions would eventually nominate Corbyn, providing crucial infrastructural support); and finally, through meetings and rallies across the country, to secure the overwhelming majority of the votes of members (old as well as new) and registered supporters.[43]

Initially, however, the main aim of the campaign, certainly as far as Corbyn was concerned, was not so much about winning the leadership as about revitalising the left. Speaking in June at a demonstration in London of some 250,000 people organised by the People's Assembly Against Austerity, which had been planned long before the Labour leadership campaign began, Corbyn was 'greeted as if he's a rock star' (in the words of his co-speaker, the comedian Mark Steel). But Corbyn did not even mention that he was running for Labour leader, let alone that those hearing him could sign up to vote for only three pounds: instead he stressed the importance of sustaining the anti-austerity movement as 'a social movement of all of us that can change our society into something good, rather than something that is cruel and divided'. In July, with the campaign in full swing, and Corbyn in the midst of speaking to literally hundreds of meetings across the country, so packed that larger and larger venues needed to be booked and still people struggled to get into them, he insisted on going to the annual Tolpuddle Martyr's Festival in Dorset (where he had first come as a fourteen-year-old with his parents) – even though the TUC had not invited him to speak because it might show favouritism. On a make-shift stage in front of the Unison tent, he was still insisting that what he really wanted his campaign to be about was: 'whatever happens, we're a force, we're a presence, we're a future, we're a hope, we're an inspiration to the next generation'.[44]

In a speech in Scotland in August, when it already looked as if his victory was assured, even in the face of a big scare campaign in the media, Corbyn doubled down on his explanation of the Labour Party's losses in Scotland as being due to its positions on austerity and Trident. Promising that as leader of the party he would ensure that the next Labour government would get rid of both, he still insisted: 'Politics isn't really about, as interesting as it is, the arithmetic in Holyrood, in Westminster, Cardiff or anywhere else . . . it's actually about what people think and do outside. Political change actually comes from the democratic base of our society.'[45]

When his victory was announced at the Labour Party conference in Liverpool in September 2015, the extent of his success could be measured: he had won 59.5 per cent of the 422,664 votes cast, including 49.6 per cent of the 245,520 members who voted, and 83.8 per cent of the 105,598 registered supporters. His closest rival, Andy Burnham, won 22.7 percent of members' votes and 5.8 per cent of registered supporters. Unite's political strategy, underpinned by a campaign that drew a million pounds out of its political fund, was vindicated by its persuading as many as 100,000 of its members to sign up directly to the party. Nothing like this had ever happened in the history of the Labour Party. But the project of transcending the party's traditional parliamentarism and fashioning it into an agency for socialism in the twenty-first century had barely begun. While Unite members no doubt accounted for a majority of the 57 per cent of individually affiliated union votes cast for Corbyn, trade unionists accounted for only 17 per cent of all the votes cast; and even Unite, whose influence with the leadership of the party would now prove immense, had far to go in democratising itself, let alone politically educating its membership.

As for the party apparatus, the role it had played throughout the leadership campaign – worrying over, rather than welcoming, the massive influx of new members – spoke volumes about the transformation it would have to go through before it could become an agency of socialist policy formation, political education and popular mobilisation. Yet, as always with the Labour Party, it was the parliamentary party that would be the hardest nut to crack. Tom Watson, who so clearly did not share Corbyn's project and had a track record of making Labour leaders' lives difficult, was elected as deputy leader, which in itself did not bode well for party unity under Corbyn in the years to come. Meanwhile, of the thirty-six MPs who had signed Corbyn's nomination papers, only fourteen had voted for him.[46]

9

'For the Many, Not the Few': Broadening the New Left Project

Jeremy Corbyn was a veteran of the last sustained attempt to make the Labour Party capable of leading a socialist transformation. He knew that a reversion to social democracy, such as Ed Miliband had attempted, would once again end in defeat, and that the aim must be a radical restructuring of society, the economy and the state. He also understood that this project would face challenges even greater than those that had defeated Miliband. These included, crucially, the challenge of democratising the Labour Party itself, which New Labour had left more deeply integrated than ever with the capitalist economy and the state – a situation that Miliband had failed to change.

The next three years would be an object lesson in just how acute this challenge was. Not only was the leadership group small and unprepared, but within a year the Brexit referendum result would also divide the party, pulling areas of core Labour support towards right-wing nationalism rather than socialism. The victory of the Leave campaign by 52 to 48 per cent over Remain in the 2016 referendum posed especially acute electoral difficulties for Labour. While some 80 per cent of Labour members were for Remain, two-thirds of Labour MPs represented constituencies where an often large majority had voted to leave. Corbyn himself had campaigned for remaining in the EU, making no less than 123 media appearances.[1] But his lack of charisma, and the emphasis he placed on the need to reform the EU as it stood, left Remainers feeling that Corbyn's stance was insufficiently enthusiastic, and too complicated for voters. On top of this, Corbyn's long-standing dissent from many of the ruling tenets of Atlanticism, on areas ranging from Trident to Palestine, would add to the strength of opposition against him. In the face of all these immediate difficulties, Corbyn and his allies needed to consolidate their position in the party, building a democratic base capable of sustaining the socialist project, while simultaneously making plans for winning an election and implementing major reforms. Their opponents in the PLP lost little time in making their task even more difficult.

A Very Labour Party Coup

The referendum result provided the occasion for the first internal challenge to Corbyn's leadership. A large majority of the membership supported him, but a large majority of the PLP did not. Many of them were unreconciled to having as leader someone they looked on with condescension and whose socialist politics they disliked, and they thought that the party members who had elected him – especially the 200,000 new members who had flocked to join the party when he was nominated – were unrepresentative of Labour voters. David Cameron's resignation immediately following the referendum meant a new Conservative leader, and in all likelihood an early general election; with Corbyn as Labour leader, many of them thought the party would lose badly, and they might lose their seats.[2] In late June 2016, just three days after the referendum, most of his shadow cabinet resigned. By resigning, they intended to show him that he could not lead. At a full PLP meeting, supported by a large majority of backbenchers, they told him so to his face, in language that freely expressed their hostility and contempt. For the sake of the party, they insisted, he had to go.

But word had got out, and when Corbyn emerged from the PLP meeting he was met in Parliament Square by a rally of ten thousand people, alerted within hours by Momentum.[3] To intense enthusiasm, he made it clear there was no question of his resigning: he had been elected by the membership, not the PLP. Indeed, the composition and purpose of the rally confirmed Tony Benn's intuition in 1999 that a time was coming when it would be possible to envisage reconnecting socialist politics and radical social movements. Yet at another PLP meeting the following month, Neil Kinnock (now a peer) invoked the whole history of the Labour Party to explain why it was precisely this radical reconnection that meant that Corbyn had to go. The party's founders, he insisted, had made

> a deliberate, conscious, ideological choice that they would not pursue ... the revolutionary road – it was a real choice in those days – they would pursue the parliamentary road to socialism ... remember that history, remember the people when they join the Labour party they are joining a party committed to a parliamentary role and that makes it crucial to have a leader who enjoys the support of the parliamentary Labour party.[4]

The attempted coup may have been precipitated by the Brexit referendum result, but it had been much longer in gestation.[5] The aim was to force a fresh leadership election in which Corbyn would this time not be able to get the required number of nominations from MPs, and so would not be able to stand. Given the scale of his victory the year before, this idea could only have seemed plausible to MPs living in a Westminster dream-world, but it was strongly promoted by the party's general secretary, Iain McNicol.[6] Nevertheless, with firm union support, the NEC ruled that the incumbent leader was automatically on the ballot. Even so, as soon as Corbyn and some of his supporters had left the meeting following this decision, those who remained passed a resolution that in order to take part in the new leadership contest, party members had to have been members for at least six months, thus excluding an additional 130,000 who had joined within weeks of the coup in June.

This did not prevent Corbyn being re-elected in September with an increased majority, even without the help of these new members. Corbyn's victory in this second leadership contest over Owen Smith, one of the shadow cabinet ministers who had resigned in June, especially reflected the growing impact of Momentum, the new organisation of Labour activists that had emerged from among the many thousands of people who flocked to campaign for him in his first leadership bid the year before. When Corbyn's re-election was announced in September 2016 during the Labour Party conference in Liverpool, the energy and creativity of the activists who mobilised to re-elect him were fully registered at a new four-day festival called 'The World Transformed'; its events, paralleling the conference, combined strategic political discussions with radical art, music and culture, attracting enormous activist, delegate and media attention. The contrast with the trade-show atmosphere of conferences during the New Labour years was striking. And, although in 2016 most Momentum activists were enjoying themselves too much at The World Transformed to pay attention to the resolutions and reports in the conference hall, Momentum would go on to surpass the CLPD's successes in mobilising delegates to vote for the left's resolutions, making annual party conferences once again well-attended and passionate affairs.

But the whole episode of the second leadership election that was forced on Corbyn, and the party staff's support for the parliamentarians' attempted coup, showed that the Corbyn team could not avoid a radical shake-up of the party apparatus. This would become even clearer the following year, when Cameron's successor Theresa May called a snap election to try to take advantage of the divisions in the PLP. But neither her political advisers nor the commentariat, who universally agreed that Labour under Corbyn was electorally weaker than it had been at any point since 1983, had registered the scale of the shift in public opinion against austerity, or the potential of Momentum. May fought the election solely on a platform of offering 'strong and stable' government, with virtually no programme of domestic reform to address the legacy of the crash, justifying this in terms of the need for a large parliamentary majority to strengthen her hand in negotiating the terms of the UK's exit from the EU.

The focus on Brexit, which was identified as a Conservative project and which had commanded 52 per cent of the referendum vote, initially worked to May's advantage. But the situation was transformed by Labour's election manifesto, whose title, *For the Many, Not the Few*, became an instant hit with the public.[7] So, more substantively, did its 'distinctive themes [of] collectivism and universalism, after years of individualism and means-tested entitlements', which represented a conspicuous turn away from the accommodation to the Thatcherite legacy practised by New Labour, and the acceptance of austerity under Ed Miliband's leadership.[8] A draft of the manifesto was leaked a week ahead of its scheduled release, which meant that voters got to hear about Labour's pledges a week early, and with the high level of coverage that leaks always attract – while the fact that it had been leaked, presumably to damage Corbyn, galvanised the membership, and not least Momentum, into a new phase of intense campaign activity.

Momentum now perfected the techniques its activists had developed in the two leadership campaigns, enlisting the support of musicians and comedians, releasing hundreds of videos, and swarming canvassers into nearby marginal seats at short notice by the skilful use of social media. One of Momentum's most brilliant videos linked the issue of inequality to Labour's anti-austerity message, and was viewed by no less than a third of all Facebook users in Britain. It featured a home care-worker, a firefighter and a policeman on the job; after each of these turned to the camera to say 'I am paid too much', it ended with a man in a pinstriped suit and bowler hat turning to the camera just before entering his London mansion to complain 'I am not paid enough'. The sudden reinvestment of hope, energy and creativity in the Labour Party under Jeremy Corbyn's leadership was also epitomised by the filmmaker Ken Loach, who in 2013 had led yet another futile attempt to launch an electoral alternative to the Labour Party (Left Unity). By 2017 Loach was making official Labour Party campaign videos featuring a broad range of working people demanding 'the full fruits of our labour'. And once the rules governing television and radio coverage of election campaigns kicked in, allowing Corbyn himself to speak directly to voters, unmediated by the views of journalists, his popularity shot up. Labour's support rose from around 25 per cent six weeks earlier to 40 per cent of the votes cast on the day of the election. This yielded a net Labour gain of thirty seats. The Conservatives lost their majority and were forced into an unsavoury deal with the Democratic Unionist Party in order to remain in office.

It was not a victory, but it was an unprecedented leap of support in a single election campaign, and the largest increase in Labour's share of the vote since 1945. It might even have been a victory if the party's headquarters had shared the faith of the leader's office that a range of seats that party officials saw as unwinnable could have been won by taking the party's new message to voters who had never voted, and dramatically increasing the turnout. Instead, the officials devoted resources to Labour-held seats they considered at risk, but which were in fact won comfortably, thanks to the shift in public opinion that had taken place. The party machine's defensive strategy revealed once more the 'great incompetence' which, as we saw in Chapter 5, Corbyn had complained about back in 1983. Momentum, in contrast, mobilised and trained campaigners in thirty selected marginal constituencies, giving priority to those areas where there was an activist base that could be further built up. It also developed a website, used by over 100,000 Labour members and supporters across the country, which directed them to 'My Nearest Marginal'.[9]

Perhaps the most significant aspect of the June 2017 election, in good part due to Momentum, was the greatly increased turnout by young people to vote Labour. This was achieved despite almost two years of constant denigration of Corbyn by many of his own MPs, amplified across the mainstream media, as well as against the drag of a central party machine more concerned with vetting than welcoming new members. With the strongest electoral support coming not only from students but also from working-class voters under thirty-five, and especially from the semi-skilled, unskilled and unemployed among them, this gave the Labour electorate a remarkably young cast, and marked an important shift in the class composition of its young voters.[10] As we saw in Chapter 2, the last time anything like this had happened was a half-century before, in the two elections of the mid 1960s, when a new generation of working-class voters belied the widespread notion that political differentiation by class was a thing of the past by voting Labour in large numbers.

The renewal of the Labour new left project, which many activists now came to call the 'Corbyn project', was still inherently fragile, due to its unanticipated, almost accidental nature. But the election result had earned it a reprieve from being cut short by its opponents in the PLP. The massive influx of new members, which had continued through the election campaign, had brought the party's total membership up from just under 200,000 in 2010 to over 550,000 by the end of 2017, making it the largest party in Europe.[11] But the attack was soon resumed by the same alliance of Corbyn's PLP opponents and the mainstream media, including the *Guardian*, that had been central to the defeat of the Labour new left three decades earlier.

What was most distinctive about the new left's surprising comeback, and most critical for the future, was the renewed commitment to democratisation. From Corbyn's initial decision to consider standing for the leadership, through his refusal to step down when told to do so by the majority of Labour MPs, to the unprecedented success of his election campaign, it was the support of thousands of people in the streets that was critical to Corbyn's success. This was partly due to his personality and style – calm, unassuming, honest, likeable – but, as we have seen, also to his conception of politics. Unlike some left-wing leaders in other European countries, his appeal was 'not centred on himself as a charismatic leader'.[12] He was always most at home among social activists and when speaking with ordinary people, inviting them to contribute to party policy and become participants in helping to get it enacted and implemented.

And this marked his leadership as much after the 2017 election as before. A slightly envious complaint by a senior colleague needing decisions on urgent strategic issues was that 'Jeremy is touring four days a week'. This was more than a personal preference: it was a point of principle, adopted by his mentor Tony Benn during the Labour new left's rise in the 1970s, and reinforced after its defeat in the early 1980s, as a way of responding to the heavy top-down party management that sought to stifle internal dissent and distance the party from radical positions and mobilisations over the subsequent decades. This style of leadership drove the Westminster-focused media to new levels of hostility, aided by briefings from his critics in the PLP. Whereas thirty years earlier the new left's parliamentary critics had been worried that Benn's charisma would enable him to persuade people beyond the ranks of party activists, they now sensed, not unjustifiably, that Corbyn's lack of charisma could not – and they were, in some ways paradoxically, unhappy about this, too. Within the first few months of 2018, Corbyn was accused, first, of having been a spy for Czechoslovakia, then of being an ally of Putin, and finally of condoning antisemitism. The press and the BBC persistently gave top coverage to this last canard, alleging that the Labour Party was a hotbed of antisemitism and that Corbyn condoned it. It was left to progressive websites to point to the lack of evidence for this claim, to the deliberate equation of support for Palestine with antisemitism, and to the evidence of Israeli government efforts to encourage elements in the Labour Party to reduce the chances of Corbyn becoming prime minister. The initial timing of media criticism of Corbyn was clearly aimed at influencing the impending local government elections in May, and it was credited with having prevented Labour from gaining control of at least one of the two remaining Conservative-controlled councils in London.

The charges that Corbyn had spied for Czechoslovakia or was an ally of Putin were quickly disproved, and were so patently absurd they probably backfired in his favour. In spite of overwhelming evidence to the contrary, the media succeeded in making the charge that Corbyn was antisemitic stick and continued to support the allegations that the party was not dealing adequately with the problem. His opponents in the party and the media saw that Corbyn – who suffered painfully from the travesty of reality involved in accusing him of 'condoning antisemitism', and refused ever to respond in kind to personal attacks – was vulnerable to being smeared, especially if his famous reputation for high principle could be tarnished.

Under enormous pressure, the party succumbed by stages to an acceptance that opposing Israeli policy in Palestine was antisemitic, to the point where no party member could express an opinion unacceptable to Labour Friends of Israel without risking suspension and possible expulsion. A former Scottish MP, Jim Sheridan, was forced to apologise for saying: 'For all my adult life I have had the utmost respect and empathy for the Jewish community and their historic suffering. No longer, due to what they and their Blairite plotters are doing to my party and the long-suffering people of Britain who need a radical Labour government.' But his apology did not satisfy the critics, who called for his suspension to be re-imposed. It even became antisemitic to object to this: a prominent Corbyn supporter, Chris Williamson MP, felt forced to apologise for saying that the party had been 'too apologetic' about antisemitism in the party (which was hardly an illegitimate opinion), but was nonetheless suspended. Yet such evidence as there was made it clear that claims that the party was 'riddled with antisemitism', let alone 'institutionally antisemitic', were thoroughly disingenuous.[13]

The way Corbyn addressed these allegations in his 2018 conference speech should have nailed them once and for all:

I say this to all in the Jewish community: This party, this movement, will always be implacable campaigners against antisemitism and racism in all its forms. We are your ally. And the next Labour government will guarantee whatever support necessary to ensure the security of Jewish community centres and places of worship, as we will for any other community experiencing hateful behaviour and physical attacks. We will work with Jewish communities to eradicate antisemitism, both from our party and wider society. And with your help I will fight for that with every breath I possess.[14]

Later in the speech, when dealing with Labour's foreign policy, Corbyn was equally firm in making it clear that principled opposition to antisemitism did not preclude principled opposition to Israeli-government policy:

And let me next say a few words about the ongoing denial of justice and rights to the Palestinian people. Our Party is united in condemning the shooting of hundreds of unarmed demonstrators in Gaza by Israeli forces and the passing of Israel's discriminatory Nation-State Law. The continuing occupation, the expansion of illegal settlements and the imprisonment of Palestinian children are an outrage. We support a two-state solution to the conflict with a secure Israel and a viable and secure Palestinian state ... And in order to help make that two-state settlement a reality we will recognise a Palestinian state as soon as we take office.

The attacks on Corbyn were of a piece with the general systematic bias of the media against the socialists in the Labour Party.[15] The shift of readers from print to online news and comment, and from major broadcasters and newspapers to social media, could sometimes work to the advantage of the left – the 2017 election has been described as the first 'post-tabloid' election, in which the hysterical attacks on Corbyn by the *Daily Mail* and other right-wing papers had no detectable impact. But over time the bias against Corbyn shown by the BBC and the *Guardian*, as well as the right-wing press, was a serious political handicap. Unlike New Labour's modernisers, however, Corbyn was not afraid of the media. In a major speech he pointed to a survey which showed that

the British press is the least trusted press in Europe, including non-EU countries like North Macedonia and Serbia. Let that sink in for a moment. The owners and editors of most of our country's newspapers have dragged down standards so far that their hard-working journalists are simply not trusted by the public. It's a travesty. A free press is essential to our democracy, but much of our press isn't very free at all ... Just three companies control 71 per cent of national newspaper circulation and five companies control 81 per cent of local newspaper circulation ... One of the more radical and interesting ideas I've heard, which limits the power of unaccountable media barons without state control, is to give journalists the power to elect editors and have seats on boards for workers and consumers when a title or programme gets particularly large and influential.[16]

Corbyn went on to make some bold and imaginative proposals for 'a free and democratic media in the digital age'. Yet the fact that they were put forward in a Corbyn speech, rather than in an NEC policy document, underlined the general difficulty the party had in developing policies while under incessant attack. The distraction was particularly damaging since there was such an acute need to focus on ways of implementing the policies the leadership had championed while also transforming the party into an organisation capable of winning popular support for them.

The Gestation of Policy

It is said that when Margaret Thatcher's close lieutenant, Sir Keith Joseph, first took office as secretary of state for industry in 1979, he gave his senior civil servants a list of key neoliberal texts, such as Hayek's *The Road to Serfdom*, and told them to read them, so that they would understand the radical shift in policy they were going to be expected to implement after thirty-five years of social democracy. It was not obvious what would be on an equivalent reading list that Corbyn's team might give senior civil servants following an election victory.[17] And, unlike in the early 1970s, when the Labour new left's control of the NEC's policy committees provided a reasonably coherent and comprehensive programme for a Labour government, Corbyn and his team inherited nothing of that nature either. Experts in a wide variety of fields had many creative ideas for progressive policies that a Labour government could use, including on macroeconomic policy, banking, taxation, pensions, debt, higher education and ways of restoring the primacy of the public interest in the funding and management of the public infrastructure. But the party machine had hardly tapped into them, and it was not clear how far many of them had reached, or been pursued by, Corbyn's reconstructed shadow cabinet by the time Theresa May called her snap election in April 2017.[18]

The 2017 manifesto, hastily drafted when the election was called, largely drew on policy proposals the unions had put forward in previous years. Hardly revolutionary, it was nonetheless radical enough: the privatisation of the NHS would end, tuition fees for higher education would be abolished, union and workers' rights would be restored, public utilities and the railways would be returned to public ownership. The manifesto set out an industrial strategy to create an 'economy that works for all' through the strategic use of public procurement and national and regional investment banks. Although much of this was cast as a 'new deal for business', oriented towards making British industry more regionally balanced and internationally competitive, and underpinned by a 'successful international financial industry', the emphasis was on state actions and on changes to company law that would require finance and industry to make their activities respond to the needs of workers, consumers and communities. A *Daily Mirror* opinion poll showed that ending tuition fees for students, lifting the austerity-driven pay cap for public-sector workers, protecting the state pension from erosion, and closing the gender and racial pay gaps also found wide support. But so had even more radical proposals:

> Renationalising the railways, the Royal Mail and the energy industry ... each had the support of roughly half the public, with only about a quarter opposed. Seventy-one percent wanted zero hours contracts banned. Sixty-three percent supported the radical idea of requiring any company bidding for public contracts to adopt a maximum pay ratio of 20:1 between their highest and lowest paid staff. Taxing the rich, for so long taboo in British politics, turned out to be a big hit. Sixty-five per cent liked the idea of raising the income tax of those earning over £80,000, including a majority of Tory voters.[19]

How far the programme would prove feasible in practice would depend on whether its radical break with austerity and extensive programme of social-democratic measures could be carried through in the face of predictably intense resistance – from shareholders and investors, the Conservative Party, the media, the City of London, the

Treasury and the civil service, the 'deep state', the US state, and NATO – in the context of a corporate sector highly integrated with global markets. Yet, despite being instantly denounced as Stalinist, economically illiterate, incoherent and unaffordable, it was clearly a programme that could be made to seem 'plain common-sense'. It offered to improve the lives of ordinary people in important ways that people cared about, and it included 'landmark' measures whose radical nature was clear. When implemented, they would symbolise a new order. The tax increases to pay for them were to fall on corporations whose tax avoidance had become notorious, and on the rich, who had done well out of both the boom and the crisis. The long list of measures to restore workers' rights implied a significant shift in the social balance of power, potentially beginning to restore working-class confidence, shattered by years of unemployment and trade-union decline.

The manifesto contained plenty of omissions and weaknesses, some due to the speed with which it had to be composed. Whole areas of policy clearly needed far more radical measures, not least 'a radical reorientation of economic priorities away from the industrial capitalist obsession with economic growth' if ecological catastrophe is to be avoided.[20] The manifesto's statement that 'Labour supports the renewal of the Trident nuclear deterrent' could be largely explained by Unite's determination to protect its members' jobs; but it also revealed the absence of an alternative policy for the conversion of defence production in general, and the Trident nuclear weapons programme in particular. Already in 2016 Corbyn, in spite of his own long-standing opposition to nuclear weapons, had assigned his shadow defence spokesman, Clive Lewis, the task of telling the conference Labour delegates that the new leadership accepted the party's existing position on this. The political and ideological confusion sown by Lewis's attempt to defend this position by equating the labour movement's 'fundamental value of solidarity' with NATO's 'collective responsibility' only made matters worse.

A crucial element missing from the manifesto was any significant move towards democratising the state. There was a promise to establish a Constitutional Convention 'to examine and advise on reforming of the way Britain works at a fundamental level', as well as commitments to an elected upper house of parliament and reducing the voting age to sixteen, but nothing more. There was no proposal to have a written constitution, or to make the electoral system more democratic, or to end the exercise of unaccountable executive power through the royal prerogative and other archaic devices. There was nothing on ending the corporate capture of the state – the rampant influence of unregulated lobbying, the 'revolving door' between the senior civil service and leading business enterprises, or the 'executive boards' that had been set up for each government department, largely filled with private-sector personnel. There was no proposal to end government reliance on corporate management consultancies, or to deal with the undemocratic nature of the BBC, nominally a politically neutral public service but in practice a key component of the capital-ist state. There was no suggestion of ending subsidies to the private schools through which the rich constantly renew their dominant positions in the state and corporate elites.

All this said, the circumstances of the manifesto's production meant that it did not fully reflect the Corbyn team's developing project. John McDonnell, in particular, had assembled a policy team engaged in the search for new radical policies, as could be seen in the *Alternative Models of Ownership* report, commissioned by McDonnell and released a few days before the election. Though not official party policy, the stress this document placed on the role of municipal public ownership and procurement policies to seed and nurture worker and community cooperatives was designed to encourage broad discussion of new socialist strategies.[21] This picked up from the thinking of the Labour new left about new forms of public ownership that could draw directly on the expertise and insights of ordinary people, on the lines pioneered by the Lucas Aerospace shop stewards in the 1970s and the Greater London Council in the 1980s. Yet the emphasis on decentralised forms of common ownership skirted the crucial question of how to integrate and coordinate enterprises, sectors and regions through democratic economic planning processes.[22]

The *Alternative Models of Ownership* report also revived the concern, voiced by the Labour left ever since the nationalisations of the 1945 Labour government, to avoid top-down corporate management in publicly owned enterprises by encouraging new forms of industrial democracy, as well as accountability to 'diverse publics'. McDonnell's team continued to work on this, as he signalled in an important speech in February 2018:

We should not try to recreate the nationalised industries of the past . . . we cannot be nostalgic for a model whose management was often too distant, too bureaucratic and too removed from the reality of those at the forefront of delivering services. Taking essential industries away from the whims of the market is an opportunity to move away from profit as the driver of investment and hiring decisions. But just as importantly it's an opportunity for us to put those industries in the hands of those who run and use them.[23]

In his speech to the 2018 party conference McDonnell went even further:

Democracy is at the heart of our socialism – and extending it should always be our goal. Our predecessors fought for democracy in Parliament, against the divine right of kings and the aristocracy. They fought for working people to get the franchise. Our sisters fought for women's suffrage in the teeth of ferocious opposition and our movement fought for workers to have a voice at work. The trade unions founded this party to take that democratic vision even further. So in 2018 I tell you that at the heart of our programme is the greatest extension of economic democratic rights that this country has ever seen. It starts in the workplace.[24]

Since it was 'not just the employees of a company that create the profits it generates . . . it's the collective investment in infrastructure, education and research and development that we as a society make', worker representatives would have a third of the seats on company boards. In addition, legislation was being prepared for 'Inclusive Ownership Funds', which all large companies (covering some 40 per cent of the private-sector workforce) would be required to create. Shares would be transferred to these funds, which would be managed collectively by the workers. After the distribution to the workers of the dividends from these shares (up to maximum of £500 a year each) the balance in the funds would be treated as a social dividend which, over time, would 'mobilise billions that could be spent supporting our public services and social security'.[25]

This kind of reform is obviously not in itself transformational. Like their counterparts in Germany going back to the 1950s, or even the more radical reforms advanced by the Swedish unions in the 1970s, reforms of this kind can lead to management co-optation of workers to the end of enhancing the firm's competiveness. On the other hand, insofar as McDonnell explicitly stressed the importance of these proposals for recovering 'the hope and optimism of our people', they could be seen as a key part of a broader strategy for restoring the working-class confidence needed for the achievement of more transformative ends. As Barnaby Raine suggested:

McDonnell has no intention of abandoning the British proletariat as a radical political subject. On the contrary: unlike Keynes and those postwar social democrats for whom boosting effective demand was an end in itself – returning large populations to well-paid, stable jobs and thus, perhaps, to docility – it seems to me that McDonnell wants the return of good jobs for a quite different reason: they might grant the working class the footing to rise out of docility. McDonnell wants to create the conditions of possibility for a new working class that can agitate and advocate for itself, empowered and emboldened by the novel experience of running firms democratically. He wants to make the state a lever from above for reigniting industrial politics from below, which has long been dormant.[26]

In fact, James Schneider, one of the cofounders of Momentum, who became head of strategic communications in the leader's office, summarised the project (speaking in a personal capacity) even more broadly:

> The long-run aim is to achieve a radical shift in the balance of power, income and wealth, transforming the political, economic and social levels. You then work backwards on how to get there. A basic and necessary step is winning elections within the current system and balance of forces, so as to be able to make major changes that noticeably improve the lives of the overwhelming majority. With power, you have to make more fundamental, structural and institutional changes: politically, by democratising the state; economically, by expanding the commons, shifting the distribution of ownership towards the majority and giving workers and communities control over work and economic life; and socially, through a concerted shift in the balance of social forces, with race and gender justice playing a vital role.
>
> From this analysis, it follows that you must pass three categories of measures in the first term of office – and get the balance right. The first is a broad swathe of immediate ameliorative measures, mainly using the state's existing policy levers, such as tax and spend, to improve lives noticeably and swiftly. There must be several major measures that fall into the second category of contributing to shifting hegemony – they must be radical, and attract opposition; not reforms by stealth, like Brown's tax credits, which are being undone, but like the minimum wage, which can't be. The third category is non-reformist reforms, those which push at the boundaries of the possible and therefore open up new horizons, such as the NHS in the 1940s or expanding workers' ownership and control. The number of reforms of the third kind that can be achieved will depend more on the balance of forces in society and within the movement itself than on capacity within the administration.[27]

The sophistication of this formulation is striking, with its blend of strategic and tactical considerations, its integration of the struggle for hegemony – Gramsci's 'war of position' – with planning for the short term (the 'war of movement'), and its strong emphasis on democracy, both in the organisation of the state and the economy, as well as in the struggle itself. All these elements are important, and combining them in this way had no parallel in the thinking of previous Labour leaderships. Nonetheless, whether it could realise its promise would depend on how far a strategy could be developed to transform state as well as party institutions to make them capable of implementing it.

10

Implementing the New Left Project: Possibilities and Limitations

Labour's dramatic advance in the 2017 election raised the serious prospect of a Labour government and posed the hard question of what implementing the project of the Labour new left would now involve. A general problem would be the unconscious absorption by most existing public servants of a professional mind-set geared to neoliberal values and processes. Moreover, the 'new public management' and austerity had reduced the British civil service by a fifth between 2008 and 2017; and the senior (policymaking in the civil service had been hollowed out to the point where it lacked both planning and implementation capacity.[1] Even liberal commentators recognised that the degraded version of a representative state that by this time existed in Britain had been responsible for a catalogue of policy failures by successive governments, on a scale that a socialist-led Labour government could not afford.[2] New forms of accountability at all levels of the state and public services would be needed to restore a 'public realm' that had been corrupted by spin and disinformation.

Preparing Labour for government was the remit of Jon Trickett, Corbyn's shadow minister for the cabinet office. A core strategy group met in the leader's office each month, consisting of Corbyn, MacDonnell, Trickett and Diane Abbott, the shadow home secretary, plus Seumus Milne, the party's director of strategic communications, and Andrew Murray, the chief of staff of Unite, who had been seconded to assist in the leader's office during the 2017 election campaign. But with no set agenda, or secretariat, this was hardly adequate to the strategic challenge that Labour under Corbyn had set itself.

This was sobering, especially in light of what had already transpired with the Syriza government in Greece in 2015, which created such socialist enthusiasm when it was elected, and such disappointment less than six months later. One of Syriza's former leading cadres, Andreas Karitzis, has argued that this reflected not just the unequal strength of the Syriza government and Greece's creditors; it was also a failure of strategic planning, which must 'not only involve the government, but requires methods of social and political mobilisation at multiple levels and of a different nature than movements of social resistance and actions for attaining government power'. Perhaps the most serious consequence of failing to do this was that grassroots participation exhausted itself – 'in protest or support demonstrations, rather than in substantive and productive engagement'.[3] This was itself related to the fact that both before its election and again once the government was elected,

> the party did not focus on its basic duty: developing plans of action to address the difficult 'how?' of a different policy in the framework of an asphyxiated political environment. The obsessive adherence to lists of demands that are not attached to plans of action, and the acceptance of difficulties as a reason for adopting a more conventional governance mindset, did not advance the party's operational capability, and did not serve its political strategy.[4]

In and Against the State?

Labour's need to develop implementable plans was all the more important because resistance from capital, from both domestic and multinational corporations, and from the purchasers of government bonds, was predictable and very difficult to deflect. The UK economy was already weak from decades of low investment, running an unsustainable balance-of-payments deficit, and consequently very dependent on the foreign-exchange earnings of its global financial services sector.[5] Whether a Corbyn government would be able to borrow at an affordable rate of interest, and whether corporations would resume investment in the context of a determined social-democratic economic policy, were known unknowns – as was the possibly severe economic cost of Brexit. A Labour government would thus face acute difficulties in delivering on any policies that entailed significant costs.

Once again, a necessary condition of success would be understanding and support from the public; but there was as yet no clear public 'narrative' of what would be involved in restoring the state's capacity to manage the economy, or to insulate some aspects and sectors from exposure to market forces and embark on rebuilding the country's capacity to export – a precondition of socialist transformation. A further risk was that the trade unions – and not least Unite, which occupied a strategic position in the party, besides having members in key sectors of the economy – could withdraw their support if implementing a Labour government's policies appeared to threaten their members' jobs in the short term, even if the long-term results looked to be beneficial for jobs in general.

Yet McDonnell's speeches at the 2018 party conference and The World Transformed were more substantial. They offered a sharp commentary on how little previous Labour governments – including the 1945 Labour government – had done in terms of democratising the state and preparing it for the challenge to capital. Recapping the Greater London Council's practice in the 1980s of drawing on popular knowledge, in which he had been centrally involved, McDonnell sounded very much like Karitzis in the quotation above. But in terms of specific strategic proposals for changing state apparatuses there was little on offer beyond his determination, expressed in his speech to the party conference, to 'reprogram the Treasury, rewriting its rule books on how it makes decisions about what, when, and where to invest', so as finally to bring to an end its being used 'as a barrier against putting power back into the hands of the people'. The one concrete change he mentioned pertained to setting up a 'Public and Community Ownership Unit' in the Treasury, which would 'bring in the external expertise we will need'.[6]

More detailed plans for structural changes at the Bank of England were outlined in an independent report, commissioned by McDonnell, which proposed 'restructuring and relocating core Bank of England functions [to] provide a counterweight to the dominance of London'.[7] This would not only involve establishing regional offices 'to ensure that productive lending is geared towards local businesses', but moving some of the main Bank of England offices, even including the Monetary Policy Committee, to Birmingham, where it would sit alongside the offices of the National Investment Bank and the Strategic Investment Board, responsible for generating and allocating investment under Labour's industrial strategy, and the National Transformation Fund, responsible for Labour's infrastructure programme. This geographic shift was seen as essential for realising the report's main policy proposals: beyond setting a modest 3 per cent productivity growth target, these included establishing credit guidelines to shift private bank lending away from property; discretionary corporate bond purchasing, to stimulate investment and reduce the cost of the infrastructure programme; and aiding the National Investment Bank by using the still mainly publicly owned Royal Bank of Scotland as its banking arm.

But these plans were still far from anything that might be called a socialist strategy for structural change. This was not because of the report's sensible insistence that decision-making must reflect the views of 'scientists, researchers, engineers and technology experts', nor because it said that 'private sector investment is critical', and that all the institutions involved 'must encourage an entrepreneurial spirit'. Rather, it was because the foreign models it offered for a Labour government's industrial strategy to emulate went so far beyond social-democratic Norway or even Germany as to include such uncompromisingly capitalist regimes as Singapore, South Korea, Japan – and most of all, the United States. Lurking here was perhaps the most problematic aspect of Labour's industrial strategy: its silence on the question of how the promotion of internationally competitive export enterprises within the framework of global capitalism relates to the development of a transformational socialist strategy.[8]

McDonnell's public silence on the equally difficult question of how and when to introduce controls over the movement of capital was entirely understandable, given its political sensitivity and the importance of the financial sector's foreign-exchange earnings. But policies on this issue were no less necessary than industrial policies if the government was to be able to direct investment where it was needed, and prevent capital flight. The logical response to a refusal by companies to invest for long-term productivity growth would be to introduce capital controls and investment planning. But this could not be done without developing the state's capacity to transform financial services, Britain's dominant economic sector, into a public utility – even taking advantage of the possibility of starting with the Royal Bank of Scotland, still largely in public ownership after having been rescued in the wake of the 2007–08 crisis. Yet this would have major consequences for the global role of the City of London and would require the cooperation of other states. McDonnell told participants at The World Transformed in 2017 that plans were in hand to deal with capital flight or a run on the pound but he did not indicate what they were.[9]

To draw the contrast with the Labour new left policies advanced in the 1970s, when there was much greater willingness to discuss these questions openly, is not to suggest that confronting capital in these ways is easy, but only that these issues need to be explicitly addressed. As Tony Benn told the 1979 Labour Party conference, any serious socialist strategy has to begin from 'the usual problems of the reformer: we have to run the economic system to protect our people who are locked into it while we change the system'.

Transforming the Party?

By late 2017, the NEC finally had a pro-Corbyn majority, due to successful efforts by Momentum to get support for its slate in the election of the CLP section – a majority including, most notably, Jon Lansman, who had played a central role in the struggle to democratise the party over the previous four decades. Iain McNicol, the party's general secretary, had also been replaced by one of the new generation of left-wing trade-union officers, Unite's Jennie Formby, a strong supporter of Corbyn; four of the five national directorates were now headed by left-wing officials; and a start had been made in replacing right-wing regional directors.[10] The struggle to get resources and even responses from resistant headquarters officials, which had consumed much of the Corbyn team's time and energy between 2015 and 2017, finally appeared to be over, although the task of loosening the grip of the right wing on lower levels of the party apparatus had barely begun to be executed.

The significance of the change at the top of the party was illustrated in February 2019, when MPs demanded that the new general secretary, Jennie Formby, give them a detailed report on progress in dealing with allegations of antisemitism, for which responsibility had recently been transferred from the regions to the centre. She declined, reminding them that she was accountable to the NEC, not the PLP, and had to respect the party's privacy rules.[11] At the same time, the way she had been appointed was hardly very democratic, being the product of a behind-the-scenes stitch-up between the leader's office and the leadership of Unite, which the NEC was expected to rubber-stamp. This so smacked of the old manner of running the party that Lansman announced that he would also put his name forward; but he withdrew it again in face of the insistence by the rest of the team that it was finally the turn of a woman. In terms of Lansman's unparalleled understanding of Labour's internal procedures and relationships, he was by far the most qualified for the job among the team that had brought Corbyn to the leadership. In fact, the manner of the appointment made the case that the general secretary should be elected by the party's membership. The fear that this would establish conflicting claims to democratic legitimacy and would prove distracting and confusing to the Corbyn project was understandable. But against this was the longer-term strategic consideration that electing the general secretary would provide an alternative source of democratic protection for the project in face of the many compromises that Corbyn would be under pressure to make, in light of the balance of forces in the PLP, let alone the more powerful forces of capitalist, media and bureaucratic opposition.

Given the gap in attitudes between so many MPs and the party's membership, there was a strong case for reintroducing 'open' – i.e. routine – reselection of all MPs, which, as we have seen, had been secured by the Labour new left in 1979, but abandoned after the left's defeat in the 1980s. The leadership under Corbyn, however, ruled it out, evidently fearing that overcoming PLP resistance to it would consume energies when other issues had higher priority, and risk splitting the party at a time when they were not strong enough to face down resistance.[12] But it was a continuing source of tension between activists and the union leadership, in particular, and came to a head at the 2018 party conference when the NEC pre-empted a widely supported motion to introduce open selection with a motion to make reselection easier, but only on a case by case basis. As Michael Calderbank reported,

> From now on 33 per cent of CLP branches or affiliates (trade unions or affiliated socialist societies such as the Co-Op or Fabians) can trigger such a process. This lowers the hurdle for MPs to be triggered, but still requires a negative campaign to trigger an open contest. In some ways this is much more likely to spark destabilising internal feuding than simply requiring all MPs to re-contest the nomination alongside other candidates. This reform might well need to be revisited in favour of Open Selection.[13]

Momentum avoided being drawn into a bout of media-fuelled hysteria over this issue, as the CLPD had been in the 1970s. But it worked hard to get Momentum-backed candidates nominated as parliamentary candidates, with the result that about half of the one hundred or so candidates who had been selected for winnable seats by mid 2019 were on the left. It also tried to do the same with candidates for local council seats, as well as for key positions inside the party, such as the Conference Arrangements Committee, the NEC, CLP chairmanships, and so on, in order to build support for further moves towards democratising the party. In this respect, Momentum was certainly a force to be reckoned with, although its denigration by the right as a gang of Marxist fanatics intent on a 'power grab', and its constant vilification in the mainstream media, besides being a travesty, attributed more influence to it than it really had.

But democratising the party was only one of Momentum's two main aims. The other was to reach out and mobilise the electorate. Initially it had difficulty in combining these aims, but after some conflict a constitution was adopted in early 2017 that went a long way towards resolving the tensions.[14] And when Theresa May's decision to call a general election in 2017 reinvigorated its outward-facing energies, Momentum's paid-up membership grew to over 40,000, giving it a budget of about £500,000 and a paid staff of twenty. Only some 2,000 to 3,000 Momentum members made political activism a major commitment; but the coordination provided by Momentum's national office gave these members a confidence and weight beyond their numbers, and the digital skills of the younger members, especially, gave the organisation a considerable impact.

In the words of its national coordinator, Laura Parker, 'Momentum was born as a sort of praetorian guard for Jeremy – to get him elected and keep him there', but 'it shouldn't be seen as rent-a-rally, but as an innovator, developing new ways of campaigning':

> We should be working out the role of a party in the 21st century in which so many people live precarious lives – on short-term contracts, struggling with money and housing, but also much more fluid lives – people no longer grow up reading just one newspaper, watching just two or three TV channels – how does the party relate to this? People don't have time to go to party branch meetings – where is the return for doing that? They need to feel they can actually shape politics – whether doing it from home on their laptop, or out on the street. We have to be strong and focussed so as to keep going after Jeremy goes – the transformational agenda he has set out isn't the work of just one parliamentary term.[15]

In practice, however, Momentum concentrated primarily on doing more and better what the CLPD used to do inside the party. Much less was done in the way of political education or the development of people capable of getting their CLPs to engage in local struggles of all kinds and link up struggles in different domains, from tenants' rights to union rights to immigrants' rights, setting them in the context of a broader socialist vision of society. The Momentum leadership was aware that this work was essential, both in the long run for the democratisation of everyday life, and immediately, for maintaining members' morale and activism, but far too little of it was actually undertaken.

That said, a major concern of the Momentum leadership was to get the party to take up this agenda. At first Corbyn's team 'seemed unsure of what to do with its new recruits' beyond the 'highly impressive get-out-the-vote operation', as Tom Blackburn, a leading Momentum activist in Salford, argued in the *New Socialist* immediately after the 2017 election. Noting that 'the Corbynite base as a whole remains somewhat inexperienced' – especially in terms of its ability 'to actively cultivate popular support for a radical political alternative, rather than assuming that there is sufficient support already latent, just waiting to be tapped into' – Blackburn argued that 'the leadership must now start to provide its rank and file supporters with clear guidance and encouragement if this project is to progress further'. What this especially required was

> 'clarity and honesty about the scale of the task facing Labour's new left, and the nature of that task as well – to re-establish the Labour Party as a campaigning force in working-class communities, to democratise its policymaking structures and to bring through the next generation of Labour left cadres, candidates and activists.

Members looking to open up local parties and experiment with new methods of organising needed support from Labour's HQ for this. But this did not mean that they should just sit around and wait for help from on high before organising in their communities. Indeed, there is already a great deal of highly useful and relevant experience of grassroots organising among Labour members – the hands-on experience of anti-cuts campaigners and trade-union activists is already substantial. Rank-and-file initiative can make substantial achievements. But for this sort of approach to take hold solidly nationwide, an attentive and supportive central party apparatus will be invaluable.[16]

The party's establishment of a new forty-strong 'Community Organising Unit' to work with constituency Labour parties and trade unions in key marginal constituencies, as well as so-called 'held back' (de-industrialised and abandoned) constituencies where Labour had lost trust, augured well for this.[17] Yet the problem pointed out by Max Shanly in relation to the youth wing of the party also applied to the party as a whole:

> The consistent defeats faced by our movement laid waste to the once-vibrant socialist culture that existed in our working class communities and areas. Political networks and grounded sentiments of collective resistance and counter-authority to the ruling order, built up over generations by the labour movement, are no longer as significant or influential as they once were. As Labour retreated from day-to-day engagement with ordinary people, our traditional base of support became increasingly detached from us, and often dropped out of voting or turned to the far-right for political answers and practical solutions.[18]

But, Shanly argued, 'political education – the very bread and butter of the socialist movement – has been put on the backburner; when our members are taught, they are taught to follow, not to lead'. In so far as the new mass membership now allowed for changing this situation, the change would have to go right down to the level of constituency parties in order to remould them into 'hubs of ongoing discussion, education and culture', so as to end the party's old 'alienation from ideas . . . Alongside recruitment and retention, our task must be to build the political and organisational quality . . . to both understand and resist capitalism'. Political education, to give activists a wider framework within which to understand their work and analyse its challenges, was thus a task which both the party and Momentum needed to make a priority.

The first report of the intra-party Democracy Review set up by the NEC in 2017 under the direction of Katy Clark, previously Corbyn's political secretary, was presented to the 2018 conference after submissions from some 10,000 members, and following well-attended meetings across the country. It was disappointing. As Calderbank concluded, it had

> delivered little real meat, beyond a long-overdue shake up in the way BAME Labour is organised. The change to the process for Leadership candidates getting on the ballot paper spurned the opportunity to reduce the Parliamentary Party's ability to act as gatekeeper, merely introducing the additional need for 10 per cent of either CLPs or affiliates. Again this passed as an NEC proposal which meant more radical rule changes from the membership fell. Other key changes – not least over democratising Labour structures at Local Government level, or the overhaul of the party's policy making process – have been kicked into next year.[19]

In the event, hopes that with the balance in the NEC becoming more favourable to the left, more extensive proposals for change might be included in a second iteration of the Democracy Review, and endorsed by the NEC, were not realised. In 2017 the NEC had rejected a widely supported motion from CLPs to abolish the National Policy Forum, which even with elected members was still seen as a means by which party managers could prevent members' views being properly ventilated at the conference – an echo of the NEC's resistance to OMOV for the NPF in 2009. So, in 2018, the CLP representatives on the NEC, led by Lansman, proposed setting out clear terms of reference for the respective powers of the NEC and the NPF, along with five other proposals for greater democratic accountability of party organs. All but one were rejected, with the union delegates notably lining up against them.[20]

This revealed an old problem confronted by the Labour new left in the 1970s. Under New Labour a new generation of left-wing union leaders had been crucial in challenging the leadership, supporting the revival of internal party democracy and vehemently opposing any compromise with Tory austerity – all of which paved the way for Corbyn's leadership. The key role in all this of Unite, in particular – including providing experienced left-wing personnel to fill key posts in the leader's office and party headquarters – brought the party leadership increasingly close to that union's leadership. Yet it was a relationship that now seemed to provide little impetus for the transformation of the party into an active agent of political education and democratic mobilisation. It is important to recall that the earlier attempt to transform the Labour Party, in which people like Jeremy Corbyn and Jon Lansman first cut their teeth politically, was halted when the left-wing union leadership, which had supported it through their block vote at the party conference, pulled the plug on it in the face of the inevitable divisions it created inside the party and the labour movement as a whole. By 2018 it was once again becoming clear that transforming the Labour Party would have to involve much deeper changes in the party–union relationship than those that had led to Corbyn's election as party leader.

The obstacles to changing the extra-parliamentary party reinforced the tendency of the leader's office to replicate the old practice of 'social-democratic centralism'. And, with the centre of gravity of policy preparation firmly located in McDonnell's policy team, the media were even more encouraged to treat what was happening inside the 'Westminster bubble' as the real locus of action. After the failure of the PLP coup against Corbyn and Labour's strong showing in the 2017 election, a realignment in the PLP could first of all be seen in the founding of a new Tribune Group, as the self-described 'centre-left' home of some seventy MPs. These MPs broadly supported the social-democratic aspects of Corbyn's policy agenda, while expecting Corbyn's team to take a strong stand against rank-and-file pressures pushing for reselections. Their basic orientation, very much following the line set out in the break with New Labour by Ed Miliband (who had now joined the new Tribune group), echoed his 'One Nation' theme by defining their own project as fulfilling the 'British Promise'. Labour's fundamental political task, the Tribune MPs said, was to 'convince people that it is our core values that they want to see applied in government'.[21]

The realignment took further shape amid the Brexit convulsions that shook Westminster through February and March 2019. When nine Labour MPs broke from away from Labour, blaming the party's 'lurch to the left' under Corbyn, Tony Blair hastened to praise their politics, declaring that the Labour Party he had once led was 'in thrall to left-wing populists';[22] and the centre-left MPs, concerned above all with the need to 'focus debate in our party on how we grow and achieve government', quickly issued a Tribune Group pamphlet called *Healing the Divide*, including essays by eleven MPs on 'how we build a future that brings together leavers and remainers'.[23] Not to be outdone, centre-right MPs followed suit. While fanning the 'not-enough-is-being-done-about-antisemitism' flames, the deputy leader, Tom Watson (who after the 2017 election had pronounced Corbyn 'completely secure as Labour's leader for years to come'), now called for yet another new internal grouping of MPs as the only way to hold the party together. This provided a platform to those 'whose views were not currently represented in Jeremy Corbyn's shadow cabinet', affording 'a chance for them to discuss and shape policy'. The resulting Futures Britain Group was launched at a meeting attended by 130 'parliamentarians', of whom some seventy were MPs – including some of those in the Tribune Group. The meeting was addressed by Lords Mandelson and Kinnock, Dame Margaret Hodge, and Hilary Benn: the 'theme of the night' was 'stay and fight'.[24]

There was, in fact, considerable overlap between these groups. What united them above all – despite mild differences on certain domestic policies, and their degree of commitment to retaining the formal link with the EU and inclusion in the informal American empire in the international arena – was the defence of the PLP's privileged position in the party, and especially opposition to the reselection of MPs. Their fury at some of their number being subjected to sectarian name-calling on social media was understandable; but that made all the more unacceptable their refusal to stand up to the scurrilous attacks on Corbyn by some of their own in the House of Commons, as when Margaret Hodge venomously called him 'a racist and antisemite', and had her intended effect of securing top headlines in all the mainstream media.

Although these opponents of the Corbyn leadership described themselves as 'social democrats', what they actually stood for in policy terms was exceedingly unclear, even compared with the 'third way', let alone the postwar concept of social democracy set out with the intellectual heft of a Tony Crosland. In any case, as Jon Trickett pointed out in a timely response from the leadership team, making a strong case for democratic socialism, even Crosland's 'noble ambition of achieving equality within capitalism has now clearly foundered . . . Crosland singularly overstated the scope for capitalism to be reformed . . . We can win the argument and go on to elect a pioneering, radical and transformative government.'[25] Nor was this implausible. In mid March 2019, a poll by Survation, which alone among the pollsters had correctly registered the swing to Labour in the 2017 election, showed Labour at 39 per cent (a rise of 3 per cent since a month earlier), ahead of the Tories at 36 per cent (a fall of 5 per cent). For the vast majority of Labour MPs – who were not in any case very comfortable parsing the distinction between a democratic-socialist strategy and social-democratic pragmatism – that was what really counted. For serious supporters of the attempt to revive the new left project, however, the verdict of Ben Sellers was more relevant:

> If you'd asked me five years ago what the plan was, I would have said: build locally in CLPs, win policy arguments, organise at conference; get more representative MPs; win the leadership – in

that order. I would have talked in terms of a 10-year plan at a minimum. Instead, we did it back to front, winning the leadership in an extraordinary summer. None of that gave us time to educate, organise and agitate in the rest of the party and movement.[26]

11

The Brexit Conjuncture and Corbyn's Defeat

The 2017 election had appeared to show that the Labour new left's democratic-socialist project was finally in sight of at least electoral success. In striking contrast to the 1983 manifesto, contemptuously dismissed by the party's right wing as 'the longest suicide note in history', Corbyn was able to credit the 2017 manifesto with having armed Labour with 'the programme of a modern, progressive social-ist party that has rediscovered its roots and its purpose, bucking the trend across Europe'. As he told the party conference after the election:

> It is often said that elections can only be won from the centre ground. And in a way that's not wrong – so long as it's clear that the political centre of gravity isn't fixed or unmovable, nor is it where the establishment pundits like to think it is. It shifts as peo-ple's expectations and experiences change and political space is opened up . . . A new consensus is emerging from the great eco-nomic crash and the years of austerity, when people started to find political voice for their hopes for something different and better. 2017 may be the year when politics finally caught up with the crash of 2008 – because we offered people a clear choice. We need to build a still broader consensus around the priorities we set in the election, making the case for both compassion and collective aspiration. This is the real centre of gravity of British politics. We are now the political mainstream.[1]

The 2019 election would show that this claim was seriously over-stated. Nevertheless, Corbyn was right to insist that what had been achieved in 2017 was remarkable at a time when all around the world democracy is facing twin threats. One is the emergence of an authoritarian nationalism that is intolerant and belligerent. The second is apparently more benign, but equally insidious. It is that the big decisions should be left to the elite, that political choices can only be marginal and that people are consumers first, and only citizens a distant second. Democracy has to mean much more than that. It must mean listening to people outside of election time.

What this meant, above all, Corbyn insisted, was that 'For people to take control of their own lives, our democracy needs to break out of Westminster into all parts of our society and economy where power is unaccountable.'

Yet, as would become painfully clear over the next two years, the Labour new left under Corbyn's leadership faced even greater difficulties than before. In depriving Theresa May's government of its majority, Labour had left May dependent on the far-right Brexiteers in the Commons, who held out for terms in any Brexit agreement with the EU that the other parties could not accept. This now meant that the next phase of politics would take place in Westminster, not in the country at large – the precise opposite of what Corbyn saw as the all-important next step for the left's democratic advance. And as Corbyn himself inevitably became immersed in the arcane complexities of parliamentary procedure around Brexit, his personal political profile was transformed, from the inspiring leader of a mass repudiation of both Thatcherism and New Labour to a rather desultory performer at the despatch box, 'stuck in the House of Commons where the ambience and rituals reek of institutional power on somebody else's terms'.[2] All the pressures that have traditionally trapped Labour leaders in the 'Westminster bubble' took on an even greater significance in the Brexit conjuncture. Corbyn's promise, in his 2017 party conference speech, to use 'the process in parliament [and] keep up pressure in parliament [against] a government in disarray', produced its own backlash, as UKIP and the Conservative Brexiteers

235

came to hold parliament itself responsible for thwarting 'the will of the people'.

For many people in Labour's traditional working-class base, the 2017 manifesto's vision of a reconstructed society and economy was overwhelmed by the fraudulent but deeply emotive appeal of 'taking back control' by 'getting Brexit sorted', as the right wing relentlessly fanned Leave voters' feeling that their vote was not being respected. Meanwhile the call for a second referendum was advanced by many inside the Labour Party who were also hoping to see Corbyn deposed from the leadership. The balance of forces in the PLP was still heavily stacked against the project of the Labour new left – even after the 2017 election, the Socialist Campaign Group had only some twenty members out of over 260 Labour MPs. The intellectual, strategic, tactical and organisational burdens of carrying forward the new left project all fell on a small handful of socialists in Corbyn's team, who were necessarily anxious to avoid a party split – not least since winning elections was indeed crucial to the project. Corbyn's opponents in the PLP were ready to exploit this weakness, in some cases organising openly to frustrate him, preferring to see the party remain in opposition than to see him become prime minister. In 2019 a few undistinguished Labour MPs went so far as to leave the party. Corbyn's more substantial opponents remained in the PLP, and hoped to achieve by a steady stream of attacks what the 2016 coup had failed to accomplish. In all this, the charges of mishandling (if not 'facilitating') Brexit, and still not doing enough about antisemitism, as partisan weapons to be wielded against the left, were new; but the underlying politics, encapsulated in the claim by one of those who resigned that the party had been 'hijacked by the machine politics of the hard left',[3] were not.

Brexit

At the time of the 2016 referendum hardly any of the grave issues it raised, and still less the issues it raised for socialists, had been seriously debated. The EU was unarguably a capitalist construct, whose 'uniform rules for market activity operated across borders, overriding national legislatures' looked very much like the regional federations neoliberal thinkers like Hayek had called for in the 1930s; indeed, by the time Britain joined in 1971, the EEC had already 'surpassed their blueprints. Competition law became the linchpin of this supranational order, a model of "multilevel governance"'.[4] As the Labour new left had recognised in 1973, important parts of its industrial strategy would have fallen foul of the rules of the EEC, which was a major reason why Tony Benn had joined Michael Foot and other senior figures on the party's old left in campaigning for the Leave side in the 1975 referendum. Over the ensuing decades, a strong current of left opinion continued to advocate leaving the EU, as for example in an 'alternative economic and political strategy' manifesto published in 2012 by a group that included Seumas Milne and Andrew Murray, who would become key figures on Corbyn's team. They made the case for withdrawal from the EU and 'a reorientation of the UK's priorities globally [to] enable Britain to take an independent approach to political and economic issues . . . with greater potential to design and implement an economic and social policy, which could embrace full employment and social solidarity'.[5] Corbyn largely shared this view, yet when Cameron pledged to hold a referendum on EU membership in 2012 Corbyn immediately foresaw – long before anyone dreamed that he might become the Labour leader – that 'it would be a mistake to leave the EU under conditions determined by the Eurosceptic right, who would then be in a strong position to reshape Britain's internal and external relations'.[6]

At the same time, in the wake of the economic crisis, disenchantment with the EU was being advanced on very different grounds by reactionary forces in Britain, for whom even the Cameron government's austerity did not go far enough. This was seen not only in the rise of UKIP, but also within the Conservative Party itself, in the shape of a group of young Tory MPs very much on the rise. Three of these – Priti Patel, Dominic Raab and Liz Truss – who would later hold important positions in Boris Johnson's cabinet, co-authored a book in 2012 entitled *Britannia Unchained*, which argued that Britain 'rewards laziness', that British workers were 'the worst idlers in the world', and that 'too many people in Britain prefer a lie-in to hard work'. Businesses were deterred from hiring people, they claimed, because of EU employment laws that made them fear 'taking a risk and hiring new staff'.[7] The goal of allowing Britain to emulate the East Asian capitalist 'tigers' by relieving itself of EU labour standards was the underlying basis of the alliance that was forged over the rest of the decade between this new Tory right and xenophobes still further to the right. The protections the EU offered to the citizens of its member-states, and which had always made socialists less willing to oppose it, were precisely what UKIP and Tory Brexiteers were primarily concerned to be rid of.

Corbyn's position on Brexit, after he became leader, would come to be one of the most controversial, and most misrepresented, aspects of Labour's handling of the question. Because he had foreseen the need to resist a right-wing Brexit, Corbyn felt quite comfortable, as Labour leader in 2016, campaigning in the referendum to remain in the EU, while also calling for it to be reformed. Yet, in subsequently deciding that the referendum result must be accepted, he was recognising that, for all its faults, it had expressed what 17 million voters said they wanted. This also reflected a concern for the likely electoral cost of ignoring people's views in the Labour-held constituencies that had voted to leave (well over half of the 230 seats Labour had won in 2015 had Leave majorities),[8] whose support would be needed if the project of the Labour new left was to have any chance of being implemented.

Corbyn's speech to the 2017 party conference provides a good measure of his consistency on Brexit. Insisting that 'how Britain leaves the European Union is too important to be left to the Conservatives and their internal battles and identity crises', he vowed that Labour would 'never follow the Tories into the gutter of blaming migrants for the ills of society'. Posing a clear choice between a 'shambolic Tory Brexit driving down standards, or a Labour Brexit that . . . establishes a new co-operative relationship with the EU', Corbyn pointed out:

A cliff-edge Brexit is at risk of becoming a reality. That is why Labour has made clear that Britain should stay within the basic terms of the single market and a customs union for a limited transition period. It is welcome at least that Theresa May has belatedly accepted that. But beyond that transition, our task is a different one. It is to unite everyone in our country around a progressive vision of what Britain could be, but with a government that stands for the many not the few. Labour is the only party that can bring together those who voted leave and those who backed remain and unite the country for a future beyond Brexit. What matters in the Brexit negotiations is to achieve a settlement that delivers jobs, rights and decent living standards.

At this time, almost all of those who had joined in the attempted coup against Corbyn after the June 2016 referendum, on the ostensible grounds that he had not campaigned for Remain enthusiastically enough, also took the position that the party could not ignore 'the clear decision the British people made back in June', as the deputy leader Tom Watson put it, promising that he personally would 'never ignore the democratic will of the British people'. In early 2017 Chukka Umunna, the most prominent of the Labour MPs who would leave the party in 2019, declared: 'We must abide by the national result, which is a clear choice to leave the EU. To stand against the decision of the country would be to deepen Labour and the country's divisions.' [9] Thus, in the 2017 election, Brexit did not divide the Labour Party. But by 2019 Umunna, Watson and others in the PLP whose main preoccupation was trying to see which way the wind was blowing, had changed their minds, declaring with even greater fervour that a second referendum was a democratic necessity.

As May's negotiations dragged on, the clamour for a second referendum grew, buoyed by polling results which suggested that another referendum might possibly reverse the 2016 result, and led to the formation in April 2018 of a cross-party 'People's Vote' campaign, in which Chukka Umunna, alongside Peter Mandelson, was a leading figure. At the Labour Party's 2018 conference a compromise motion was agreed that kept a second referendum as an option if there was no possibility of fighting an election. To be sure, most party members who had voted for Corbyn as leader were pro-Remain, even if a number of those who were prominently aligned with his leadership, such as Unite's Len McCluskey and the party chairman Ian Lavery, were not. Notably, the MPs at the core of Corbyn's team were themselves inclined towards taking somewhat different positions on Brexit. Jon Trickett, especially sensitive to the strong working-class pro-Brexit sentiments in the Midlands and the north, was strongly in favour of Leave; on the other hand, the London-based Diane Abbott was a Remain supporter, and John McDonnell was increasingly inclined in that direction.

Corbyn still took every opportunity to make it clear that Labour's support for leaving the EU was conditional on securing a withdrawal agreement that would safeguard jobs and working conditions. And he consistently called for a general election, so that Labour could form a government and negotiate a trade agreement that would include a UK–EU customs union and give the UK the fullest possible access to the single market. But lacking a parliamentary majority, there was little Corbyn could do except repeat this; and it still fell to parliament, not the electorate, to determine what form the UK's long-term relationship with the EU would be.

Yet against party policy, and often in a manner clearly designed to damage Corbyn, more and more Labour MPs joined the call for a second referendum in which the party should campaign unambiguously for Remain. The party's members had no role to play in this: it was the PLP, with its anti-Corbyn majority, which called the shots, and the divisions over Brexit added to the mix of complaints against Corbyn's leadership that were fundamentally driven by opposition to his commitment to socialism and anti-imperialism. This was the position that would now be promoted not only by those, like Umunna, who quit the party in February 2019, but also by Tom Watson who, even while remaining deputy leader, organised 130 parliamentarians into a new group determined to 'stay and fight' against Corbyn at the very height of the parliamentary Brexit battle in the spring of 2019 (see Chapter 10). By then the position Corbyn had consistently articulated was increasingly being presented in the mainstream media as evidence of either an antiquated 'Old Labour' hostility to the EU or an inability to 'come off the fence' – in other words, to be willing to accept the reduction of the difficult and dangerous issues at stake to a choice between two grossly simplified and often dishonestly framed alternatives.

As the March 2019 deadline approached, the risk of 'no deal' meant that almost every other dimension of politics disappeared from view, including the appeal of Labour's 2017 election manifesto. An agreement on the key terms of withdrawal from the EU had to be agreed by the end of the month: settling the UK's outstanding EU bills; defining the rights of the 3.7 million EU citizens in the UK and the 1.3 million UK citizens in the EU; and agreeing a means of keeping open the EU's border between the Irish Republic and Northern Ireland, to which both the UK and the Irish Republic were committed. Mrs May agreed with the EU to pay the bills and secure the rights of EU and UK citizens, and to keep the UK in the customs union until some alternative way of keeping the Irish border open could be found and agreed. Everything else in the future relationship between the EU and the UK would be negotiated by whichever party was in office over the next two years. But right-wing Conservative MPs refused to support the agreement because it involved keeping the UK indefinitely in the EU customs union. The great majority of the PLP also opposed it, whether in the hope of securing a second referendum or from a belief that in the negotiations to come the Conservative government could not be trusted to keep the UK in the customs union, retain access to the single market, and defend crucial workers' rights and protections. As a result, the prime minister's 'deal' was heavily defeated in parliament three times, leading to a humiliating extension of the deadline from March to October, and a belated offer of cross-party talks from Mrs May. In retrospect, it can be argued that, had the Corbyn team been willing to face down the opposition in the PLP and put more effort into making these talks succeed, a deal on a protracted soft Brexit might have left the Tories divided, sustained Corbyn's coherent position on accepting the outcome of the referendum, and kept faith with Leave voters in the Labour heartlands.

Meanwhile, because the UK was still a member of the EU, it had to take part in the European Parliament elections to be held in late May. On a low turnout of 37 per cent, Nigel Farage's Brexit Party won 30.5 per cent of the vote, the Liberal Democrats 19.6 per cent, and Labour only 13.7 per cent, leaving the Conservatives with a derisory 8.8 per cent. This seemed to spell electoral disaster for the Tories in the next general election unless they could win back Leave voters from the Brexit Party. Theresa May resigned as Conservative leader, and was replaced by Boris Johnson, whose overriding aim became to leave the EU on the 31 October deadline, if necessary without any withdrawal agreement at all. Johnson pitched himself as the voice of the people against 'the elite', and took the unprecedented step of using the royal prerogative to prorogue – or suspend – parliament for five weeks, to prevent it from scrutinising his negotiations (or lack of them) with the EU.

Over the course of the summer, in the face intense PLP and media pressure, Corbyn acceded to the demand that a Labour government should call a second referendum after concluding new negotiations with the EU. But, on this as on so much else, the more Corbyn gave way, the more intense became the pressure on him to go further. Just before the party conference in September, Tom Watson called for Labour to back a second referendum before, not after, a general election was held. This explicit challenge to Corbyn precipitated an unsuccessful attempt at the NEC – led by Jon Lansman, at the urging of Karie Murphy – to eliminate the position of deputy leader, which Corbyn intervened to veto. The difference between the balance of forces in the PLP, which Watson's initiative reflected, and that in the party outside parliament, was well illustrated when a substantial majority of conference delegates – including the majority of CLP delegates, who favoured remaining in the EU – supported Corbyn's position, which he spelled out clearly in his speech to the conference. Following an election, Labour would end the Brexit crisis by taking the decision back to the people with the choice of a credible leave deal alongside remain. That's not complicated . . . within three months of coming to power a Labour government will secure a sensible deal based on the terms we have long advocated and discussed with the EU trade unions and businesses: a new customs union, a close single market relationship, and guarantees of rights and protections. And within six months of being elected we will put that deal to a public vote alongside remain. And as a Labour prime minister I pledge to carry out whatever the people decide.

Although very few MPs saw fit to attend the conference, the position of most of them was articulated by Polly Toynbee in the *Guardian*. 'Corbyn's fence-sitting is preposterous' was the headline of her comment, which contained an additional barb: 'He has spent his life advocating Bennite democracy, where the party makes policy, not the leaders. Most of the party, plus the great majority of its voters, are strong remainers: how does he square that?' [10] In fact, opinion polls showed that there was no such strong majority for Remain and, as we have seen, the delegates to the Labour Party conference (reflecting the strong Leave support among voters in Labour's heartland constituencies) overwhelmingly backed Corbyn's position. Moreover, a composite resolution rejecting the leadership's position and calling for Labour to openly back Remain in another referendum was rejected by a clear majority on a show of hands (which those vociferous backing Remain took care to question from the floor and the balcony, thereby inviting the press to declare that their predictions that the conference would be 'plunged into chaos' had been confirmed).[11]

What was really at stake was forcefully expressed by Len McCluskey, whose challenge at a jointly sponsored Young Labour and Unite fringe meeting – 'Are you leavers? Are you remainers? Or are you socialists?' – brought the hundreds in attendance to their feet. Inside the conference hall, after a series of CLP delegates came to the podium and insisted that the party's task was 'not to speak to the 48 per cent or the 52 per cent, but to the 99 per cent', this was picked up by Corbyn in his closing words to the conference: 'The Conservative government as well as the far-right has fuelled division in our society ... Labour will do the opposite, we will bring people together ... We stand not just for the 52 per cent or the 48 per cent but for the 99 per cent.'

Any hope that this would be heard by many people outside the conference hall was dashed by the media's understandable focus on the Supreme Court's dramatic ruling, the same day, that Johnson's prorogation of parliament was illegal. When parliament was recalled the next day, Johnson and his front bench escalated their 'people versus parliament' rhetoric, dismissing the judgement as wrong, and accusing those who opposed his 'no deal' threat of 'surrendering to the EU'. In the face of torrential abuse and violent language, it fell to Corbyn, who had spent his life rebelling against rules and formality, to speak not only for parliamentary decorum, of all things, but also for the rule of law itself.

But the intensity of the anger and frustration in the country could not be explained purely by reference to the new issues posed by Brexit. Since at least the 1970s, if not before, the UK's archaic political system had been living on borrowed time. This was indeed one of the main messages of the Labour new left, clearly articulated by Tony Benn. The electoral system, the constitution and the state apparatus had evolved in the era of empire, and had not been significantly reformed during the post-1945 era of economic and social reform. The defeat of the new left inside the Labour Party amid the exposure of the UK economy to global market forces after 1980, and the accompanying conversion of the political elite into agents of these forces, had exposed the inherited political structure to stresses it was increasingly unable to bear.

The decision to put EU membership to a referendum, without conditions, without considering the inherent conflict between plebiscitary and representative democracy, and without any serious appreciation by the advocates of leaving of what it would really involve, was a symptom of a system in dangerous decline. The representative system itself had become fatally dysfunctional. Under the first-past-the-post electoral system, the decline of class-based party allegiance had led to governments elected by ever smaller minorities of the electorate. Increasingly fewer voters felt there was much connection between their votes in general elections and what governments did. The fact that the 2016 Brexit referendum on the EU had given every voter a choice on something really important had everything to do with the violent feelings that were aroused in many Leave voters by parliament's successive failures to implement the decision.[12]

The failure of representation was only the most obvious element in the progressive loss of coherence and workability of the country's so-called unwritten constitution, which actually consists of myriad rules and conventions embodied in statutes, precedents and commentaries that have accumulated over centuries around the central principle of parliamentary sovereignty. The lack of a written constitution meant that it was not even clear that the terms on which the country would leave the EU needed parliamentary approval. And what was true of the constitution was also true of the British state, which, as Perry Anderson once pointed out, has never acted as a 'regulative intelligence' for shaping national development.[13] When, in the wake of the crisis of the 1970s and the defeat of the Labour new left, the need for such shaping eventually became inescapable, the chosen agent of change was not the senior civil service but global market forces. The state apparatus was left to adapt the country to these forces, but with little guidance as to what this should mean except to reduce its responsibilities and size. Between 1979, when Thatcher took office, and 2015, the central civil service was cut by almost half,[14] and the recruitment and training of what remained was not reorganised to prioritise even the technical competences actually needed to support a market-driven development path. Evidence-based objections were brushed aside; ministers increasingly declined to respond to criticisms; 'spin' became the norm in the civil service itself. Large areas of public service provision were outsourced and became unaccountable. The boundary between the public interest and private interests became blurred.[15] 'Informal' government, which shades easily into corrupt government, became normalised.

In short, Brexit had exposed an 'organic' crisis. In contrast with the broad undercurrent of lost pride and anger at the political elite that Brexit reflected, the capitalist class was upset by the readiness of the neoliberal wing of the Conservative Party to leave the EU without a deal. This especially was the case with manufacturers, with their close involvement in EU-wide supply chains, who publicly condemned the government's position in increasingly vehement terms.[16] Yet for all Boris Johnson's 'fuck business' bravado, the capitalist class knew where its allegiance lay as soon as the election was called. Defeating a socialist-led Labour Party was the top priority. However much they were concerned about the impact of a no-deal Brexit, they took to heart Johnson's warning against a Corbyn government: 'These are seriously left-wing guys.'[17] The pound went up in the currency markets in parallel with the Tory rating in the polls, and millions of pounds poured into the Conservative Party's coffers during the course of the campaign.[18]

The deep state was also in no doubt as to where its allegiance lay. Immediately after the Labour leadership election of 2015, an anonymous serving general told the *Sunday Times* that, if Corbyn became prime minister and tried to scrap Trident, pull out of NATO, or announce 'any plans to emasculate and shrink the size of the armed forces . . . people would use whatever means possible, fair or foul, to prevent that. You can't put a maverick in charge of a country's security. There would be mass resignations at all levels and you would face the very real prospect of an event which would effectively be a mutiny.'[19] In fact, there was considerable evidence that in the years before the 2019 election the 'deep state' was engaged in a strategy of pre-emption, promoting a smear campaign (like other state activities this was outsourced, but in this case funded by the Ministry of Defence and the Foreign Office) as a prophylactic against the election of a Corbyn-led Labour government. [20]

They were joined in this by the mainstream media. Corbyn's election as Labour leader had 'laid bare what was only partially visible during the attacks on Miliband and Brown. Failing to accept him as the legitimate leader of the opposition, the right-wing press fear his premiership as they have feared no other Labour leader before'.[21] The nominally 'independent' BBC – better described by one of its leading analysts as representing an 'elite consensus' and being 'ultimately . . . an organisation accountable not to the public, nor even to parliament, but . . . to the heart of government' – followed suit.[22] Except for a momentary pause following Labour's success in the 2017 election, the BBC routinely showed Corbyn a level of disrespect that would have created outrage if it had been shown to a Conservative cabinet minister, let alone the prime minister. And by 2019 the shift from mainstream media to social media, which in 2017 was seen as having benefited Labour, was increasingly turned against it through political messages delivered by targeted advertising to voters identified by online data profiling. Insulated from public view, these messages traded freely in false rumours, personal smears and lies aimed at reinforcing existing sentiments and prejudices. This had a great deal to do with the extremely negative feelings about Corbyn expressed by so many voters during the 2019 election campaign.[23]

The 2019 Election

The Labour governments of the 1970s had shown that winning elections did not ensure that 'a fundamental and irreversible shift in the balance of power and wealth in favour of working people and their families' – which the Labour new left had managed to get inserted into the 1974 manifesto, and which Corbyn and McDonnell repeated frequently in their 2019 campaign speeches – would actually be put in hand. But winning elections was still essential. Labour's failure in the 2019 election certainly dashed the hopes and plans that the 2017 election result had generated.

How and why did this come about? Brexit was unquestionably a central factor. As late as March 2019, Labour was polling slightly ahead of the Conservatives, at 39 per cent; and although by July

Labour had fallen to 29 per cent, the Conservatives stood at only 23 per cent. It was only in August, after Boris Johnson had replaced Theresa May as Tory leader, and Corbyn was finally forced by the pro-Remain forces in the PLP to say he would support a second referendum after a general election, that the Conservatives' polling figure jumped ahead of Labour's. During the election campaign, as support for the Lib Dems fell away and Farage withdrew Brexit candidates in Tory-held seats, the Tories climbed steadily to over 40 per cent, while Labour only rose to just over 30 per cent.[24] Whatever other factors contributed to Labour's defeat, Johnson's embrace of so much of what Farage stood for, combined with the way Corbyn's position was undermined by the intractable divisions over Brexit inside the Labour Party, was unarguably decisive.

While the result was a huge setback, the mainstream media's characterisation of it as Labour's 'worst since 1935' was seriously misleading.[25] Labour's 32 per cent share of the vote under Corbyn in 2019 was higher than the 30 per cent it had secured under Miliband in 2015, and the 29 per cent under Brown in 2010 when Labour lost ninety-seven seats, compared with the sixty lost in 2019. One striking feature of the election was the much greater support for Labour from voters under the age of forty-four (voters between eighteen and twenty-four were actually three times more likely to support Labour than the Conservatives) – a fact that could prove very significant in the long run.[26]

Furthermore, Corbyn's claim after the 2017 election to have decisively shifted the debate on austerity was confirmed in the 2019 election. It is worth recalling that in 2015 Corbyn was alone among the candidates for the Labour leadership in insisting that the consensus on the need for austerity had to be completely broken. By the time of the 2019 election, that was close to being achieved. In Theresa May's direly misconceived 2017 election campaign she had half-heartedly declared austerity 'over'; Boris Johnson fully conceded it, supplementing 'getting Brexit done' with a total abandonment of any concern with deficits, promising lavish spending on the NHS, tens of thousands of extra nurses and police officers, £100 billion in borrowing for capital spending, and so on. Johnson thus not only stole Farage's clothes, but also at least seemed to steal some of Corbyn's. His commitment to a large programme of state investment was evidence of the Labour new left's success in challenging neoliberal ideology at a time when the German Social Democrats, still in a coalition government committed to zero deficits, were down to 11 per cent support in the polls; and when President Macron in France was facing general strikes and massive protests against his neoliberal fiscal and pension reforms.

The fact was that all of Labour's main economic and social policies, including measures to restore public ownership of the national infrastructure, were remarkably popular – and not only with Labour voters.[27] That said, the 2019 manifesto's scope and size (at over a hundred pages) gave the impression of a list of promises which, however popular individually, came across as bids in a spending auction. Many voters were prone to respond with the deeply ingrained Thatcherite question: 'Where is the money coming from?' – and voters in Leave constituencies were suspicious of being offered a bribe to overlook Labour's equivocations on Brexit. Above all, perhaps, there was a failure to distinguish between the manifesto as a statement of Labour's vision of an alternative future and the need for a few key policies on which to fight the election, and a failure to frame both the vision and the policies in an emotionally convincing 'narrative'.[28]

This was especially damaging in historic Labour-voting constituencies where large majorities had voted Leave. Whereas Labour's ambitiously radical policies 'were so remote from everyday experience of government that, for a lot of voters, [they] felt abstract and utopian', as Richard Seymour aptly commented, nationalism was 'such an established script in this country that its abstractions can be experienced as intimate, concrete'.[29] Of course the whole history of working-class formation in Britain, as in most other places, is one of the intertwining of class and nationalist identities, and this was reinforced by the Labour Party's original self-definition as a party representing the 'national interest'.[30] But this was always tempered by the pull of class struggles and the appeal of proletarian internationalism, both of which resonated in communities in which strong industrial unions were embedded, and where left-wing Labour and Communist shop stewards were often the most influential opinion leaders.

The Labour new left had first emerged, suffused with the ideals of participatory democracy and the new social movement spirit of the 1960s, at a time of great working-class militancy, although the union leaders of the time eventually agreed to join the party leadership in opposing the new left in the name of party unity. After disillusion with New Labour led to the emergence of new left leaders in the unions, as well as in the myriad social movements, they played a key role in the election of Corbyn as party leader. But by the time this occurred Farage had exposed deep cultural differences between these activists and a large segment of voters in working-class communities, whose disgust with the existing political system was expressed in their 2015 vote for UKIP. Deindustrialisation, coupled with the massive political defeats of trade unionism, had left these communities open to the spread of the individualist competitive mind-set already exhibited by the Nottingham miners in the 1980s. Meanwhile, the persisting need for collective identity partly manifested itself in 'make-Great-Britain-great-again' nationalism.

All of these trends had been reinforced, rather than countered, by New Labour, whose continuing influence was reflected in the inability, or refusal, of so many in the PLP, and even in the shadow cabinet, to hear what Jon Trickett and Ian Lavery were telling them throughout 2018 and 2019 – namely, that in many old working-class communities the call for a second referendum was being taken as an expression of profound political disdain. The identification of Corbynism with the 99 per cent, with 'the many not the few', proved popular and energising in ways Labour Party politics had rarely been; but it also covered over the fact that, as Ursula Huws observed, 'real divisions within the working classes, based on structural as well as cultural differences, cannot be wished away ... by glib sloganizing'.[31] This was ultimately what made it so difficult for Corbyn and his team to hold on to his initially coherent position on Brexit. Tom Blackburn summarised the problem accurately:

> It may be that the contradictions within Labour's electoral coalition . . . simply could not be reconciled on this issue when it came to the crunch, and had Labour persisted with its 2017 position of respecting the first referendum, it would have doubtless faced a backlash from the other side. Whether the electoral consequences of this would have been worse . . . cannot be answered definitively, but the evident nervousness of the Corbyn leadership over Brexit now looks more understandable.[32]

This nervousness was very evident during the election campaign, to the point where Corbyn appeared almost tongue-tied on the issue of Brexit in his first TV debate with Boris Johnson. But Corbyn's generally uninspiring TV performances should have surprised no one. As we saw earlier, Corbyn himself had observed back in 2016, with a touch of self-mockery, that unlike Tony Benn he had been 'monumentally unsuccessful in the conventional career pattern'.[33] Yet this was a large part of what attracted so many people to join the Labour Party in support of his candidacy – and had even appeared to work to his advantage during the 2017 campaign, when he used his TV appearances to great effect to counter the overwhelmingly negative portrayal of him in the mainstream media. But after the 2017 election, as he became ever more trapped in the Westminster bubble and his team tried to make him appear more like a normal politician, he looked less and less comfortable. On top of this, his determination 'to go high when they went low' looked like passivity in the face of the disingenuous and absurd charges that he had supported IRA terrorism and was an antisemite.[34] Corbyn could not and would not disown his anti-imperialist record; but his failure to respond to gross distortions of it cost Labour dearly in the 2019 election.

Not a Conclusion

December 2019 marked the ultimate point to which the generation formed in the 1970s had been able to carry the Labour new left project. From now on, it would fall to the new generation they had drawn into the project to discover how to take it forward. However significant the election defeat, the older generation had enabled the new one to flesh out an ambitious programme of democratic-socialist measures, unmatched anywhere since the 1970s, which could not be dismissed as a 'suicide note'.

For the reasons mentioned above, the 2019 manifesto failed to achieve the kind of impact that the 2017 manifesto had. Partly because the 2017 manifesto was leaked when the media themselves were curious about what the Labour new left actually stood for, it had a powerful and persuasive effect with its clear 'many not the few' class-struggle message. Yet the 2019 manifesto was actually more coherent and progressive – especially in making the environmental crisis, rather than the need for export competitiveness, the overarching framework for a radical industrial strategy, now called the Green Industrial Revolution.[35] Moreover, many of the radical proposals in a number of reports commissioned and published by the party came too late to be included in the 2019 manifesto. Among these, the Monbiot report's proposals for the gradual large-scale transfer of land into various forms of common ownership had the potential to be even more politically transformative than the 1944 Beveridge Report.[36]

As the *Guardian* journalist Andy Beckett noted during the course of the election campaign,

> For anyone whose sense of the party was formed during the 30 years before Corbyn took over, Labour's current boldness can still feel pretty startling. During Tony Blair's long leadership, I sat through countless New Labour election launches, always beautifully choreographed, at which Blair or one of his lieutenants would energetically announce the party's intention not to upset the status

quo very much . . . Corbyn's party has done precisely the opposite. The shape of the economy, the distribution of wealth, the future of work, the role of the state, the purpose of foreign policy – all these and other awkward questions have been thrown into the everyday political debate.[37]

Besides this ambitious shift in the policy agenda, the signal organisational achievement of the Corbyn years was the creation of Momentum. This turned what might have been a transient enthusiasm for the election of Corbyn as leader in 2015 into a significant intra-party and electoral force of the kind needed to take the project of the Labour new left forward. Momentum's ability to shift the composition of the NEC and other party bodies to the left, to advance radical resolutions to the party conference, to secure the nomination by CLPs of left-wing parliamentary candidates, to help staff the party's new Community Organizing Team with experienced activists, and to play a very active and independent role in the 2019 election campaign, all attest to its ongoing creative potential. Yet Momentum still had serious problems to overcome, not least its own dearth of democratic structures and procedures, and a tendency to focus on internal party issues and electoral campaigning at the expense of engagement in class-based struggles, organising and education.

This tendency was aggravated by Momentum's relative weakness in the post-industrial regions where the need for engagement in class struggles, organising and education was most acute. There was a risk that Momentum would simply enable a 'fast-track route for activists into representative politics, which is not the same as helping to reshape politics from the bottom up'.[38] That task calls, instead, for activists to commit themselves to the long hard road of what now needs to be called 'working-class re-formation'. This above all entails engaging directly in struggles and activities at the level of the community as well as the workplace, and fostering the social as well as political networks to create links across diverse working-class communities and workplaces. In the very different world of the twenty-first century – where, indeed, the 'real divisions within the working classes, based on structural as well as cultural differences, cannot be wished away' – this would be analogous to what those activists who created the original base for mass working-class parties were themselves engaged in.

To be sure, Labour's defeat in 2019 underlined the limits of what could be done in this respect without fundamental changes in the party itself, very little of which had been accomplished during the Corbyn years, along all the dimensions discussed in Chapter 10. Moreover, a growing 'bunker mentality' in the leader's office, in face of the relentless hostility of so many Labour MPs, let alone of the media, combined with the lack of strategic clarity to produce 'its own story of dysfunction'.[39] The effects of the failure to transform the national party apparatus were seen in the persistence of 'social democratic centralism' at party headquarters, reinforced by the preponderance of senior union personnel in key roles (this was especially registered in the run-up to the snap December 2019 election, when union-backed candidates were imposed on a significant number of CLPs). The fact that party staff remained far more concerned with routine administration, than with mobilising members and turning them into 'leaders not followers', proved especially costly at the constituency level, not least in the working-class constituencies lost in the 2019 election. Most of the vast increase in membership during the Corbyn years occurred through affiliations at the national level rather than through a local constituency party. And very few of the new members, including Momentum activists, attended regular local party meetings.

What this meant was that even if Corbyn had won the 2019 election, the manifold obstacles to accomplishing much would have included not only opposition from among his own MPs, but also the fact that the Labour new left project had so far achieved, at best, 'a tenuous counter-hegemony' – even at the base of the party.[40] In this light, Corbyn's defeat could be read as confirming the view that continuing with the attempt to convert the Labour Party into an effective force for democratic socialism is a 'crippling illusion', as Ralph

Miliband put it in the mid 1970s,[41] which can only exhaust the energies of the new generation of activists who have been drawn into the party. Yet given the difficulties experienced everywhere in establishing new socialist parties with any prospect of electoral success, and the fact that even those that have had some success have often ended up as at best minor partners in coalitions with mainstream social democratic parties, it seems unlikely that the new generation of activists will quickly see any other way forward than continuing the struggle inside the Labour Party, so as to fundamentally change it.

In face of the contradictions being generated by twenty-first-century capitalism, discovering and developing new political forms adequate to addressing them, and the popular capacities needed to overcome them, will take time. And yet, given the scale and intensity of these contradictions – political, economic, cultural, and not least ecological – time is short. This is the central dilemma for democratic socialists, not just in Britain but everywhere.

Notes

1 Beyond Parliamentary Socialism

1. Ralph Miliband, *Parliamentary Socialism: A Study in the Politics of Labour* (London, 1961).

2. Ralph Miliband, 'Moving On', *The Socialist Register 1976* (London, 1976), p. 128. Until the early 1980s – after the Labour new left had already been defeated at the national level of the party – there were few links between the Labour new left and most of the original new left's leading intellectual figures, including E. P. Thompson, John Saville, Raymond Williams, Miliband himself, Stuart Hall and later editors of *New Left Review*.

3. Stuart Hall, 'The Great Moving Right Show', *Marxism Today*, January 1979. See also 'Thatcherism – A New Stage', *Marxism Today*, February 1980.

4. Tony Crosland, *Socialism Now and Other Essays* (London, 1974), pp. 27, 72–3.

5. Tony Benn, *The New Politics: A Socialist Reconnaissance*, Fabian Tract 402, September 1970, pp. 8–9. It is also worth noting that Benn's pamphlet of 1970 anticipates in all essentials the argument of Hall's 'Great Moving Right Show', at the end of the decade.

6. Michael Crozier, Samuel P. Huntington and Joji Watanuki, *The Crisis of Democracy: Report on the Governability of Democracies to the Trilateral Commission* (New York, 1975).

7. Wolfgang Streeck, *Buying Time: The Delayed Crisis of Democratic Capitalism* (London, 2014).

8. David Hine, 'Leaders and Followers: Democracy and Manageability in the Social Democratic Parties of Western Europe', in William E.

Patterson and Alastair H. Thomas, eds, *The Future of Social Democracy* (Oxford, 1986), pp. 278–89.

9. Quoted in R.W. Johnson, *The Long March of the French Left* (New York, 1981), p. 159.

10. See Stefano Bartolini, 'The Membership of Mass Parties: The Social Democratic Experience, 1889–1978', in H. Daalder and P. Mair, eds, *Western European Party Systems: Continuity and Change* (London, 1983), esp. pp. 185–91.

11. Ralph Miliband, 'A State of De-Subordination', *British Journal of Sociology* xxix: 4 (December 1978), pp. 399–409.

12. Trevor Blackwell and Jeremy Seabrook, *A World Still to Win* (London, 1985), pp. 113–14.

13. See Leo Panitch, 'The Developmentof Corporatism in Liberal Democracies', *Comparative Political Studies* 10: 1 (April 1977); and 'Trade Unions and the State', *New Left Review* I/125 (January–February 1981).

14. See R. Cayrol, 'The Crisis of the French Socialist Party', *New Political Science* 12 (Summer 1983), pp. 11–16; Daniel Singer, *Is Socialism Doomed? The Meaning of Mitterrand* (New York, 1988).

15. See M. Spourdalakis, *The Rise of the Greek Socialist Party* (London, 1988), esp. Chapter 6.

16. Jonas Pontusson, *The Limits of Social Democracy: Investment Politics in Sweden* (Ithaca/London, 1992), esp. Chapter 7.

17. Tony Benn, 'Fabian Autumn Lectures', 3 November 1971, in *Speeches by Tony Benn* (Nottingham, 1974), p. 275.

18. Robert Michels, *Political Parties: A Sociological Study of the Oligarchical Tendencies of Modern Democracy* (New York, 1962 [1915]).

19. Max Weber, quoted in G. Carchedi, *Class Analysis and Social Research* (Oxford, 1987), p. 12.

20. Lewis Minkin, *The Labour Party Conference: A Study in the Politics of Intra-Party Democracy* (London, 1978), p. 14.

21. R.T. McKenzie, *British Political Parties: The Distribution of Power Within the Conservative and Labour Parties* (London, 1955).

22. Ralph Miliband, 'Party Democracy and Parliamentary Government', *Political Studies* VI (1958), pp. 170–4.

23. Robert McKenzie, 'Power in the Labour Party: The Issue of Intra-Party

Democracy', in D. Kavanagh, ed., *The Politics of the Labour Party* (London, 1982), pp. 196–7.

24. Perry Anderson, 'The Antinomies of Antonio Gramsci', *New Left Review* 1/100 (November 1976–January 1977), pp. 28–9.

25. Raymond Williams, Edward Thompson, Stuart Hall and Ralph Miliband had noted as early as 1968 that past efforts by the Labour left had always bogged down in the same way: the left 'becomes of necessity involved in the same kind of machine politics, the same manipulation of committees in the name of thousands ... It is also ... directing energy into the very machines and methods which socialists should fight ... And this has prevented the outward-looking and independent long-term campaign.' Raymond Williams, ed, *The May Day Manifesto* (Harmondsworth, 1968), pp. 173–4.

26. Fritz W. Scharpf, *Crisis and Choice in European Social Democracy* (Ithaca, NY, 1991).

27. Donald Sassoon, *One Hundred Years of Socialism* (London, 1996), p. 702. See also pp. 505, 740. Sassoon's judgement that the Labour left's defeat was inevitable because of its 'profound conservatism' on both the constitution and on international issues was not a 'polemical exaggeration', but wrong – as Sassoon himself half recognised when he acknowledged that Benn, as leader of the Labour left, was not a constitutional conservative but a radical democratiser, as well as a proponent of a written constitution. And insofar as Sassoon admitted that overcoming the European Community's undemocratic capitalist character would be 'a momentous enterprise whose outcome is uncertain', his silence with regard to how this momentous enterprise could be tackled makes the position of the Labour new left in the 1970s look quite clear-sighted and practical.

28. Among European socialists, the Labour new left was particularly admired for its combativeness and political creativity. Even in 1984 the Swedish sociologist Göran Therborn could still call on Neil Kinnock to 'take care of this amazing socialist combativeness in the British Labour Party, so different from the demoralised gloom nearly everywhere else'. Göran Therborn, 'Britain Left Out', in James Curran, ed., *The Future of the Left* (London, 1984), p. 7.

29. For a vivid, but ultimately unresolved analysis of this problem, as presented by the 1988 Rover factory strike at Cowley, in Oxford, see David Harvey, 'Militant Particularism and Global Ambition: The Conceptual Politics of Place, Space and Environment in the Work of Raymond Williams', *Social Text* 42 (1995).

30. For a survey of the practical problems recognised at the time, see Hilary Wainwright's concluding chapter in Sheila Rowbotham, Lynne Segal and Hilary Wainwright, *Beyond the Fragments* (London, 1979). For their subsequent work with the Labour new left in the 1980s, especially in the Greater London Council, and its ongoing contemporary relevance, see their introductions to the third edition of this book (London, 2013).

31. But for an example of how creatively some new left theorists were thinking about democracy, see Raymond Williams, 'An Alternative Politics', in Ralph Miliband and John Saville, eds, *Socialist Register 1981* (London, 1981), pp. 1–10.

32. The Labour new left's critics have not done any better in this respect. For example, Eric Shaw's generally outstanding *The Labour Party Since 1979: Crisis and Transformation* (London, 1994) criticises reselection of MPs for having transferred so much power to local activists that the party became 'paralysed', since 'a party . . . requires a degree of internal order and centralised direction' and a leadership able to respond flexibly to 'external challenges' (pp. 22–3). Leaving aside the question of whether the degree of power that reselection gave to local activists was really incompatible with these requirements, it is noteworthy that, later in the book (p. 220), Shaw laments the loss of incentives for activism that the post-1983 reforms entailed, because 'a core group of activists constitutes the driving force for recruiting, organising and motivating a wider involved membership'. Many of Labour's 'modernisers', of course, would not see any problem, as they wanted a wider membership but not an involved one.

33. Peter Mandelson and Roger Liddle, *The Blair Revolution* (London, 1996), pp. 2, 214. See also Tony Blair's commentary on the BBC's series, 'The Wilderness Years', *Observer*, 17 December 1995.

34. 'They have not won their political battles; they have not carried their main points, they have not stopped their adversaries' advance; but they

have told silently upon the mind of the country, they have prepared currents of feeling which sap their adversaries' position when it seems gained, they have kept up their communication with the future'. Matthew Arnold, quoted in Fred Inglis, 'The Figures of Dissent', *New Left Review* I/215 (January–February 1996), p. 82.

35. While it was through these institutions that a senior Labour minister, such as Stafford Cripps in 1949, could direct an appeal to workers for wage restraint in the name of 'Christian values' as well as the 'national interest', the same institutions provided the space where a woman cleaner in Whitehall, a delegate of the Transport and General Workers Union, could take the floor to proclaim that, while the vegetarian Cripps might 'live on orange juice and radish tops ... the workers of Great Britain cannot be expected to follow his example to that extent'. From the *1949 TUC Report* as quoted in L. Panitch, *Social Democracy and Industrial Militancy* (Cambridge, 1976), p. 30.

36. See Peter Mair, 'Partyless Democracy', *New Left Review* I/2 (March–April 2000).

37. See Sam Gindin and Leo Panitch, 'Transcending Pessimism: Rekindling Socialist Imagination', in Leo Panitch and Colin Leys, eds, *Necessary and Unnecessary Utopias: Socialist Register 2000* (London, 1999).

38. See the National Party Forum's Report to the 2000 Labour Party Conference, esp. pp. 7, 18–21.

39. Alan Simpson, 'Inside New Labour's Rolling Coup: The Blair Supremacy', *Red Pepper*, 1 December 2014.

40. See Stephanie L. Mudge, *Leftism Reinvented: Western Parties from Socialism to Neoliberalism* (Cambridge, MA, 2018); David F. Patton, *Out of the East: From PDS to Left Party in Unified Germany* (Albany, NY, 2011); Michael Spourdalakis, 'Left Strategy in the Greek Cauldron: Explaining Syriza's Success', *Socialist Register 2013* (London, 2012), pp. 98–119.

41. Alex Nunns, *The Candidate: Jeremy Corbyn's Improbable Path to Power*, 2nd edn (London, 2018), p. 68.

2 The Roots of Labour's New Left

1. Martin Jacques and Francis Mulhern, eds, *The Forward March of Labour Halted?* (London, 1981), p. 18.

2. 'Election Agenda', *Socialist Commentary*, May 1962, p. 5 (emphasis in original).

3. Labour Party Conference *Report* (hereafter *LPCR*), 1961, p. 155.

4. TUC *Report*, 1964, p. 383.

5. Swansea, 25 January 1964. Reprinted in Harold Wilson, *The New Britain: Labour's Plan, Selected Speeches* (London, 1964), p. 19. On Benn's contribution to this speech, see Robert Jenkins, *Tony Benn: A Political Biography* (London, 1980), p. 99.

6. *LPCR*, 1963, p. 198.

7. See esp. *Tribune*, 8 January, 5 and 19 February, 23 April, 28 May 1965.

8. Perry Anderson, 'Problems of Socialist Strategy', in Perry Anderson and Robin Blackburn, eds, *Towards Socialism* (Ithaca, NY, 1966), pp. 222, 261, 284.

9. After the first breakthrough in Labour's vote to over 30 per cent, in the 1920s, and the second breakthrough to over 40 per cent, in the 1940s, Labour's support showed no tendency to a steady rise or fall until the experience of the 1966 Wilson government. Labour's percentage of the vote fell from an historic high in 1951 of 48.8 per cent (when they lost the election) to 46.4 per cent in 1955 and 43.9 per cent in 1959. But in its standing in the opinion polls between elections, it pretty consistently ran ahead of the Tories through the 1950s, hovering around the percentage of the vote it had obtained in 1951. The first Wilson government, in 1964, was elected on 44.1 per cent of the vote, and the second, in 1966, by 48.1 per cent of the vote – barely less than in 1951, and distributed in such a way this time as to yield an overwhelming majority in the House of Commons. (The longitudinal data employed in this discussion are mainly drawn from A. Heath, R. Jowell and J. Curtice, *How Britain Votes* [Oxford, 1985], Tables 1.2 and 3.1 and Diagram 1.3, pp. 3–5, 30.) The class voting patterns in the mid 1960s remained strong enough to seem to justify leading psephologists, with their typical tendency to extrapolate the present into the future, in the view that

Labour was being invested by demographic changes with a permanent majority. See, for example, David Butler and Donald Stokes, *Political Change in Britain* (London, 1969).

10. Their first findings were published as John H. Goldthorpe and David Lockwood, 'Affluence and the British Class Structure', *Sociological Review*, July 1963.

11. Mark N. Franklin, *The Decline of Class Voting in Britain: Changes in the Basis of Electoral Choice* (Oxford, 1985), p. 174. David Weakliem's subsequent study confirms that the critical moment in determining the decline in working-class voting for the Labour Party took place between 1964 and 1970, when the party lost a similar degree of support among what he identifies as 'class-conscious' working-class voters as among those whom he defines as 'class-aware'. (The views that were expressed by 'class-aware' voters are similar to the new working-class consciousness Goldthorpe and Lockwood identified as 'instrumental collectivism'.) See David Weakliem, 'Class Consciousness and Political Change: Voting and Political Attitudes in the British Working Class, 1964 to 1970', *American Sociological Review* 58: 3 (1993), esp. pp. 391–5.

12. Jenkins, *Tony Benn* (London, 1980), p. 109.

13. Trevor Blackwell and Jeremy Seabrook, *A World Still To Win* (London, 1985), p. 133.

14. Cynthia Cockburn, *The Local State* (London, 1977), p. 5. See also John Gyford, *The Politics of Local Socialism* (London, 1985), p. 25.

15. Interview with Ken Livingstone, in David Kogan and Maurice Kogan, *The Battle for the Labour Party* (London, 1982), p. 122.

16. See Dennis Healey, *The Time of My Life* (London, 1989), p. 444; Tony Benn, *Against the Tide: Diaries 1973–76* (London, 1989), pp. 521–2.

17. Ian Mikardo, 'Watch the Unions: That's My Tip', *Tribune*, 8 October 1965.

18. Lewis Minkin, *The Labour Party Conference* (London, 1978), p. 294.

19. See Lewis Minkin's definitive account, *The Contentious Alliance: Trade Unions and the Labour Party* (Edinburgh, 1991), esp. Chapters 5 and 6.

20. Eric Shaw, *Discipline and Discord in the Labour Party* (Manchester, 1988), p. 296.

21. See Minkin, *Labour Party Conference*, esp. pp. 125–6.

22. *LPCR*, 1968, pp. 127, 149, 153.

23. Jenkins, *Tony Benn*, p. 214.

24. The most significant instances of disaffiliation took place among the railway, miners, textile and sheet metal workers' unions. Moreover, although the unions maintained the level of block affiliations to the party, the actual number of individuals who contracted out of the political levy portion of their dues also increased (most markedly from 240,616 in 1966 to 320,983 in 1970 in the engineers' union).

25. Jack Jones, 'Keeping Trade Union Links with Labour', *Tribune*, 9 February 1968.

26. Quoted in Geoffrey Goodman, *The Awkward Warrior, Frank Cousins: His Life and Times* (London, 1979), p. 515.

27. Interviews with Michael Foot, 5 August and 11 November 1971, conducted by Leo Panitch for *Social Democracy and Industrial Militancy: The Labour Party, The Trade Unions and Incomes Policy, 1945–74* (Cambridge, 1976).

28. Tony Benn, *A New Course for Labour*, Institute for Workers' Control pamphlet, (Nottingham, 1976), p. 10.

29. Official figures on individual party membership were notoriously inflated, not least because they reflected from 1963 to 1979 the introduction of a new party rule requiring constituencies to affiliate on the basis of a minimum figure of 1,000, although most CLPs had memberships far less than that. The 680,000 figure around which the party's individual membership hovered by the end of the 1960s probably needed to be discounted by at least one-half, perhaps by as much as two-thirds. See *Report of the Committee on Financial Aid to Political Parties*, Cmd.6601 (London, 1976); Paul Whitely, *The Labour Party in Crisis* (London, 1983), Chapter 3.

30. See Stefano Bartolini, 'The Membership of Mass Parties: The Social Democratic Experience, 1889–1978', in H. Daalder and P. Mair, eds, *Western European Party Systems: Continuity and Change* (London, 1983), Figure 7.3 (p. 188).

31. Quoted in Patrick Seyd and Lewis Minkin, 'The Labour Party and Its Members', *New Society*, 20 September 1979, p. 614.

32. There was a loss of 150,000 members from 1964 to 1969. Once the inflated official 680,000 membership figure of 1969 is appropriately discounted (i.e. at least by half), we can see that Ken Livingstone's estimate that the party lost half its members in these years may not have been too much of an exaggeration.

33. Seyd and Minkin, 'The Labour Party and Its Members', p. 613.

34. David Widgery's *The Left in Britain 1956–68* (Harmondsworth, 1976) provides a useful glossary of left-wing groups and publications up to the early 1970s (pp. 477–505).

35. Marjorie Mayo, 'Radical Politics and Community Action', in M. Loney and M. Allen, eds, *The Crisis of the Inner City* (London, 1979), pp. 132–5.

36. See P. Abramson, 'Intergenerational Mobility and Partisan Preferences in Britain and Italy', *Comparative Political Studies* 6 (1973), pp. 221–34.

37. 'Weighing 'Em Up', *Labour Organizer* 50: 578 (January 1971), pp. 3–4.

38. Peter Paterson, *The Selectorate: The Case for Primary Elections in Britain* (London, 1967), pp. 65–6.

39. Shaw, *Discipline and Discord*, p. 295.

40. See Blackwell and Seabrook, *World Still to Win*, p. 53. The same might be said of Stuart Hall's writings on the rise of Thatcherism.

41. At least not until the Campaign Group of MPs in the mid 1980s, by which point the Labour new left's project of the 1970s had been defeated.

42. The term is Minkin's, from *Labour Party Conference*, p. 329.

43. 'Secrecy and the National Executive', *Tribune*, 15 June 1973, reprinted in *Speeches by Tony Benn* (Nottingham, 1974), p. 302. Benn concluded this book with these words.

44. See Ben Pimlot, *Harold Wilson* (London, 1992), p. 150; Benn, *Against the Tide*, pp. 12, 692.

45. Tony Benn, *Talking About Socialism* (Glasgow, 1996) – based on an interview with John Foster.

46. Tony Benn, *Out of the Wilderness: Diaries 1963–67* (London, 1987), p. 459.

47. 731 *HC Debates*, 14 July 1966, cols 1789.

48. Leo Panitch interview with Tony Benn, 10 October 1985. For Benn's

rather different account in his diary on the day, see *Office Without Power: Diaries 1968–72* (London, 1988), pp. 154–5.

49. Tony Benn, *The New Politics: A Socialist Reconnaissance*, Fabian Tract 402, September 1970, p. 9.

50. Ibid., p. 12.

51. 'Democratic Politics', Fabian Autumn Lecture, 3 November 1971, in *Speeches by Tony Benn*, pp. 277–9 (emphasis added).

52. Ibid., p. 278.

53. Interview with Tony Benn in Alan Freeman, *The Benn Heresy* (London, 1982), pp. 174–5.

54. Frank Allaun, Ian Mikardo and Jim Sillars, 'Labour – Party or Puppet?', July 1972.

55. Simon Hoggart and David Leigh, *Michael Foot: A Portrait* (London, 1981), p. 163.

56. Quoted in Michael Hatfield, *The House the Left Built* (London, 1978), p. 114.

57. TUC *Report* (Brighton, 1972), pp. 401–2.

58. Ibid., p. 285.

59. Benn, *Office Without Power*, p. 454. For Jones's view in this respect, see Minkin, *Contentious Alliance*, esp. pp. 180–1; and Jones's autobiography, Jack Jones, *Union Man* (London, 1986), esp. pp. 220–7.

3 The Limits of Policy

1. Michael Hatfield's valuable book, *The House the Left Built* (London, 1978), was not so much on the structure of the 'house' as on the process of painting it red. For its part, David Coates's *Labour in Power? A Study of the Labour Government 1974–79* (London, 1980) saw the attempt to change the party almost entirely in terms of economic policy victories of the new left alliance in the party ('a series of clear policy commitments more radical in tone and in aspiration than any the Party had endorsed since 1945'), which he judged as inadequate in terms of the crisis of international capitalism. See also Mark Wickham Jones, *Economic Strategy and the Labour Party: Politics and Policy-Making, 1970–83* (London/New York, 1996).

2. Quoted by John Campbell, *Roy Jenkins: A Biography* (London, 1983), p. 141.

3. *LPCR*, 1971, p. 236.

4. Lewis Minkin, *The Labour Party Conference: A Study in the Politics of Intra-Party Democracy* (London, 1978), p. 406 n. 16.

5. Tony Benn, *Against the Tide: Diaries 1973–76* (London, 1989), p. 40.

6. See Peter Taaffe, *The Rise of Militant: Militant's Thirty Years* (London, 1995), pp. 53–5; Andy McSmith, *Faces of Labour* (London, 1996); Michael Crick, *The March of Militant* (London, 1986); John Callaghan, *British Trotskyism: Theory and Practice* (London, 1984) and *The Far Left in British Politics* (London, 1987); Patrick Wintour, 'Militant's Resolutionary Socialism', *New Statesman*, 18 January 1980.

7. Hilary Wainwright, *Labour: A Tale of Two Parties* (London, 1987), p. 153. When Benn met Ted Grant, Militant's leader, for the first time (one of the very few times they ever met), at a debate staged between them by the LPYS in 1973, Benn came away 'feeling that he is really a theological leader . . . He is absolutely rational, logical and analytical up to a point and then he just goes over the top and keeps talking about "the bloody settlement that the capitalists are preparing for the workers"'. In the debate Benn directly criticised this revolutionary posturing: 'If I believed it, we wouldn't be here passing resolutions, we would be planning guerilla warfare. If the young people, with all their passion and idealism were diverted to thinking in civil war terms, it would weaken rather than strengthen their influence.' Benn, *Against the Tide*, pp. 20–1.

8. The resolution was endorsed and passed on a show of hands without a card vote.

9. Quoted in Hatfield, *House the Left Built*, p. 216.

10. Benn, *Against the Tide*, p. 46. Jones makes no mention of the twenty-five companies episode in his autobiography, *Union Man*; but, to confirm Benn's impression, see Lewis Minkin, *The Contentious Alliance: Trade Unions and the Labour Party* (Edinburgh, 1991), pp. 172–3.

11. Benn's diaries show clearly the private despondency he felt at his almost complete isolation among the leadership. See *Against the Tide*, pp. 45–82.

12. Ibid., pp. 115, 118.

13. Paul Whiteley, 'The Decline of Labour's Local Party Membership and Electoral Base, 1945–74', in D. Kavanagh, ed., *The Politics of the Labour Party* (London, 1982), p. 132.

14. Cited in Hatfield, *House the Left Built*, pp. 228–9.

15. Benn's paper was published in its entirety in *The Times*, 23 May 1974.

16. Quoted in Barbara Castle, *The Castle Diaries 1974–1976*, London, 1980, p. 103.

17. Quoted in Benn, *Against the Tide*, p. 194. See also Edmund Dell, *A Hard Pounding: Politics and Economic Crisis, 1974–1976* (London, 1991), p. 97.

18. The White Paper was published as Cmnd. 5710, 15 August 1974.

19. Harold Wilson, *Final Term: The Labour Government 1974–76* (London, 1979), p. 34. See also Simon Hoggart and David Leigh, *Michael Foot: A Portrait* (London, 1981), p. 173; Eric Heffer, *Labour's Future: Socialism or SDP Mark 2?* (London, 1986), p. 12; Benn, *Against the Tide*, pp. 212–14.

20. See Wilson, *Final Term*, p. 98, and *The Governance of Britain* (London, 1976), Appendix III; and James Callaghan, *Time and Change* (London, 1988), pp. 303–7, 316–18.

21. Wilson threatened in this context to resign as leader of the party (but not as prime minister, thus raising, as Wilson later put it, 'a most interesting constitutional situation'). See Wilson, *Final Term*, pp. 104–8; Castle, *Castle Diaries*, pp. 346–50; Hoggart and Leigh, *Michael Foot*, pp. 178–9.

22. Midway into the referendum campaign, the pertinent issues of the debate and the debate itself almost seemed to be reduced to the simple question of whether you were 'for' or 'against' Tony Benn. Benn was portrayed by the press as personifying the entire anti-EEC movement and, in the final days before the vote, press reports consisted almost entirely of quotes by pro-marketeers who accused Benn of lying about the effect of EEC membership on employment. The *Daily Mirror* labelled Benn the 'Minister of Fear'. See Mark Hollingsworth, *The Press and Political Dissent* (London, 1986), pp. 47–50.

23. In May 1975, Wilson had already tipped off the *Daily Telegraph*'s political correspondent, Harry Boyne, of his plans to sack Benn from Industry. See Hollingsworth, *Press and Political Dissent*, pp. 45–6.

24. On Foot's opposition to Wilson's cabinet reshuffle, see Hoggart and Leigh, *Michael Foot*, pp. 180, 182–3. On Jones's opposition to the 'victimisation' of Benn – and his failure to do anything about it when it nevertheless happened – see Hatfield, *House the Left Built*, pp. 148–9.

25. Joe Haines, *The Politics of Power* (London, 1977), p. 31. See also Benn, *Against the Tide*, pp. 390, 525, 547; Dennis Healey, *The Time of My Life* (London, 1989), p. 446; and Benn, *Against the Tide*, p. 525; Marcia Falkender, *Downing Street in Perspective* (London, 1983), pp. 169–70, 209–10.

26. Quoted in Ian Mikardo, *Back-Bencher* (London, 1988), pp. 195–6.

27. Kathleen Burk and Alec Cairncross, *'Goodbye, Great Britain': The 1976 IMF Crisis* (New Haven, CT/London, 1992), p. 19.

28. *LPCR*, 1976, pp. 188–9. See also Callaghan, *Time and Change*, pp. 425–7.

29. Andrew Gamble, *Britain in Decline: Economic Policy, Political Strategy and the British State*, 4th edn (London, 1994), p. 185.

30. See Benn, *Against The Tide*, pp. 303, 324–5.

31. The others included the maintenance of price controls, selective assistance to industry on a larger scale, work-sharing and temporary employment subsidies, progressive tax increases, cuts in overseas defence spending, and a further downward float of sterling.

32. Benn, *Against the Tide*, pp. 325–6 (see also pp. 302–3).

33. John Eaton, Michael Barratt Brown and Ken Coates, *An Alternative Economic Strategy for the Labour Movement*, Spokesman Pamphlet No. 47, February 1975, p. 12. Francis Cripps also saw the alternative economic strategy primarily in terms of its contribution to building a participatory form of democracy. See his 'The British Crisis – Can the Left Win?' *New Left Review* I/128 (July–August 1981). For the most remarkably detailed and inspiring version of the strategy presented in these terms, see Raymond Williams, 'An Alternative Politics', *The Socialist Register 1981* (London, 1981).

34. See Castle, *Castle Diaries*, pp. 420–8; Benn, *Against The Tide*, pp. 403–4.

35. See Benn, *Against the Tide*, pp. 165–6.

36. Ibid., p. 380. See also Eaton, Barratt-Brown and Coates, *Alternative Economic Strategy*, p. 3.

37. Cambridge Political Economy Group, *Britain's Economic Crisis*, Spokesman Pamphlet No. 44, September 1974.

38. See Anthony P. Thirlwall, *Nicholas Kaldor* (Brighton, 1987), pp. 250–4, 281; Benn, *Against the Tide*, p. 657; Burk and Cairncross, 'Goodbye, Great Britain', p. 89; and Dell, *Hard Pounding*, pp. 126–9, 259.

39. Benn, *Against the Tide*, p. 518 (see also p. 498).

40. When Michael Meacher, Benn's parliamentary undersecretary at the Department of Industry, wrote an article on saving jobs at the beginning of 1975 that included reference to the 'anarchy of capitalist markets that had developed after 1970', Sir Anthony Part objected to Benn on the grounds that this was a political phrase and inappropriate for use by a government minister. Benn, *Against The Tide*, pp. 294, 329.

41. Ibid., p. 313.

42. Benn's main contribution as energy minister to the broader struggle was that of leading by example: demonstrating that a radical minister could run a department efficiently with much less secrecy and much more participation than was the norm in Whitehall. See Robert Jenkins, *Tony Benn: A Political Biography* (London, 1980), pp. 232–7, 242–54.

43. This work bore fruit in the publication of three important and influential books by the turn of the decade: the CSE London–Edinburgh Weekend Return Group's *In and Against the State*, in November 1979; the CSE State Apparatus and Expenditure Group's *Struggle Over the State: Cuts and Restructuring in Contemporary Britain*, in December 1979; and the LCC and CSE's joint publication, *The Alternative Economic Strategy* – an elaboration of the London CSE Group's 'Crisis, the Labour Movement and the Alternative Economic Strategy', *Capital & Class* 8 (Summer 1979).

44. Exemplified by Geoff Hodgson, *Socialism and Parliamentary Democracy* (London, 1977), by Ralph Miliband, *Marxism and Politics* (London, 1977) and by Sheila Rowbotham, Lynne Segal and Hilary Wainwright, *Beyond the Fragments* (London, 1979).

4 A Crisis of Representation

1. 'CLPD Priorities for 1979', Discussion Paper prepared by the Secretary, 17 December 1978, p. 1. The following account is based on original CLPD documents and interviews with CLPD activists, including Vladimir and Vera Derer. See also Patrick Seyd, *The Rise and Fall of the Labour Left* (London, 1987), esp. pp. 83–9, 103–21; David Kogan and Maurice Kogan, *The Battle for the Labour Party* (London, 1982), esp. Chapters 5 and 6; A. Young, *The Deselection of MPs* (London, 1983), esp. chapters 7 and 8.

2. 'CLPD Priorities for 1979', p. 1.

3. Nicholas Costello, Tony Cutler, Vera Derer, Irene Hong and Seumas Milne, *The Case for Public Ownership: A Campaign for Labour Party Democracy Pamphlet* (September 1986).

4. 'Secretary's Statement', *CLPD Bulletin*, 11 January 1986, pp. i–x.

5. The quotations in this paragraph and the two quotations which follow are from 'Paper No. 2', which Vladimir Derer prepared for a Labour Left Liaison meeting in the Summer of 1988.

6. As a cabinet minister, Benn had to keep his distance, of course. But he had in any case been wary of concentrating on precise constitutional formulae in advancing the case for internal party democracy. Within the NEC, especially after 1976, he became one of the strongest supporters of the CLPD's campaign.

7. Robert Michels, *Political Parties* (New York, 1962 [1915]).

8. Patrick Seyd and Lewis Minkin, 'The Labour Party and Its Members', *New Society*, 20 September 1979, p. 614.

9. Campaign for Labour Party Democracy, 'Statement of Aims', June 1973.

10. 'CLPD Priorities for 1979', pp. 1–2.

11. Eric Shaw, *Discipline and Discord in the Labour Party* (Manchester, 1988), p. 199.

12. Indeed, upon his election to the leadership, a profile in the *New Statesman* ('Lucky Jim', 9 April 1976, pp. 460–1) had likened Callaghan to Mayor Daley of Chicago. But, very much unlike Daley, Callaghan at the same time affected the demeanour of the quintessential statesman.

13. LPCR, 1976, pp. 193–4.

14. Stuart Hall, Chas Critcher, Tony Jefferson, John Clarke and Brian Roberts, *Policing the Crisis* (London, 1978), pp. 313–14.

15. Tony Benn, *Conflicts of Interest: Diaries 1977–80* (London, 1990), p. 359.

16. Andrew Ross, *Parliamentary Profiles* (London, 1984), pp. 295–6.

17. 'Williams Notices a Swing to Centre', *Financial Times*, 21 February 1979. See also Alison Young, *The Reselection of MPs* (London, 1984), pp. 132–3.

18. Lewis Minkin, *The Contentious Alliance: Trade Unions and the Labour Party* (Edinburgh, 1991), p. 303.

19. David Hine, 'Leaders and Followers: Democracy and Manageability in the Social Democratic Parties of Western Europe', in William E. Patterson and Alastair H. Thomas, eds, *The Future of Social Democracy* (Oxford, 1986), p. 279.

20. Michael Rustin, 'The New Left and the Present Crisis', *New Left Review* I/121 (May–June 1980), p. 66. In a subsequent article, however, Rustin would show a more nuanced appreciation for what was involved in the Labour new left's constitutionalism. See his excellent essay, 'Different Conceptions of Party: Labour's Constitutional Debates', *New Left Review* I/126 (March–April 1981).

21. 'Secretary's Statement', CLPD *Bulletin* 11 (January 1986), p. iii.

22. Perry Anderson, 'The Antinomies of Antonio Gramsci', *New Left Review* I/100 (November 1976–January 1977), pp. 28–9.

23. Although Labour Party identification among the middle classes and nonmanual workers had actually continued to rise through the 1970s (standing at over 30 per cent among the latter by 1979), it had declined by the end of the decade to only 50 per cent of skilled and unskilled manual workers. See Ivor Crewe, 'On the Death and Resurrection of Class Voting: Some Comments on How Britain Votes', *Political Studies* 34 (1986), pp. 620–38; A. Heath, R. Jowell and J. Curtice, 'Trendless Fluctuations: A Reply to Crewe', *Political Studies* 35 (1987), pp. 256–77.

24. Patrick Seyd and Lewis Minkin, 'The Labour Party and Its Members', *New Society*, 20 September 1979, p. 615.

25. 'Thatcherism – A New Stage?', *Marxism Today*, February 1980, p. 27. See also Leo Panitch, 'Socialists and the Labour Party – A Reappraisal',

in Ralph Miliband and John Saville, eds, *The Socialist Register 1979* (London, 1979).

26. All these words, and the quotations that follow, are from John Soper's biography, *Tony Blair: The Moderniser* (London, 1995), pp. 50–1. Soper anchored BBC party conference broadcasts.

27. Benn, *Conflicts of Interest*, p. 533.

28. See Seyd, *Rise and Fall*, p. 86; Kogan and Kogan, *Battle for the Labour Party*, p. 52.

29. Shaw, *Discipline and Discord*, pp. 249–51.

30. For the most thorough documentation of the media's tendency to cover the conflict in the party in 1980 and 1981 'almost exclusively from the point of view of the right wing of the Labour Party', see Greg Philo, John Hewitt, Peter Beharrell and Howard Davis, *Really Bad News* (London, 1982).

31. Benn, *Conflicts of Interest*, p. 508.

32. Tony Benn, *Arguments for Democracy* (London, 1981), Preface.

33. Ibid.

34. See especially Hilary Wainwright, *Labour: A Tale of Two Parties* (London, 1987), Chapter 4.

35. Ken Livingstone, *If Voting Changed Anything They'd Abolish It* (London, 1987), p. 91.

36. Benn, *Arguments for Democracy*, p. 168.

37. Ibid., p. 171.

38. *LPCR*, 1979, pp. 292–3.

39. Peter Hain, ed., *The Crisis and the Future of the Left: The Debate of the Decade*, London 1980, p. 50.

40. Ibid., pp. 47–8.

41. See Tony Benn, 'Britain: Lessons for the Left – An Interview with Leo Panitch', *Studies in Political Economy* 13 (Spring 1984), p. 11.

42. Benn, *Conflicts of Interest*, p. 538.

43. *LPCR*, 1980, p. 13.

44. Ibid., p. 31.

45. Ibid., pp. 194–5.

46. See Kogan and Kogan, *Battle for the Labour Party*, p. 101.

5 Disempowering Activism

1. Hilary Wainwright describes how 'socialists with a few exceptions, everywhere (those over 30, at least), inside the Labour Party and outside, felt some elation at the news of his election'. Hilary Wainwright, *Labour: A Tale of Two Parties* (London, 1987), p. 82.

2. Michael Foot, 'The Labour Party and Parliamentary Democracy', *Guardian*, 10 September 1981.

3. Raymond Williams, 'An Alternative Politics', in Ralph Miliband and John Saville, eds, *The Socialist Register 1981* (London, 1981), p. 1.

4. For accounts of the labyrinthine complexity that governed the voting and the outcome at Wembley, see David Kogan and Maurice Kogan, *The Battle for the Labour Party* (London, 1982), pp. 94–7; Patrick Seyd, *The Rise and Fall of the Labour Left* (London, 1987), pp. 118–21; and Lewis Minkin, *The Contentious Alliance: Trade Unions and the Labour Party* (Edinburgh, 1991), pp. 200–2.

5. Jon Lansman, *The Future of the Rank and File Mobilising Committee*, CLPD discussion paper, February 1981.

6. Ibid.

7. Quoted in Kogan and Kogan, *Battle for the Labour Party*, p. 106.

8. Quoted in Tony Benn, *The End of an Era: Diaries 1980–1990* (London, 1994) p. 77.

9. Bill Keys, speaking at the final meeting of the Commission of Enquiry in July 1980.

10. Benn, *End of an Era*, p. 116.

11. See especially Daniel Egan, 'The Local State, Capital and Opportunities for Local Autonomy: A Reassessment of the Greater London Council's Local Economic Strategy', *Research in Political Sociology* 8 (1998), pp. 165–87, based on his PhD dissertation, 'Relative Autonomy and Local Socialism: The Greater London Council's Local Economic Strategy', Department of Sociology, Boston College, 1994.

12. Wainwright, *Tale of Two Parties*, pp. 97, 99.

13. *Sunday Times*, 30 August 1981.

14. Ken Livingstone, *If Voting Changed Anything They'd Abolish It* (London, 1987), p. 177.

15. W.L. Miller, 'There Was No Alternative: The British General Election of 1983', *Parliamentary Affairs*, vol. 38, 1984, p. 376.

16. Ibid., p. 383. Compare Michael Foot, *Another Heart and Other Pulses* (London, 1984), esp. pp. 87, 161.

17. Mark Wickham-Jones, *Economic Strategy and the Labour Party: Politics and Policy-making, 1970–83* (London and New York, 1996), pp. 114–15.

18. Benn, *End of an Era*, p. 296.

19. Hobsbawm's interventions in this period are collected in his *Politics for a Rational Left: Political Writing 1977–88* (London, 1989).

20. Most notoriously expressed by Patrick Seyd in his 'Bennism Without Benn', *New Socialist*, May 1985. Excellent accounts of this realignment are given in Richard Heffernan and Mike Marqusee, *Defeat from the Jaws of Victory: Inside Kinnock's Labour Party* (London, 1992), esp. pp. 62ff; and Eric Shaw, *The Labour Party Since 1979: Crisis and Transformation* (London, 1994), pp. 160–6.

21. Labour Coordinating Committee, *Reconstruction: How the Labour Party – and the Left – Can Win*, March 1984.

22. Author interview with Ken Livingstone, June 1987.

23. Donald Sassoon, *One Hundred Years of Socialism* (London, 1996), p. 692.

24. Quoted in Benn, *End of An Era*, p. 308.

25. Shaw, *Labour Party Since 1979*, p. 163.

26. The number of individual CLPD members fell from 1,203 in 1982, through 668 in 1984, to 474 in 1986. Over the same period, CLP affiliations fell from 153 to 101 to 68; and trade union branch affiliations fell from 105 to 77 to 43. See Seyd, *Rise and Fall of the Labour Left*, Table 4.2 (p. 87).

27. Raymond Williams, 'Mining the Meaning: Key Words in the Miners' Strike', *New Socialist* 5 (1985), p. 7, cited in Andrew J. Richards, *Miners on Strike: Class Solidarity and Division in Britain* (Oxford/New York, 1996), p. 231.

28. See Seumus Milne, *The Enemy Within: The MI5, Maxwell and the Scargill Affair* (London, 1994).

29. *The Times*, 10 December 1985.

30. Larry Whitty, speech to the 1987 Labour Party Conference, quoted in Patrick Seyd and Paul Whiteley, *Labour's Grass Roots: The Politics of Party Membership* (Oxford, 1992), p. 201.

31. Seyd and Whiteley, *Labour's Grass Roots*, p. 201.

32. See John Rentoul, *Tony Blair* (London, 1995), pp. 337–9.

33. Henry M. Drucker, *Doctrine and Ethos in the Labour Party* (London, 1979).

34. See Rentoul, *Tony Blair*, esp. Chapters 3–4.

35. See Seyd and Whiteley, *Labour's Grass Roots*, pp. 54, 101.

36. *Guardian*, 8 August 1995.

37. The figures are from an official Labour Party survey of a thousand new members in May 1995, reported by Anthea Davey in *Red Pepper*, February 1996, pp. 22–3. Of the new members, 10 per cent were in blue-collar jobs and 47 per cent in white-collar jobs; 9 per cent were unemployed, 9 per cent were students, and 25 per cent were retired.

38. Tony Blair interviewed by Martin Kettle in the *Guardian*, 13 March 1995.

39. *Guardian*, 28 May 1995.

40. In 1995 the unions' block vote was weighted at 70 per cent of the total vote cast. Only one union, the Communications Workers, balloted all its members on the issue. The change was supported by 90 per cent, while MORI polls found the same proportion of AEEU (Engineers' union) members supporting change, and 85 per cent of trade-union members generally. This suggested that, in the unions as in the constituencies, the rank-and-file were much more sympathetic to the modernisers than to the activists; the modernisers' strategy had paid off. Constituency parties were not required to ballot their members, but under strong urging from party headquarters 501 did so. The 'turnout' or response rate in the first 133 constituency party ballots averaged 54 per cent. With 79 CLPs still to report results on the eve of the special conference, the percentage of individual members voting for the new Clause IV was 85.25; in only three of the constituencies that balloted their members was there a majority against change. The unions casting their conference vote against the change were the TGWU, UNISON, RMT, GPMU, NUM, FBU, EPIU, BFAWU, ASLEF and

UCATT (data from the *Observer*, 23 April 1995 and the *Guardian*, 29 April 1995).

41. *Guardian*, 1 May 1995.

42. Tony Blair announced this in a speech to the annual conference of the GMBU in June 1995 (*Guardian*, 8 June 1995).

43. Tony Benn interviewed by Patrick Wintour and Michael White, *Guardian*, 1 May 1995.

44. Patrick Wintour and Larry Elliott, *Guardian*, 28 March 1996.

45. Ballots were also sent to 2.6 million affiliated trade-union members, of whom 24 per cent responded, 90 per cent of them voting in favour (*Guardian*, 5 November 1996).

46. The first to be threatened with deselection on these grounds (for allegedly 'heckling at meetings and badgering Mr Blair as he attended a reception' at the 1996 party conference) was the MEP Hugh Kerr, a veteran critic of New Labour. The New Labour leader of the Labour MEPs said: 'He is being made an example of' (*Guardian*, 18 December 1996).

47. *Guardian*, 30 January 1997. In one of several symptomatically curious formulations, *Labour into Power* envisaged that, after two successive reviews by the Policy Forum, policy documents would be published, in advance of the annual conference, by the 'NEC, including NEC members of the JPC'. See *Labour into Power: A* Bill Keys, speaking at the final meeting of the Commission of Enquiry in July 1980. Ibid., p. 116 – compare p. 62. *Framework for Partnership*, January 1997, p. 16.

48. Ibid., p. 14.

49. *Guardian*, 13 September 1996.

50. And 59 per cent of the public as a whole, according to an ICM poll (*Observer*, 15 September 1996).

51. Andy McSmith and Peter Kellner, *Observer*, 15 September 1996. Underlying this Delphic pronouncement was an important shift that had meanwhile been occurring in the party's finances. While the trade unions were still crucial, their share of party income had fallen from 77 per cent of a total of £5.8 million in 1986, to 54 per cent of a total of £12.5 million in 1995, the difference being made up by fundraising activities and donations from individuals and businesses. See David Hencke, *Guardian*, 7 September 1996.

6 New Labour in Power

1. Peter Mandelson and Roger Liddle, *The Blair Revolution* (London, 1996), pp. 17–18.

2. Michael Powers, *The Audit Explosion* (London, 1994), p. 4.

3. Author interview with Geoff Mulgan, 11 August 1995.

4. The *Guardian*'s political commentator, Hugo Young, claimed that the word 'new' occurred 137 times in Blair's speech to the 1996 Labour Party Conference.

5. For a caustic account of its brief career, apparently written by two of its participants in 2007, see 'Nexus', at powerbase.info.

6. Seumas Milne, 'My Millbank', a review of Mandelson and Liddle, *The Blair Revolution, London Review of Books*, 18 April 1996, p. 3.

7. 'People don't even question for a moment that the Democrats are a pro-business party. They should not be asking that question about New Labour. New Labour is pro-business, pro-enterprise and we believe that there is nothing inconsistent between that and a just and decent society.' Tony Blair, *Financial Times*, 16 January 1997, quoted in Wyn Grant, 'Globalisation, Big Business and the Blair Government', CSGR Working Paper No. 58/00, University of Warwick, August 2000.

8. Lewis Minkin, *The Blair Supremacy* (Manchester, 2014), p. 313. The NPF was not elected by OMOV, but consisted of representatives chosen by a wide range of organisations, among which CLPs were a large minority, but only a minority. Minkin calls the NPF the party's 'most corrupted' element.

9. Ibid., p. 196.

10. Ibid., p. 673.

11. Ibid., p. 378.

12. After the 2005 election only twenty of the thirty most 'rebellious' (i.e. left-wing) MPs remained in the House of Commons. Philip Cowley, *The Rebels: How Blair Mislaid His Majority* (London, 2005), pp. 243–4.

13. Minkin, *Blair Supremacy*, p. 138.

14. Ibid., pp. 164–5.

15. The educationist and satirist Ted Wragg popularised a character called Tony Zoffis, who was always wanting some useless new target to be set.

See Ted Wragg, 'The Greatest Foe of Tony Zoffis', *Guardian*, 15 November 2005.

16. Minkin, *Blair Supremacy*, p. 383.

17. On early instances of sleaze, see Andrew Rawnsley, *The End of the Party* (London, 2010), pp. 123–9. On the later (2006) 'cash for peerages' scandal, see pp. 357–61 and 371–4 of the same text.

18. Hugh Pemberton and Mark Wickham-Jones point out that party membership declined across Europe from 1990 onwards, and that changes in society and the role of the state affected people's incentive to join parties and be active in them, so that many factors besides disagreement with New Labour's policies are likely to have contributed to the decline in Labour membership. The decline was also a net effect of people joining as well as leaving, making overall interpretation very difficult. The case of New Labour, however, looks overdetermined by both the discouragement of activism and the adoption of capitalism instead of socialism as the party's basic principle. See Hugh Pemberton and Mark Wickham-Jones, 'Labour's Lost Grassroots: The Rise and Fall of Party Membership', *British Politics* 8: 2 (June 2013).

19. *The Times*, 31 March 1997.

20. House of Commons, Public Administration Select Committee, 'Outsiders and Insiders: External Appointments to the Senior Civil Service', 21 January 2010 (pdf available at publications.parliament.uk).

21. Sir Jeremy Haywood interviewed by Jane Dudman in the *Guardian Professional*, 6 March 2012.

22. See Colin Leys, 'The Dissolution of the Mandarins: The Sell-Off of the British State', *Open Democracy*, 15 June 2012, at opendemocracy.net. For the conflict between private and public interests in health policy, see Stewart Player, 'Ready for Market', in Jacky Davis and Raymond Tallis, eds, *NHS SOS* (London, 2013), pp. 38–61; and Tamasin Cave, 'The Health Lobbying Industry', in Jacky Davis, John Lister and David Wrigley, eds, *NHS for Sale* (London, 2015), pp. 291–9.

23. Geoff Mulgan was a particular enthusiast for this, arguing that welfare support should not 'make it too easy for [single parents] to dump their children onto the responsibility of the state'. Geoff Mulgan, *Connexity*

(London, 1997), p. 165, quoted in Ray Kiely, *The Neoliberal Paradox* (Cheltenham, 2018), p. 157.

24. David Coates, *Flawed Capitalism: The Anglo-American Condition and Its Resolution* (Newcastle, 2018), p. 164.

25. While the public debt did start to rise again after 2003, just before the crash it was still below the level Labour had inherited from the Conservatives in 1997.

26. Equality Trust, 'How Has Inequality Changed? Development of UK Income Inequality', at equalitytrust.org.uk. According to the Equality Trust, the UK's Gini coefficient rose to 0.358 in 2009–10. According to Eurostat, the UK's Gini coefficient in 2010 was 0.329, compared with the all-EU average of 0.305, not to mention Denmark's 0.269 or Norway's 0.236. See 'Gini Coefficient of Equivalised Disposable Income – EU–SILC Survey', at appsso.eurostat.ec.europa.eu.

27. John Lanchester, 'Brexit Blues', *London Review of Books*, 28 July 2016. By 2016 the situation had been aggravated by five years of cuts in public spending, but the damage done by Thatcher had been left unrepaired by New Labour.

28. David Rowland, *P.F.I.: Profiting From Infirmaries*, Centre for Health and the Public Interest (CHPI), August 2017; and Vivek Kotecha, *Dealing with the Legacy of PFI – Options for Policymakers*, CHPI, 2018 (both available in pdf form at chpi.org.uk).

29. 'There are currently over 700 operational PFI and PF2 deals, with a capital value of around £60 billion. Annual charges for these deals amounted to £10.3 billion in 2016–17. Even if no new deals are entered into, future charges which continue until the 2040s amount to £199 billion'. National Audit Office, 'PFI and PF2', report by the Comptroller and Auditor General, January 2018, p. 4 (pdf available via nao.org.uk).

30. Alan Simpson, 'Inside New Labour's Rolling Coup: The Blair Supremacy', *Red Pepper*, 1 December 2014.

31. 'Foundation' hospitals were selected on the basis of their economic viability and given freedom from central control, with the power to borrow capital and enter into partnerships with private companies. Many Labour MPs saw this as likely to disadvantage other hospitals.

32. Department of Information Services, House of Commons Library,

Labour Backbench Rebellions since 1997 (pdf available at parliament.uk).

33. David Frum, *The Right Man* (New York, 2003), quoted in Rawnsley, *End of the Party*, p. 86.

34. See Leo Panitch, Martijn Konings, Sam Gindin and Scott Aquanno, 'The Political Economy of the Subprime Crisis', in Leo Panitch and Martijn Konings, eds, *American Empire and the Political Economy of Global Finance* (London, 2009); Colin Hay, *The Failure of Anglo-Liberal Capitalism* (London, 2013); Adam Tooze, *Crashed: How a Decade of Financial Crises Changed the World* (London, 2018), pp. 80–90.

35. 'Gordon Brown's Mansion House Speech', *Guardian*, 22 June 2006.

36. The FSA's first chair described its approach to monitoring the banks as 'Consenting adults in private? That's their problem' (Tooze, *Crashed*, p. 81).

37. Leo Panitch and Sam Gindin, *The Making of Global Capitalism: The Political Economy of American Empire* (London, 2012), pp. 117–18.

38. Bank of International Settlements *Triennial Central Bank Survey: Foreign Exchange Turnover in April 2016*, Table 6 (pdf available at bis.org).

39. Tooze, *Crashed*, p. 87.

40. National Audit Office, 'Taxpayer Support for UK Banks: FAQs', August 2018, at nao.org.uk.

41. Panitch and Gindin, *Making of Global Capitalism*, p. 316. By 2018, only RBS remained even partly (62 per cent) publicly owned.

42. John Lanchester, 'Are We Having Fun Yet?', *London Review of Books*, 4 July 2013, pp. 3–8.

43. By the end of March 2019, nine people had been convicted and ten acquitted of rate rigging.

44. By 2016 the finance and insurance industry as a whole had paid bonuses totalling £13.9 billion. Sean Farrell and Larry Elliott, 'UK Bonuses Soar to £44bn Beating Pre-Financial Crash Peak for the First Time', *Guardian*, 15 September 2016.

45. Minkin, *Blair Supremacy*, p. 753.

46. Chris Mullin, *Decline and Fall: Diaries 2005–2010* (London, 2010), p. 57. In the event, a large proportion of New Labour ministers lost their seats in the 2010 election, or stood down. Two young professional

politicians who had been promoted into the government within two or three years of being elected in 2005 were cases in point: Hazel Blears ('a shiny-faced New Labour automaton', in the view of Mullin, who was especially resentful, having been dropped from the government in favour of new MPs of this kind), and Kitty Ussher ('a young upwardly mobile New Labour zealot'). But both resigned and left politics before the 2010 election, having blotted their copybooks in the parliamentary expenses scandal.

47. It is ironic that, in 1993, Blair called for a larger party membership in terms that might have been used by Tony Benn in the 1970s or Jeremy Corbyn in 2015: 'What I want to see is the Labour Party pushing itself outwards, getting back in its local community, being the party that represents people within that community'. (BBC *On The Record*, quoted in Pemberton and Wickham-Jones, 'Labour's Lost Grassroots, pp. 181–206). In Blair's case, the idea that a larger membership would assist the party to win public support rested on a misplaced confidence that New Labour's policies would prove lastingly popular. Corbyn's leadership team envisaged a very different activist and educational role for party members.

48. Minkin notes that, at the same time, CLPs were becoming less willing to accept the leadership's preferred candidates for parliament, although this could have reflected a preference for a known local candidate rather than dissatisfaction with New Labour policy (*Blair Supremacy*, p. 373).

49. Ibid., p. 262.

50. Over the ten years from 2001 (when the Electoral Commission began publishing the data) to 2010, the Labour Party received a total of £8.2 million in direct (and mostly modest) donations from companies, £40 million from individuals, and £97 million from unions. The comparable figures for the Conservatives over the same ten years were £49 million (companies) and £102 million (individuals).

51. Colin Hay seems justified in concluding that 'the government remained largely unaware of the role of easy credit, private debt and asset price appreciation in the generation of growth for which it was taking the credit' (*Failure of Anglo-Liberal Capitalism*, p. 44).

52. Andrew Pierce, 'Why Did Nobody Notice It?', *Daily Telegraph*, 5 November 2008.

7 The Left versus New Labour

1. Ruth Winston, ed., *The Benn Diaries: The Definitive Collection* (London, 2017), p. 602.
2. Paul Waugh, 'Benn Retires to Spend More Time with His Politics', *Independent*, 28 June 1999.
3. With as few as three people turning up at ward meetings in Chesterfield, the diehard party loyalists who were left dominating the local Executive Committee now insisted that when Benn criticised the Labour government he should 'make it clear that he was speaking for himself and not the Chesterfield Labour Party'. This was clearly part of the reason for his decision to stand down; indeed, not even Benn's supporters were sure he could get reselected.
4. Winston, *Benn Diaries*, pp. 462–7, 499, 507, 561.
5. Benn himself refers specifically to an incident in July 1996 when, after Corbyn had been asked to appear on the BBC's *Midnight Hour*, someone from 'Labour Party Headquarters evidently rang up and said, "If you use Jeremy Corbyn you will never get another Shadow Cabinet Minister to appear." So the TV producers pulled out.' This did not so much surprise Benn as lead him to be disappointed with the rest of the parliamentary party's subservience: 'they gripe privately and then go along with what they are told to do by the Leader who is our boss' (ibid., p. 460).
6. See W. Stephen Gilbert, *Jeremy Corbyn – Accidental Hero* (London, 2015), p. 36.
7. Joe Murphy, 'Jeremy Corbyn Will Hang On as Leader but the Battle Is Far from Over', *Evening Standard*, 21 September 2016. As Murphy explained, 'that boastful-sounding quote from Mr Blair in 1996, which attempted to reassure middle England that New Labour would not revert back to the bad old days of 1980s militancy if voters trusted it with power, did not appear in the printed interview. Why? Because Jeremy Corbyn was such a marginal figure at the time that

the idea of him taking over anything sounded ridiculous. But make no mistake: Labour's leader is deadly serious about getting his own way from now on.'

8. '"What We've Achieved So Far": An Interview with Jeremy Corbyn', by Hilary Wainwright and Leo Panitch, *Red Pepper*, 15 December 2016. Corbyn recalled first meeting Benn in the 1969–70 period, just as he was critically reflecting on his experiences as a cabinet minister; and when Corbyn was a trade union staffer in the 1970s, he worked 'very closely' with Benn on industrial democracy. He recalled thinking Benn was sometimes 'idealistically too excited . . . He'd sort of say: "Yes, it's all going to happen now."'

9. Gilbert, *Jeremy Corbyn*, p. 28.

10. Alex Nunns, *The Candidate: Jeremy Corbyn's Improbable Path to Power*, 2nd edn, (London, 2018), p. 24 (all subsequent references are to this second edition unless the first edition is indicated). See also 'Managing candidate selection' in Lewis Minkin, *The Blair Supremacy* (Manchester, 2014), pp. 368–400.

11. Winston, *Benn Diaries*, pp. 477–8. Among those who had been associated with the Bennite new left, Tony Banks, Michael Meacher and Chris Mullin held junior posts at various points from 1997 to 2005, but were kept out of the cabinet.

12. As did the 250 people attending the Campaign Group meeting at the 1999 conference who heard Benn lampooning New Labour for thinking that 'the class war had been abolished by Tony Blair'. He was followed by 'Jeremy Corbyn talking passionately about the arms trade, Alan Simpson talking about genetically modified food, and Ken Livingstone making his campaign speech for his bid as Mayor of London.' Winston, *Benn Diaries*, p. 512.

13. See Minkin, *Blair Supremacy*, pp. 411–13.

14. Ibid., p. 239.

15. Ibid., p. 248.

16. Ibid., p. 640.

17. The Campaign Group was taken seriously enough to have the governor of the Bank of England, Eddie George, come to speak at one of its meetings shortly after the 1997 election, which was seen as a 'tremendous

coup' (Winston, *Benn Diaries*, p. 516). But, apart from the kind of major speech Benn prepared for the Commons debate on the WTO, there was no statement of the group's own position on financial globalisation. Most of the group would likely have endorsed the position outlined a decade earlier in *Beyond the Casino Economy* (co-authored by the radical *Guardian* journalist Seumus Milne, who would immediately become Corbyn's right-hand man after his election as leader), which powerfully made the case that 'one of the necessary conditions for a socialist society would be to turn [the top] few hundred corporations into democratically owned and accountable public bodies'. Yet it conceded that, 'in the foreseeable circumstances of the next few years, the socialisation of all large-scale private enterprise seems highly unlikely', and that this limited 'what can plausibly be proposed as part of a feasible programme for a Labour government in the coming years – even one elected in an atmosphere of radical expectations'. Nicholas Costello, Jonathan Michie and Seumas Milne, *Beyond the Casino Economy* (London, 1989), pp. 254–5.

18. Philip Cowley, *The Rebels: How Blair Mislaid His Majority* (London, 2005), p. 171.

19. Born in working-class Liverpool, the son of a bus driver who was his TGWU branch secretary, McDonnell had worked a series of unskilled jobs before going to night school to complete his A levels, and later going on to earn a Master's degree working as union researcher, before getting elected to the Greater London Council in 1981.

20. John McDonnell, 'Campaign Group's Popular Policies' , *Guardian*, 23 July, 2007.

21. Nunns, *The Candidate*, pp. 68, 128.

22. Ralph Miliband, 'Moving On', in Ralph Miliband and John Saville, eds, *The Socialist Register 1976* (London, 1976), p. 128.

23. See especially Hilary Wainwright's in-depth study of these local activists in East Manchester and Luton, *Reclaim the State: Experiments in Popular Democracy* (London, 2003), pp. 70–84.

24. Running in 1997 in a working-class constituency against a Labour candidate who had defected from the Conservatives, Scargill got barely 5 per cent of the vote. In the 2001 general election, Scargill only

mustered 2.4 per cent running against Mandelson in Hartlepool, while the total votes cast nationally for SLP candidates peaked at one-fifth of 1 per cent.

25. Cowley, *The Rebels*, p. 170.

26. Respect was founded by George Galloway (expelled as a Labour MP for his support for Iraqi resistance to the US and British occupation), and included well-known figures like George Monbiot and Salma Yaqoob as prominent actors. Galloway won an East End constituency in London, and Respect candidates came second in three others in 2005. But the party's support peaked with the sixteen council seats it won in the 2006 local elections.

27. Alan Simpson, 'Inside New Labour's Rolling Coup: The Blair Supremacy', *Red Pepper*, 1 December 2014.

28. Winston, *Benn Diaries*, p. 540.

29. John Kelly, *Contemporary Trotskyism: Parties, Sects and Social Movements in Britain* (London, 2018), p. 212.

30. Winston, *Benn Diaries*, p. 605.

31. This phrase from the British Communist Party programme, *The British Road to Socialism*, is quoted in Miliband, 'Moving On', p. 132.

32. Andrew Murray, *A New Labour Nightmare: The Return of the Awkward Squad* (London, 2005), p. 5.

33. The quotations here are from Minkin, *Blair Supremacy*, p. 550; and Simon Hannah, *A Party with Socialists in It: A History of the Labour Left* (London, 2018), p. 207.

34. Murray, *New Labour Nightmare*, pp. 10–11.

35. Ibid., p. 36.

36. See Minkin, *Blair Supremacy*, pp. 542–3, 565–6.

37. Murray, *New Labour Nightmare*, p. x.

38. Minkin, *Blair Supremacy*, p. 598.

39. Nunns, *The Candidate*, p. 40 n. 81.

40. Sir Willian Hayden, *Strengthening Democracy: Fair and Sustainable Funding of Political Parties*, tabled by Tony Blair in the House of Commons, 15 March 2007. See Mathew Tempest, 'Phillips Review Calls for State Funding of Political Parties', *Guardian*, 15 March 2007.

41. Will Woodward and Patrick Wintour, 'Resignations and Threats: The

Plot to Oust the Prime Minister', *Guardian*, 7 September 2006.

42. Nunns, *The Candidate*, pp. 148, 151.

43. Alex Nunns, 'What Became of the Labour Left?', *Red Pepper*, 16 September 2007.

44. See Compass Organization, *A Vision for the Democratic Left* (London, 2003); and the history of Compass availaible at compassonline.org.uk /about/our-story/.

45. Winston, *Benn Diaries*, p. 625.

46. Author interview with Jon Lansman, January 2019.

47. Minkin, *Blair Supremacy*, pp. 754–5.

48. Jon Lansman, 2010 interview with Alex Nunns, in *The Candidate*, p. 343 n. 89.

8 Beyond New Labour

1. The quotations here are from Mehdi Hasan and James Macintyre, *Ed: The Milibands and the Making of a Labour Leader* (London, 2011), p. 198; and Eunice Goes, *The Labour Party under Ed Miliband: Trying but Failing to Renew Social Democracy* (Manchester, 2016), pp. 44–5.

2. See Bob Clay, 'The Campaign Group: Time to Move On?' *Left Futures*, 25 May 2010, at leftfutures.org.

3. Tim Bale, *Five Year Mission: The Labour Party under Ed Miliband* (Oxford, 2015), p. 7.

4. Hasan and McIntyre, *Ed*, pp. 151–2.

5. Quoted in Goes, *Labour Party under Ed Miliband*, p. 75.

6. Quoted in Bale, *Five Year Mission*, p. 68.

7. Ibid., p. 44. Cf. Jess Garland, 'Members Not Only', in Mark Perryman, ed. *Corbynism from Below* (London, 2019), p. 109.

8. TULO, 'Refounding Labour: The TULO Submission', p. 12 (pdf available at labourdemocracy.files.wordpress.com).

9. Goes, *Labour Party under Ed Miliband*, p. 78.

10. Bale, *Five Year Mission*, p. 86.

11. For the quotations here, see ibid., pp. 90–1.

12. Quoted in Nick Robinson, 'Ed Miliband and the TUC: Job Done?' *BBC News,* 13 September 2011.

13. See Maurice Glasman, Jonathan Rutherford, Marc Stears and Stuart White, eds, with a preface by Ed Miliband, *The Labour Tradition and the Politics of Paradox* (London, 2011).

14. Jon Cruddas and John Rutherford, *One Nation: Labour Political Renewal* (London, 2014).

15. Ralph Miliband, *Parliamentary Socialism: A Study in the Politics of Labour* (London, 1961), p. 348.

16. Andrew Murray, 'Jeremy Corbyn and the Battle for Socialism', *Jacobin*, 7 February 2016 at jacobinmag.com.

17. Hilary Wainwright 'Reporting Back from Conditions Not of Our Choosing (2013)', in Sheila Rowbotham, Lynne Segal and Hilary Wainwright, *Beyond the Fragments: Feminism and the Making of Socialism*, 3rd edn (London, 2013), pp. 58–9.

18. Nunns, *The Candidate*, p. 135.

19. 'People's Assembly Against Austerity', joint letter to the *Guardian*, 5 February 2013. If it was appropriately symbolic that Tony Benn headed the list of sixty-five signatories to this call, what was more significant was that McCluskey, Serwotka, Billy Hayes, Bob Crow and eight other trade-union leaders immediately followed. After them came the four parliamentarians on the list – first Caroline Lucas, the Green Party's sole MP, and then Katy Clark, Corbyn and McDonnell, the only Labour MPs. The list ended with the names of the leader of the Green Party, the general secretary and chair of the Communist Party, and the editor of the *Morning Star*.

20. 'The Labour Party Has Failed Us. We Need a New Party of the Left', letter to the *Guardian*, 25 March, 2013.

21. The timing of Left Unity's founding had much to do with the most devastating of a long series of crises inside the SWP, of which Loach had been a prominent member. For a powerful critique of the Left Unity initiative, as well as the tortuous attempts to analyse the SWP's crisis in Leninist terms ('there is nothing that can be adduced for or against Leninism from the crisis eroding the SWP, any more than the results obtained by the experiments of the Large Hadron Collider need verifying by observing the Duracell Bunny'), see Andrew Murray, 'Left Unity or Class Unity', in *Registering Class: Socialist Register*

2014 (London, 2013), p. 277.

22. All the quotations in this paragraph are from Nunns, *The Candidate*, pp. 69–70. On Sellers, see also Anne Coddington, 'The New Left Mediascape', in Perrymen, *Corbynism from Below*, pp. 150–3.

23. See Andrew Murray, 'Left Unity or Class Unity', pp. 280ff; Bale, *Five Year Mission*, pp. 118–19; Nunns, *The Candidate*, pp. 23–4.

24. 'How Unite Plans to Change the Labour Party', *Workers' Liberty*, 11 July, 2012, at workersliberty.org.

25. Tony Blair, 'Labour Must Search for Answers and Not Merely Aspire to Be a Repository for People's Anger', *New Statesman*, 11 April 2013; George Eaton, 'Exclusive: Len McCluskey Declares War on Shadow Cabinet "Blairites"', *New Statesman*, 24 April 2013.

26. The face-off between the leadership of the Labour Party in Scotland and the leadership of Unite was a stark reminder of how the personal was intertwined with the political. The left-wing candidate backed by Unite was Karie Murphy (who would in 2016 become Corbyn's chief of staff in the leader's office), a former chair of the Scottish Labour Party who was not only very close to McCluskey but also a thorn in the side of the current Blairite leaders of the party in Scotland, especially Douglas Alexander – an old friend of Ed Miliband's who (despite having backed David in the leadership election) was a key figure behind the accommodation to austerity in Miliband's shadow cabinet.

27. The account here draws chiefly on Nunns, *The Candidate*, pp. 25–31; and Bales, *Five Year Mission*, pp. 174–9.

28. Andrew Sparrow, 'Ed Miliband's Speech on Reforming Labour's Links with Unions', *Guardian*, 9 July 2013.

29. TULO, 'Refounding Labour', p. 6.

30. Ibid.

31. Sparrow, 'Ed Miliband's Speech on Reforming Labour's Links with Unions.

32. Ibid.

33. Jon Lansman, 'I Am Still a Bennite', *Left Futures*, 16 March 2014, at leftfutures.org.

34. Ibid. See also Lansman's reports on NEC elections in *Left Futures*, 20

June 2012 and 30 August 2014.

35. See James Foley and Pete Raymand, 'In Fear of Populism', in Leo Panitch and Gregory Albo, eds, *Socialist Register 2018: Rethinking Democracy* (London, 2017).

36. See Richard Seymour's analysis of UKIP's class base, 'Ukip and the Crisis of Britain', in Leo Panitch and Gregory Albo, eds., *Socialist Register 2016: The Politics of the Right* (London, 2015).

37. *Learning the Lessons from Defeat*, Taskforce Report by Dame Margaret Beckett, Labour Party, January 2016.

38. Andrew Grice, 'Ed Miliband Lost the Election Because He Ditched New Labour, says Tony Blair', *Independent*, 10 May 2015.

39. Nunns, *The Candidate*, pp. 66–7.

40. Quoted in ibid., p. 72.

41. 'Leading the Way Forward for Labour', *Guardian*, 15 May, 2015.

42. Nunns, *The Candidate*, pp. 62–3, 72–3.

43. Nunns, *The Candidate*, pp. 124–5, 143–4, 150–61.

44. Ibid., p. 144.

45. 'Corbyn Blames Scotland Electoral Defeat on Weak Austerity and Trident Stances', *Guardian*, 13 August 2015.

46. 'Who Nominated Who for the 2015 Labour Leadership Election?', *New Statesman*, 15 June 2015.

9 'For the Many, Not the Few'

1. 'Media coverage of the EU Referendum (Report 5)', Centre for Research in Communication and Culture, Loughborough University, 27 June 2016, Table 2.1, at blog.lboro.ac.uk.

2. Under the Fixed-Term Parliaments Act, passed in 2011, the next election was not due until 2020, but it was assumed that a new Conservative leader, who would also become the new prime minister, would seek an immediate election to capitalise on their initial advantage and secure a personal mandate.

3. Alex Nunns, *The Candidate: Jeremy Corbyn's Improbable Path to Power*, 2nd edn (London, 2018), pp. 267–8.

4. '"Remember History": Neil Kinnock's Speech to the PLP', *Politics*

Home, 8 July 2016, at politicshome.com.

5. The leading player in this was Tony Benn's son Hilary Benn. In December 2015, when serving as Corbyn's shadow foreign secretary, he had called for air strikes on Syria, in defiance of Corbyn's policy. Corbyn failed to sack him, and by June 2016 he had become the leader of a large group of backbench MPs and shadow ministers who were plotting to force Corbyn to go. On 25 June Corbyn learned of the plan, and dismissed him. For a list of internal party groups and factions, see Anoush Chakelian, 'Labour's Warring Factions: Who Do They Include and What Are They Fighting Over?', *New Statesman*, 23 October 2015.

6. When Corbyn declined to go and a new leadership election was precipitated by a formal challenge from one of his opponents, Chris Smith, McNicol pursued the idea, for which he had obtained a supportive legal opinion, at a meeting of the NEC which the party bureaucracy had used 'every trick in the book' to try to rig, including attempting to rule that Corbyn himself was not entitled to attend. See Nunns, *The Candidate*, p. 273.

7. A slightly modified form of the last line of Shelley's poem 'The Mask of Anarchy', this phase had long been a part of radical working-class political culture. Taken up as the slogan of the campaign against Thatcher's 1989 poll tax, it was already current on the left by virtue of its use in the title of an award-winning film released in 2014 on the global impact of the 2003 Stop the War demonstrations. Ironically enough, when in 1994 the Labour right finally succeeded in expunging the explicit commitment to socialism from Clause IV of the party constitution, as a sop for removing 'common ownership', the revised wording included the phrase 'the many not the few'. But with the 2017 manifesto, Corbyn's speeches infused these words with renewed socialist purpose: 'The mission of socialism in the 21st century is to lead profound change so that it benefits the many, not the few.' 'Full Text of Jeremy Corbyn's 2018 Alternative MacTaggart Lecture', 23 August 2018, at labour.org.uk.

8. Nunns, *The Candidate*, p. 314.

9. See ibid., pp. 342–3; Frederick Cotton, 'What Could Have Been', *Jacobin*, 7 July 2017, at jacobinmag.com; Chris Williamson,

'Momentum Helped Me Win My Seat – Now Labour Must Harness Its Spirit', *Guardian*, 22 June 2017; Dan Hancox, '"There Is No Unwinnable Seat Now" – How Labour Revolutionised Its Doorstep Game', *Guardian*, 13 June 2017.

10. Owen Jones, 'Armageddon Hasn't Happened – So the Labour Right Needs a Rethink', *Guardian*, 6 July 2017. See also the summary of the Ipsos Mori Poll data: Josh Holder, Caelainn Barr and Niko Kommenda, 'Young Voters, Class and Turnout: How Britain Voted in 2017', *Guardian,* 20 June, 2017. The Ipsos Mori data confirms this conclusion once the NRS 'social grades' system of demographic calculation is sensibly adjusted so that the middle-class 'C1' category (supervisory or clerical and junior managerial, administrative or professional occupations) and the 'C2' category (skilled working-class occupations) are taken together with the 'D' category of unskilled and semi-skilled, the last of whom are alone designated as 'working class' in the Mori polls. See Ipsos Mori, 'How Britain Voted in the 2017 Election', 19 June 2017, at ipsos.com.

11. *Membership of UK Political Parties*, House of Commons Library briefing paper No. SN05125, 20 July 2019 (pdf available via research-briefings.files.parliament.uk).

12. Hilary Wainwright, *A New Politics from the Left* (Cambridge, 2018), pp. 34–5.

13. For the pressure, see Equality and Human Rights Commission, 'Investigation Opened into the Labour Party Following Complaints about Antisemitism', 28 May 2019, at equalityhumanrights.com. For how disingenuous it was, see Jewish Voice for Labour, 'Journalists, Check Your Evidence on Antisemitism!', 21 May 2019, at jewishvoicefor labour.org.uk. Between April 2018 and January 2019, Jennie Formby reported, the party (which then had over 500,000 members) received 1,106 complaints of antisemitism, of which 433 were found to have nothing to do with the party, while, of the remaining 673, another 220 were dismissed for lack of evidence. Of the remaining 453, only ninety-six resulted in suspensions and twelve in expulsions, while 146 members received a first warning. Of the 307 who were suspended or notified of an investigation, forty-four left the party. Another ninety-six were referred to the party's Anti-Semitism Disputes Panel. Of these ninety-six,

only sixteen members were issued with a formal warning from the National Executive Committee, while six members' cases were referred for further investigation, twenty-five members were issued with reminders of conduct (a first written warning), and seven members' cases were closed as the full evidence suggested no further action should be taken. See BBC News, 'Labour: 673 Anti-Semitism Complaints in 10 Months', 11 February 2019. For Williamson specifically, see 'Chris Williamson Says Labour Has Been "Too Apologetic" about Antisemitism – Video', *Guardian*, 27 February 2019; and for Sheridan, see Mattha Busby, 'Jim Sheridan Suspended from Labour over Antisemitism Row Comments', *Guardian*, 18 August 2018. For a comprehensive acount, see Grey Philo et al., *Bad News for Labour: Antisematism, the Party, and Public Belief* (London, 2019).

14. For text of conference speech, see Labour Party, 'Jeremy Corbyn Speaking at Labour Party Conference Today', 26 September 2018, at labour.org.uk.

15. See Natalie Fenton and Des Freedman, 'Fake Democracy, Bad News', in Leo Panitch and Gregory Albo, eds, *Socialist Register 2018: Rethinking Democracy* (London, 2017), pp. 130–49.

16. 'Full Text of Jeremy Corbyn's 2018 Alternative MacTaggart Lecture'.

17. On the history of the neoliberal hegemonic campaign in the UK, see Richard Cockett, *Thinking the Unthinkable: Think-Tanks and the Economic Counter-Revolution, 1931–83* (London, 1994). Thatcher inherited a cadre of capable young MPs, and some civil servants, with a shared neoliberal formation.

18. See, for instance, Robin Blackburn, 'The Corbyn Project: Public Capital and Labour's New Deal', *New Left Review* II/111 (May–June 2018); and the Foundational Economy Collective, *The Foundational Economy: The Infrastructure of Everyday Life* (Manchester, 2018). The journal *Soundings* has also hosted policy proposals for a Labour government on issues such as housing, the NHS, social care and mental health services.

19. Nunns, *The Candidate*, p. 313.

20. Jeremy Gilbert, 'Leading Richer Lives', in Mike Phipps, ed., *For the Many: Preparing Labour for Power* (London, 2017), p, 175.

21. Labour Party, *Alternative Models of Ownership: Report to the Shadow*

Chancellor of the Exchequer and Shadow Secretary of State for Business, Energy and Industrial Strategy (pdf available at labour.org.uk).

22. Labour's 2016 *Digital Democracy Manifesto* might have been expected to address this, but it was instead characterised by 'a rather narrow image of technology that concentrates on the internet, end-users and "networked individuals" … an image of publicness in the form of networks that nevertheless has security and privacy at its heart'. Nina Power, 'Digital Democracy', in Panitch and Albo, *Socialist Register 2018*, p. 174.

23. The way this important speech was reported in the mainstream media illustrates the extreme difficulty faced by the Labour leadership in getting heard. The only 'broadsheet' to give it reasonable coverage was the (online) *Independent*. The BBC's coverage was minimal and negative: BBC News, 'John McDonnell: Labour Public Ownership Plan Will Cost Nothing', 10 February 2018, at bbc.co.uk. The full speech is at John McDonnell, 'The New Economics of Labour', *Open Democracy*, 25 February 2018, opendemocracy.net/en/opendemocracyuk/new-economics-labour/.

24. Labour Party, 'John McDonnell's Full Speech to Labour Conference 2018', 24 September 2018, at labour.org.uk.

25. Ibid.

26. Barnaby Raine, 'Renewed Labour: McDonnell Has a Burning Task on His Hands', *N+1* 33: Overtime (Winter 2019), at nplusonemag.com.

27. Interview with authors, May 2018.

10 Implementing the New Left Project

1. Home Employment and Labour Market People in Work Public Sector Personnel Civil Service Statistics, UK; 'Civil Service Statistics, UK: 2017', at ons.gov.uk. In 2017 the National Audit Office recognised that the civil service could no longer do all that was needed for the effective planning and administration of current policies. See National Audit Office, 'Capability in the Civil Service', 24 March 2017 (pdf available at nao.org.uk). The auditor general told MPs that 'in many parts of government the capability of even acting as a prime contractor is not

necessarily there. That is not a fault, it is decision that a number of departments have made over time.' Richard Johnstone, 'NAO Chief on How Civil Servants Should Write Submissions on Outsourcing after Carillion', *Civil Service World*, 25 April 2018, at civilserviceworld.com /articles/news/nao-chief-how-civil-servants-should-write-submissions-outsourcing-after-carillion.

2. Anthony King and Ivor Crewe, *The Blunders of Our Governments* (London, 2013).

3. Andreas Karitzis, *The European Left in Times of Crises: Lessons from Greece* (Amsterdam, 2017), pp. 23–4.

4. Ibid., pp. 30–2.

5. Although the foreign-exchange earnings of the City of London's global financial and investment banking services are a crucial offset against the UK's huge trade deficit on goods, its activities have very little to do with financing the UK's non-financial sector, and fund managers who do invest in the shares of UK-based firms are focused exclusively on their share price, and rarely have any interest in their long-term productivity plans. 'The best way to think about the City . . . is essentially [as] an off-shore phenomenon, half-way between a Caicos Island and an oil rig'. Martin Taylor, the former chief executive of Barclays bank, cited in Tony Golding, *The City: Inside the Great Expectation Machine*, 2nd edn (London, 2003), p. 5.

6. McDonnell's speech to the conference is available in full at mirror.co.uk /news/politics/john-mcdonnell-speech-full-labour-13298825.

7. Graham Turner, Peter Rice, Demetris Pachnis, Stephen Jones, Max Harris, Elizabeth Applebee and Caroline Philip, *Financing Investment: Final Report*, GFC Economics Ltd and Clearpoint Advisors Ltd, 20 June 2018, p. 102 (pdf available at labour.org.uk). Although the report was careful to make clear that it did not represent the views of the Labour Party or the shadow chancellor of the exchequer, it appeared on the Labour Party's website as soon as it was completed.

8. The *Financing Investment* report's conception of such enterprises as part of 'high-tech clusters' does not begin to address this problem. And although it was praised by McDonnell in his speech to the 2018 party conference, the final report of the IPPR's Commission on Economic

Justice, *Prosperity and Justice: A Plan for the New Economy* (September 2018) did not begin to do so either, especially with its notions of 'industrial clusters' operating amid 'more open and competitive markets' under the rubric of a 'partnership economy' between capital, labour and the state.

9. 'Labour Plans for Capital Flight or Run on Pound if Elected', *Financial Times*, 26 September 2017.

10. One of the first new regional directors was in the important West Midlands region, where for two decades several CLPs had been more or less permanently suspended for not toeing the New Labour line.

11. Rajeev Sayal, 'Labour Official Accused of Cover-Up Over Antisemitism', *Guardian*, 4 February 2019. The *Guardian* did not report the fact that Formby had found that only twenty of the 200 cases of alleged antisemitism reported with great outrage by Margaret Hodge MP involved Labour Party members. See Skwawkbox, 'Excl: Hodge's 200 "Labour" Complaints – 90% Were Not Labour Members', 12 February 2019, at skwawkbox.org.

12. Jon Lansman, as chair of Momentum's National Coordinating Group, declared that Momentum would not seek to deselect any MPs, but would not discourage local party members from trying to deselect their MP under existing party rules. See Ashley Cowburn, 'Momentum Chair: "Enthusiasm for an Alternative Government Will Grow Stronger, Not Weaker" ', *Independent*, 23 January 2018.

13. Michael Calderbank, 'What Happened at Labour Conference?', *Red Pepper*, October 2018.

14. Broad policies are laid down by the National Coordinating Group, consisting of a large minority of representatives elected online by local members, plus a small majority of nominated representatives of affiliated trade unions and other national bodies (including the CLPD, for example). But within these broad policies members can choose their local priorities and organise as they see fit.

15. Personal communication to the authors.

16. Tom Blackburn, 'Corbynism from Below', *New Socialist*, 12 June 2017, at newsocialist.org.uk.

17. Adam Klug and Emma Rees, 'How Big Organising Works', in Perry-

man, *Corbynism from Below*, pp. 132–3.

18. Max Shanly, 'Toward a New Model Young Labour', *Bullet*, 27 November 2017, at socialistproject.ca.

19. Michael Calderbank, 'What Happened at Labour Conference?', *Red Pepper*, 1 October 2018.

20. 'Report on Behalf of all NEC CLP Representatives', November 2018. Among the proposals defeated by the non-CLP majority on the NEC were a proposal to define the terms of reference of the NEC and the NPF respectively, in light of the NEC's earlier rejection of a motion, widely supported by CLPs, to abolish the NPF and a proposal to ensure that at least three NEC officers were CLP representatives.

21. Labour Tribune MPs, 'Tribune Group: Labour's British Promise', 1 April 2017 , at labourtribunemps.org.

22. Joe Watts, 'Tony Blair Backs the Independent Group as He Says "Truly Mind-Boggling" Labour Has Been Taken by Populists', *Independent*, 25 February 2019.

23. Labour Tribune MPs, 'Healing the Divide: Essays on How We Build a Future that Brings Together Leavers and Remainers', 25 February 2019 (pdf available via labourtribunemps.org).

24. BBC News, 'Labour: Disaffected MPs Asked to Join New Group by Tom Watson', 25 February 2019; Sienna Rodgers, 'Tom Watson Launches New Futures Britain Group with 130 Labour MPs and Peers', *Labour List*, 11 March 2019, at labourlist.org. See also Michael Savage, 'Jeremy Corbyn Is Now Secure as Labour Leader, Says Watson', *Guardian*, 2 July 2017.

25. Jon Trickett, 'Labour's Democratic Socialists Have Nothing to Fear from Debate with Internal Rivals', *New Statesman*, 18 March 2019.

26. Ben Sellers, 'The Dangerous Language of "Crankery" on the Labour Left', *Labour List*, 10 August 2018, at labourlist.org.

11 Crisis and Party in the Brexit Conjuncture

1. Jeremy Corbyn, 'Speech to Labour Party Conference', 27 September 2017, available at labour.org.uk.

2. Jack Shenker, *Now We Have Your Attention* (London, 2019), p. 214.

3. 'Chris Leslie's statement in full as he resigns from the Labour Party', 18 February 2009, available at nottinghampost.com.

4. Alexander Zevin, 'Every Penny a Vote', *London Review of Books*, 15 August 2019 – reviewing Quinn Slobodian's study of the origins of the EU, *Globalists: The End of Empire and the Birth of Neoliberalism* (Cambridge, MA: 2018).

5. Jonathan White, ed., *Building an Economy for the People: An Alternative Economic and Political Strategy for Twenty-First-Century Britain*, (Croydon, 2012), p. 44.

6. Daniel Finn, 'Corbyn, Labour and the Brexit Crisis', *New Left Review* II/118 (July–August 2019), p. 14 n. 18.

7. Kwasi Kwarteng, Priti Patel, Dominic Raab, Chris Skidmore and Elizabeth Truss, *Britannia Unchained: Global Lessons for Growth and Prosperity* (London, 2012).

8. Chris Hanretty, 'Areal interpolation and the UK's referendum on EU membership', *Journal of Elections, Public Opinion and Parties* 27: 4 (2017).

9. The Watson quotation is from 'Watson mocks Lib Dem Brexit "deniers" and vows Labour will not "disrespect" public by trying to overthrow EU vote', *Labour List*, 25 November 2016; the Umunna statement is from 'Chuka Umunna and West Streeting: Why we Labour Remainers voted to trigger Article 50', *iNews*, 1 February 2017. See Finn, 'Corbyn, Labour and the Brexit Crisis', p. 16.

10. Polly Toynbee, 'Corbyn's fence-sitting is preposterous', *Guardian*, 18 September 2019. Cf. Jeremy Corbyn, 'Only Labour will give the people a final say on Brexit,' *Guardian*, 17 September 2019.

11. Toby Helm and Michael Savage, 'Brexit divisions threaten to plunge Labour party conference into chaos,' *Observer*, 21 September 2019.

12. The alienating effects of the electoral system were aggravated by the Fixed Term Parliaments Act of 2011, introduced to protect the Liberal Democrats from being ditched by the Conservatives in the coalition government. Mrs May could not get her withdrawal agreement through the Commons but was able to stay in office, even though almost all other significant legislative business was at a standstill. The resulting

parliamentary paralysis, coming in the wake of the parliamentary expenses scandal of 2009, and the by now almost total professionalisation of political life, brought respect for MPs to a new low, and was beginning to put representative democracy itself at risk. In early 2019, no less than 74 per cent of people said they trusted the military to act in the public interest, compared with only 34 per cent who trusted MPs. Fifty-four per cent thought that the country needed 'a strong leader willing to break the rules', while only 23 per cent disagreed with this view. Another significant finding in the report was that even more people – 63 per cent – agreed that 'Britain's system of government is rigged to advantage the rich and powerful'. Hansard Society, *Audit of Political Engagement 16: The 2019 Report.*

13. Perry Anderson, 'The Figures of Descent', *New Left Review* I/161 (January–February 1987).

14. Alberto Nardelli, 'How the UK civil-service has changed in 10 charts', *Guardian*, 19 November 2015.

15. Colin Leys, 'The Dissolution of the Mandarins: the sell-off of the British state', *openDemocracy*, 15 June 2012.

16. Confederation of British Industry, ' "Champion business" – Open letter from CBI to all Conservative Party Leadership candidates', 30 May 2019, at cbi.org.uk; Lisa O'Carroll, 'Johnson's and Hunt's Brexit pledges irresponsible, say manufacturers', *Guardian*, 1 July 2019.

17. Heather Stewart on Twitter: 'Here's the PM, doing a kind of panto version of his stump speech', at twitter.com/Guardian, 12 December 2019.

18. The total amount donated to the Tories in the first three weeks of the 2019 electoral campaign came to more than £12 million – nearly three times as much as Labour received. Jane Merrick, 'General election 2019: Conservative Party receives more than £3.5 million in donations in one week', *Inews*, 5 December 2019.

19. Caroline Mortimer, 'British army "could stage mutiny under Corbyn", says senior serving general', *Independent*, 20 September 2015.

20. Max Blumenthal and Ben Norton, 'Inside the temple of covert propaganda: The Integrity Initiative and the UK's scandalous information war', *Grayzone*, December 17, 2018.

21. Gary Younge, 'The Tories can't win without the press. This isn't how

democracy works', *Guardian*, 15 November 2019.

22. Tom Mills, 'The BBC's fabled impartiality was only ever an elite consensus', *Guardian*, 24 November 2019.

23. See, for example, Dan Evans-Kanu, 'Reflections from the doorstep', *Medium*, 13 December 2019, at medium.com.

24. 'Election Opinion Polls Tracker: gap between Labour and Tories narrows with result in balance', *Guardian*, 12 December 2019.

25. Labour had actually gained 102 seats in 1935, having been reduced in 1931 from 297 to only 52 seats, when its leader had thrown in his lot with the Tories and the Liberals to implement draconian austerity.

26. Adam McDonnell and Chris Curtis, 'How Britain voted in the 2019 general election', YouGov, 17 December 2019.

27. Matthew Smith, 'Labour economic policies are popular, so why aren't Labour?', YouGov, 12 November 2019.

28. See James Meadway, 'Labour's Economic Plans: What Went Wrong', *Novara Media*, 17 December 2019.

29. Richard Seymour, 'No False Consolations', *Novara Media*, 13 December 2019.

30. Leo V. Panitch, 'Ideology and Integration: The Case of the British Labour Party', *Political Studies* XIX: 2 (June 1971).

31. Ursula Huws, 'The Unwoke are Awake', *Bullet, Socialist Project*, 17 December 2019.

32. Tom Blackburn, 'No Final Defeat', *New Socialist*, 14 December 2019.

33. See Chapter 7, note 8, above; and Hilary Wainwright and Leo Panitch, '"What We've Achieved So Far": An Interview with Jeremy Corbyn', *Red Pepper*, 15 December 2016.

34. That these charges could even appear credible almost beggars belief when it comes to someone whose only crimes were to be so much in advance of Major and Blair in wanting to meet with Sinn Fein's leaders at the time of the civil war in Northern Ireland and to have sat beside Hamas and Hezbollah leaders in support of Palestinian rights and against Israeli government actions, even while constantly taking courageous public stances in defence of Jewish communities – as a local councillor in London, for example, against a neo-Nazi March in Wood Green, and as an MP, advancing dozens of early-day motions to defend

Jewish communities not only in the UK but also in Iran, Turkey, France, Russia and Eastern Europe; to denounce Holocaust deniers; to commemorate Jewish resistance to fascism; and to pressure the police to do more to protect synagogues.

35. For a highly positive view of the process of producing the manifesto, see Sienna Rodgers, 'Writing Labour's manifesto was a messy process. But it's bolder and better for it', *Guardian*, 26 November 2019.

36. George Monbiot, ed., *Land for the Many: Changing the Way Our Fundamental Asset Is Used, Owned and Governed*, Labour Party, June 2019, p. 44 (available at labour.org.uk).

37. Andy Beckett, 'Win or lose, Labour's radicalism has redefined what's possible in British politics', *Guardian*, 16 November 2019.

38. Shenker, *Now We Have Your Attention,* p. 210.

39. 'The fact that among a close group of comrades someone shared that memo with the Murdock press tells its own story of dysfunction'. These words are Andrew Fisher's, the executive director of policy in the leader's office and principal author of both the 2017 and 2019 manifestos, referring to his memo criticising the operation of the office, leaked to the *Sunday Times* during the 2019 party conference. Andrew Fisher, 'There is a lot to criticize. But Corbyn and McDonnell have transformed Labour', *Guardian,* 17 December 2019.

40. See Tom Blackburn, 'Office Without Counter-Power', *New Socialist*, 15 October 2019.

41. See Chapter 1, note 2, above. Ralph Miliband, 'Moving On', *Socialist Register 1976* (London, 1976), p. 128.

Index

Brown, Michael Barratt, 32, 74
Burk, Kathleen, 71
Burnham, Andy, 196, 199
Bush, George W., 151, 152
Butskellism, 65
Byers, Stephen, 130
Byrne, Liam, 180

Cabinet, 21, 38, 48, 50, 51, 55, 56, 62, 64–78, 81, 101, 102, 104, 105, 107, 111, 116, 117, 128, 129, 141, 151, 156, 177, 180, 182, 188, 202, 203, 211, 219, 231, 237, 247, 250
Cabinet Industrial Policy Committee, 67
Cairncross, Alec, 71
Calderbank, Michael, 225, 229
Callaghan, Jim, 2, 8, 67, 69, 71, 73, 78, 79, 85, 86, 89, 102–5, 112, 130
Campbell, Alastair, 138
Cameron, David, 188, 202, 204, 237
Campaign for Democratic Socialism, 46
Campaign for Labour Party Democracy (CLPD), 81–5, 89–92, 94, 95, 105, 106 108, 113, 116, 117, 163, 164, 174, 175, 193, 196, 198, 204, 225, 227
Castle, Barbara, 39, 41, 69
CBI (Confederation of British Industry), 18, 67, 72, 169
Chamberlain, Neville, 54
Chesterfield Labour Club, 161
Chesterfield Socialist Conferences, 170
CinemaAction, 44
Civil Service Union, 165, 169
Clark, Katy, 229
Clause Four, 30, 35, 49, 51, 59, 98, 120, 125–7, 133, 166
Clinton, Bill, 148
Clintonism, 31
CLP (Constituency Labour Party), 47, 60, 105, 106, 113, 116, 117, 130, 139, 140, 141, 156–8, 161, 163, 175, 177, 187–90, 194, 223, 225, 227, 229, 232, 242, 243, 253, 254
CND (Campaign for Nuclear Disarma-

ment), 185
Coates, David, 148
Coates, Ken, 74
Cold War, 10, 37, 38, 60, 174
Collins, Ray, 189, 192–4, 196
Collins Review, 192–4
Communist Party (also CP), 5, 18, 20, 34, 35, 38, 49, 87, 97, 114, 168, 169, 250
Compass, 173, 174, 180
Confederation of Shipbuilding and Engineering Unions (CSEU), 66
Conference Arrangements Committee, 63, 84, 108, 225
Conference of Socialist Economists, 79
Conservative, 6, 21, 22, 24, 30, 33, 35, 46, 47, 54, 123, 125, 126, 127, 132, 134– 6, 143, 145, 148, 149, 158, 159, 202, 204, 205, 208, 212, 235, 237, 238, 241, 242, 244, 246–8
Cook, Robin, 102
Co-Op, 225
Cooper, Yvette, 147, 196
Corbyn, Jeremy, 2, 3, 5, 28, 29, 113, 132, 152, 161, 162, 165–70, 175, 177, 180, 183, 184, 195, 197–211, 213, 214, 219, 220, 223–5, 227, 229–32, 234–44, 246–54
Corbynism, 250
Corbynite, 227
Cousins, Frank, 31, 32, 38, 41, 42, 50, 51
Cripps, Francis, 64, 74–6
Crosland, Anthony (Tony), 6, 25, 39, 43, 61, 76, 77, 232
Crow, Bob, 170
Cruddas, John, 173, 174, 180
CWU (Communication Workers Union), 169, 177

Daily Mail, 210
Daily Mirror, 212
Daly, Lawrence, 38
Deans, Stevie, 189
Democracy Review, 229
Democratic Unionist Party, 206